WordPerfect® 5.1 SmartStart

Jean S. Insinga
Middlesex Community-Technical College

Kathie-Jo Arnoff

que College

WordPerfect 5.1 SmartStart.

Copyright © 1993 by Que® Corporation

All rights reserved. Printed in the United States of America. No part of this book may be used or reproduced in any form or by any means, or stored in a database or retrieval system, without prior written permission of the publisher except in the case of brief quotations embodied in critical articles and reviews. Making copies of any part of this book for any purpose other than your own personal use is a violation of United States copyright laws. For information, address Que Corporation, 11711 N. College Ave., Carmel, IN 46032.

Library of Congress Catalog No.: 93-83865

ISBN: 1-56529-246-4

This book is sold *as is*, without warranty of any kind, either express or implied, respecting the contents of this book, including but not limited to implied warranties for the book's quality, performance, merchantability, or fitness for any particular purpose. Neither Que Corporation nor its dealers or distributors shall be liable to the purchaser or any other person or entity with respect to any liability, loss, or damage caused or alleged to be caused directly or indirectly by this book.

96 95   4

Interpretation of the printing code: the rightmost double-digit number is the year of the book's printing; the rightmost single-digit number, the number of the book's printing. For example, a printing code of 93-1 shows that the first printing of the book occurred in 1993.

Screens reproduced in this book were created using Collage Plus from Inner Media, Inc., Hollis, NH.

WordPerfect 5.1 SmartStart is based on WordPerfect 5.1 for DOS.

Publisher: David P. Ewing

Associate Publisher: Rick Ranucci

Product Development Manager: Thomas A. Bennett

Operations Manager: Sheila Cunningham

Book Designer: Scott Cook

Production Team: Jeff Baker, Claudia Bell, Danielle Bird, Julie Brown, Jodie Cantwell, Paula Carroll, Brad Chinn, Lisa Daugherty, Brook Farling, Wendy Ott, Linda Seifert, Donna Winter, Michelle Worthington

About the Authors

Jean Insinga is professor of information systems and accounting at Middlesex Community-Technical College in Middletown, Connecticut. She has an extensive background in the computer programming and application software fields. She is also the author of *The Prentice Hall Computerized Accounting Practice Sets*. Jean has earned B.S. and M.S. degrees from Central Connecticut State University. She also holds a C.A.I.S. (Computer Applications Information Systems) certificate from the University of New Haven.

Kathie-Jo Arnoff is a product development specialist at Que Corporation. She is the author of *WordPerfect 5.1 QuickStart* and a contributing author to *Introduction to Business Software* and *1-2-3 Release 2.2 QuickStart*.

Title Manager
Carol Crowell

Senior Editor
Jeannine Freudenberger

Production Editor
Gregory R. Robertson

Editorial Assistant
Elizabeth D. Brown

Formatter
Jill Stanley

Trademarks

All terms mentioned in this book that are known to be trademarks or service marks have been appropriately capitalized. Que cannot attest to the accuracy of this information. Use of a term in this book should not be regarded as affecting the validity of any trademark or service mark.

> Microsoft, Microsoft Word for Windows, Microsoft Excel, Microsoft Windows, and Microsoft Word are registered trademarks of Microsoft Corporation. IBM is a registered trademark of International Business Machines Corporation. WordPerfect is a registered trademark of WordPerfect Corporation. 1-2-3 and Lotus are registered trademarks of Lotus Development Corporation.

Composed in *Garamond* and *MCPdigital* by Que Corporation

Give Your Computer Students a SmartStart on the Latest Computer Applications

Que's SmartStart series from Prentice Hall Computer Publishing combines the experience of the Number 1 computer book publisher in the industry with the pedagogy you've come to expect in a textbook.

SmartStarts cover just the basics in a format filled with plenty of step-by-step instructions and screen shots.

Each SmartStart chapter ends with a "Testing Your Knowledge" section that includes true/false, multiple choice, and fill-in-the-blank questions; two or three short projects, and two long projects. The long projects are continued through the book to help students build on skills learned in preceding chapters.

Each SmartStart comes with an instructor's manual featuring additional test questions, troubleshooting tips, and additional exercises. This manual will be available both on disk and bound.

Look for the following additional SmartStarts:

Windows 3.1 SmartStart	1-56529-203-0
Word for Windows SmartStart	1-56529-204-9
Excel 4 for Windows SmartStart	1-56529-202-2
MS-DOS SmartStart	1-56529-249-9
Lotus 1-2-3 SmartStart (covers 2.4 and below)	1-56529-245-6
dBASE IV SmartStart	1-56529-251-0

For more information call:

1-800-428-5331

or contact your local Prentice Hall College Representative

Contents at a Glance

Introduction 1
1 Getting Started 5
2 Editing 37
3 Working with Blocks 59
4 Formatting Lines and Paragraphs 75
5 Formatting Pages 109
6 Proofreading 133
7 Printing 153
8 Merging Documents 167
9 Sorting and Selecting 193
A Graphics 211
   Index 219

Table of Contents

Introduction 1
    What Is WordPerfect? 1
    What Does This Book Contain? 2
    Who Should Use This Book? 2
    What Is in This Book? 2
    Where To Find More Help 3
    Conventions Used in This Book 3

1 Getting Started 5
    Objectives 5
    An Overview of WordPerfect Features 6
    Objective 1: To Start WordPerfect 8
    Objective 2: To Get Acquainted with WordPerfect's Keyboard,
        Mouse, and Menus 10
    Objective 3: To Change the Default Directory 15
    Objective 4: To Create a Document 15
    Objective 5: To Preview and Print a Document 26
    Objective 6: To Save, Exit, and Clear a Document 28
    Chapter Summary 32
    Testing Your Knowledge 32

2 Editing 37
    Objectives 37
    Objective 1: To Retrieve Files 38
    Objective 2: To Use the List Files Screen 39
    Objective 3: To Insert Text 45
    Objective 4: To Delete Text 47
    Objective 5: To Display and Delete Hidden Codes 52
    Chapter Summary 55
    Testing Your Knowledge 55

3 Working with Blocks 59
Objectives 59
Objective 1: To Define a Block of Text 60
Objective 2: To Move, Copy, and Delete Text 63
Objective 3: To Save, Print, and Append a Block of Text 66
Objective 4: To Boldface, Underline, and Center a Block
   of Text 69
Chapter Summary 71
Testing Your Knowledge 71

4 Formatting Lines and Paragraphs 75
Objectives 75
Objective 1: To Change Left and Right Margins 76
Objective 2: To Change Line Spacing 81
Objective 3: To Set Tab Stops 82
Creating Tables 86
Objective 4: To Indent Text 88
Objective 5: To Use Justification 91
Objective 6: To Enhance Text 100
Chapter Summary 105
Testing Your Knowledge 105

5 Formatting Pages 109
Objectives 109
Objective 1: To Choose Paper Size and Type 110
Objective 2: To Change Top and Bottom Margins 117
Objective 3: To Design Headers and Footers 120
Objective 4: To Number Pages 122
Objective 5: To Control Page Breaks 126
Chapter Summary 128
Testing Your Knowledge 128

6 Proofreading 133
Objectives 133
Objective 1: To Search for a Word or Phrase 134
Objective 2: To Replace a Word or Phrase 137
Objective 3: To Use the Speller 141
Objective 4: To Use the Thesaurus 147

  Chapter Summary 149
  Testing Your Knowledge 149

7 Printing 153

  Objectives 153
  Objective 1: To Print from the Screen 154
  Objective 2: To Print from Disk 156
  Objective 3: To Control the Printer 159
  Objective 4: To Preview a Document 160
  Chapter Summary 164
  Testing Your Knowledge 164

8 Merging Documents 167

  Objectives 167
  Understanding the Basics 168
  Merging Text Files 169
  Objective 1: To Create a Secondary Merge File 170
  Objective 2: To Create a Primary Merge File 173
  Objective 3: To Merge the Primary and Secondary Files 175
  Objective 4: To Merge from the Keyboard 178
  Objective 5: To Address Envelopes 181
  Objective 6: To Print Mailing Labels 186
  Chapter Summary 190
  Testing Your Knowledge 190

9 Sorting and Selecting 193

  Objectives 193
  Objective 1: To Understand the Sort Screen 194
  Objective 2: To Sort Lines and Paragraphs 197
  Objective 3: To Sort Secondary Merge Files 202
  Objective 4: To Choose Particular Data 203
  Chapter Summary 206
  Testing Your Knowledge 207

A Graphics 211

  Choosing the Box Type 212
  Importing a Graphics Image 216

Index 219

Introduction

WordPerfect 5.1 SmartStart is designed for a hands-on computer course in word processing, enabling you to structure your topics within the time frame of your curriculum. The book takes you through WordPerfect with step-by-step exercises within the chapters, describing all the fundamentals you need to know about the software. The text supplies essential information, provides comments on what you see, and describes abstract ideas. Many illustrations guide you through procedures or clarify difficult concepts.

What Is WordPerfect?

WordPerfect is one of the most popular word processing programs. Why is WordPerfect so popular? Because it has all the "basic" features you expect in a word processing package, plus a full complement of advanced features. The program is suited to your needs, whether they entail short memos or complex documents.

"What makes WordPerfect attractive is that it gets out of your way," explains W. E. "Pete" Peterson, executive vice president of WordPerfect Corporation. "It's like a well-mannered houseguest who is kind enough not to disrupt your life or the way you do things."

An editing screen uncluttered by menus or cryptic codes, an abundance of features, support for a wide range of printers, and unparalleled customer assistance are just a few of the reasons why WordPerfect enjoys the prominence it so rightly deserves.

WordPerfect 5.1 SmartStart

What Does This Book Contain?

Each chapter in *WordPerfect 5.1 SmartStart* focuses on a particular WordPerfect operation or set of operations. At the end of each chapter, the student can work through questions and projects in the "Testing Your Knowledge" section. Overall, the book's movement reflects the steps typical in the creation of any document, from entering text to formatting, proofreading, and printing.

Who Should Use This Book?

WordPerfect 5.1 SmartStart is an easy guide for anyone just starting with WordPerfect 5.1. The book is intended for new users or for people who have not yet been able to understand WordPerfect. Basic information is presented to help a first-time user get started quickly. And enough essential information is provided so that a more experienced user can use the book as a reference tool.

What Is in This Book?

Each chapter in *WordPerfect 5.1 SmartStart* focuses on a particular task or set of tasks. Overall, the book's movement reflects the steps typical in the creation of any document, from entering text to proofreading and printing. Later chapters concentrate on more specialized topics.

Chapter 1, "Getting Started," shows you how to start WordPerfect and introduces you to the editing screen, keyboard, and mouse. You learn the basics of using the program: typing text, moving the cursor, making a menu selection, printing and saving a document, clearing the screen, and exiting.

In Chapter 2, "Editing," you learn to retrieve a file and modify it by inserting and deleting text. You also investigate WordPerfect's hidden codes and two document windows.

Chapter 3, "Working with Blocks," shows you how to highlight a block and manipulate it in several ways; for example, you learn to move, copy, delete, print, and save a block of text. You also learn how to enhance a block by adding boldfacing or underlining or by centering the block.

Chapters 4 and 5 cover formatting. First, you work with formatting lines and paragraphs. You change the margins, change line spacing, set tab stops, indent and align text, and use hyphenation. You also gain more experience enhancing text and learn to work with fonts. Then, in Chapter 5, you move to formatting pages. You choose the paper size, change the top and bottom margins, design headers and footers, number pages, and control page breaks.

Chapter 6, "Proofreading," not only introduces you to WordPerfect's built-in Speller and Thesaurus but also demonstrates how to use the Search and Replace features. In Chapter 7 you learn to print your documents. You learn to select a printer and to print from the screen or disk.

Chapter 8, "Merging Documents," guides you through the steps for creating personalized form letters, addressing envelopes, and printing mailing labels. Chapter 9 introduces sorting. You learn how to work with sort keys and to select data for sorting. Finally, the Appendix gives you an overview of WordPerfect's graphics capabilities.

Where To Find More Help

After you learn the fundamentals presented in this book, you may want to learn more advanced applications of WordPerfect. Que Corporation has a full line of WordPerfect books you can use. Among these books are *Using WordPerfect 5.1*, Special Edition; *WordPerfect Tips, Tricks, and Traps*, Third Edition; *WordPerfect Quick Reference*; and *WordPerfect Applications Library*.

If you find yourself stymied at a particular point, WordPerfect's Help feature may be able to answer your questions.

Should all else fail, WordPerfect Corporation provides toll-free telephone support: 1-800-541-5096. The telephone staff is helpful and knowledgeable. The line is open from 7 a.m. to 6 p.m., Mountain Standard Time, Monday through Friday.

Conventions Used in This Book

Certain conventions are used throughout the text and graphics of *WordPerfect 5.1 SmartStart* to help you understand the book.

The keys you press and text you type appear in **boldfaced blue** type in the numbered steps and in **boldfaced** type elsewhere. Key combinations are joined by a plus sign: **Shift**+**F5** in numbered steps and **Shift**+**F5** elsewhere.

WordPerfect 5.1 SmartStart

Function-key commands are identified both by name and by keystrokes—for example, Ctrl+F2 (Spell). To choose this command, you press and hold down the Ctrl key while you then press the F2 key. Menu options are referred to by the name of the option, usually followed by the number of the option in parentheses—for example, Line (1). You also can press the highlighted key to activate the commands. For example, you can press L or 1 to choose the Line (1) option.

Commands accessed through WordPerfect's pull-down menu system are identified by a 🖱. An instruction marked by this icon provides an alternative to using WordPerfect's function-key commands. Although the icon used in this book is a mouse, you can access the pull-down menu commands with either the mouse or the keyboard.

DOS commands, file names, and directory names are written in all capital letters. Options, commands, menu names, and dialog box names are headline style. On-screen prompts and messages are in a `special typeface`. DOS commands, file names, and directory names are written in all capital letters. Options, commands, menu names, and dialog box names are headline style.

Getting Started

This chapter begins with the basics of WordPerfect: starting the program, examining the editing screen, learning the keyboard, and using the Help feature. You learn some fundamental skills for using a word processor, including how to type text, move around the editing screen, make a menu selection, print and save a document, and exit WordPerfect.

Before you learn these basic skills, the chapter gives you a brief overview of WordPerfect's features. Because this book is a *SmartStart* for those just learning WordPerfect, some of the advanced features are not covered. You do, however, quickly learn to perform a variety of word processing tasks with WordPerfect's many features.

Objectives

1. To Start WordPerfect
2. To Get Acquainted with WordPerfect's Keyboard, Mouse, and Menus
3. To Change the Default Directory
4. To Create a Document
5. To Preview and Print a Document
6. To Save, Exit, and Clear a Document

Getting Started

1

Key Terms in This Chapter	
Defaults	Standard WordPerfect settings that are in effect each time you start the program.
Status line	The bottom line on the WordPerfect editing screen. The status line indicates the disk drive, file name, and position of the cursor on-screen. From time to time, the WordPerfect status line displays system messages and prompts.
Cursor	An on-screen marker that indicates where a character will appear when you type. The cursor also marks the location where a hidden code will be entered.
Word wrap	A WordPerfect feature that eliminates the need to press the ⏎Enter (Return) key each time you reach the right margin. With word wrap, you need to press ⏎Enter only when you come to the end of a paragraph or a short line, or you enter a command.
Soft return	The code inserted at the end of each line when the text reaches the right margin and is automatically wrapped to the next line.
Hard return	The code for a carriage return, inserted when you press ⏎Enter at the end of a line.
File name	A descriptive title that you assign to a file before storing it in system memory.

An Overview of WordPerfect Features

WordPerfect offers a range of features for making your word processing tasks convenient and efficient. These features enable you to create and edit text documents, enhance the basic appearance of the text, check the spelling, print documents, and manage files.

The more specialized features covered in this book enable you to merge text files, create mailing labels, and sort and select data.

An Overview of WordPerfect Features

Basic Features

One of the first features you notice when you start WordPerfect is the uncluttered editing screen. Many word processors display a number of indicators and codes while you edit, but WordPerfect keeps these to a minimum—freeing most of the screen for text. In addition, the document shown on-screen looks very much the way it will appear when printed.

WordPerfect commands are easy to access with either the keyboard or a mouse. When you use WordPerfect, you will appreciate WordPerfect's on-line Help feature, which provides context-sensitive information about WordPerfect's commands and keys. Even though you can access all WordPerfect commands with the function keys, you also have the option of using WordPerfect's system of pull-down menus to access the same commands. The pull-down menus, particularly when you access them with the mouse, are often easier to use when you are just learning WordPerfect.

Using the program's Block feature, you can designate a specific portion of a document on which you want certain commands to have an effect. For example, you can use Block to move or copy a sentence or paragraph, to display a certain portion of text in boldface, or to delete a particular passage.

A number of formatting features enable you to enhance the appearance of text. You can adjust margins, use boldface and italic, center text, justify text, hyphenate words, change the line spacing, design headers and footers, activate page numbering, and control where pages break.

The built-in Speller and Thesaurus give you access to a 115,000-word dictionary, as well as lists of synonyms and antonyms you can access from the editing screen. Among the special printing features is View Document, which enables you to preview a document on-screen before you print it.

You can handle file management efficiently through the List Files screen. From that screen, you can manipulate files and directories from within WordPerfect much more extensively than most word processors allow.

Specialized Features

WordPerfect's Merge feature enables you to merge text files and thereby save valuable time for other tasks. For example, you can merge data from an address list into a form letter, or you can piece together complicated reports. Other tools for handling data are WordPerfect's Sort and Select features. Using these features, for example, you can sort phone lists or extract certain ZIP codes from a mailing list.

Getting Started

Objective 1: To Start WordPerfect

This section shows you how to start WordPerfect on a hard disk system and on a dual-floppy disk system.

Exercise 1.1: Starting WordPerfect on a Hard Disk System

Follow these steps to start WordPerfect on a hard disk system:

1. Be sure that the drive door of the floppy drive(s) is open.
2. Turn on your computer.
3. If necessary, respond to the prompts for date and time. The opening screen appears, showing either a menu or a C:\> prompt.
4. If a menu appears, choose the corresponding number for WordPerfect and press ⏎Enter to start WordPerfect 5.1. You are now ready to become acquainted with WordPerfect. See "Objective 2: To Get Acquainted with WordPerfect's Keyboard, Mouse and Menus."
5. If your computer does not list WordPerfect as a menu option and the C:\> prompt appears instead, you need to change to the subdirectory where WordPerfect 5.1 files are located and press ⏎Enter. Depending on the subdirectory name used on your classroom computer, you probably type **cd\wp51** or **cd\wp**.
6. Type **wp** and press ⏎Enter.

   You should see the opening screen for a few seconds, and then the editing screen appears (see fig. 1.1).

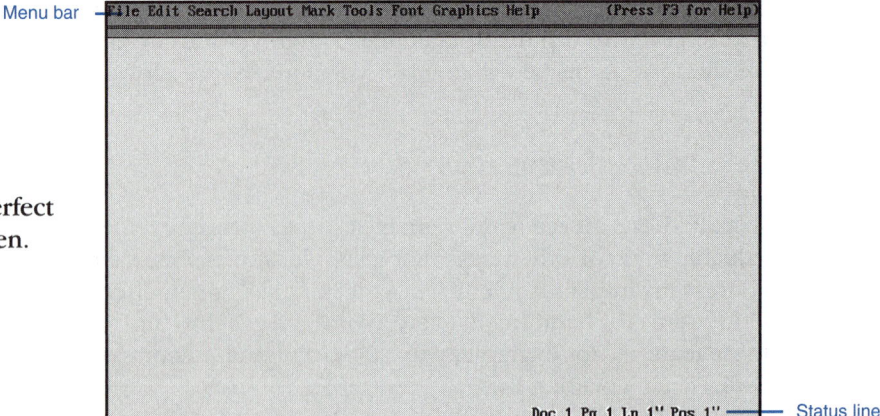

Menu bar → File Edit Search Layout Mark Tools Font Graphics Help   (Press F3 for Help)

Fig. 1.1
The WordPerfect editing screen.

Doc 1 Pg 1 Ln 1" Pos 1" —— Status line

To Start WordPerfect

Note: If you start WordPerfect and the power fails, the following prompt appears at the bottom of the screen when you restart the program:

```
Are other copies of WordPerfect currently running? (Y/N)
```

Press N in response to this prompt.

Exercise 1.2: Starting WordPerfect on a Dual-Floppy System

Follow these steps to start WordPerfect on a dual-floppy disk system:

1. Insert the DOS disk into drive A. Be sure to close the disk drive door every time you insert a disk into a floppy drive.
2. Turn on your computer.
3. If necessary, respond to the prompts for date and time.
4. Insert your working copy of the Program 1 disk into drive A.

    Note: If you are using an IBM Personal System/2 computer, the main program files are combined on one 3 1/2-inch disk labeled Program 1.

5. Insert a formatted data disk into drive B and close the drive door.
6. When the A:\> prompt appears, type **b:** and press [Enter].

    Drive B is now the default drive, which means that any data you save to disk is saved to the disk in drive B.

7. Type **a:wp**, and press [Enter].

    WordPerfect's opening screen appears. This screen contains WordPerfect copyright information, the version number of your copy, and an indication of the default directory used by the operating system.

    WordPerfect prompts you to insert the Program 2 disk.

8. Remove your working copy of the Program 1 disk from drive A, and insert your working copy of the Program 2 disk into drive A.
9. Press any key. The editing screen appears (refer to fig. 1.1).

Objective 2: To Get Acquainted with WordPerfect's Keyboard, Mouse, and Menus

Before you begin to use WordPerfect, you should take a few minutes to become familiar with WordPerfect's screen display, keyboard, mouse, and menus.

Understanding the Editing Screen

Look again at figure 1.1, which shows WordPerfect's editing screen. Notice that the entire screen is available for typing text. Before typing anything, however, it is important for you to become familiar with the menu bar across the top of the screen and the status line in the lower right corner of the screen. If your screen does not display the menu bar, you can change the screen display by using the Se**t**up command on the **F**ile menu.

You can access the menu bar with a mouse or with the Alt key. Later in this chapter, you learn more about the menus.

At the bottom of the screen is the *status line*, which contains the following information, which describes the cursor's status:

- Doc indicates which of two available documents is currently displayed on-screen. WordPerfect is capable of holding two documents in memory simultaneously. The documents are identified as Doc 1 and Doc 2.

- Pg identifies the number of the page on which the cursor is currently located.

- Ln indicates the cursor's vertical position in inches (the default) from the top edge of the paper.

- Pos tells you the cursor's horizontal position in inches (the default) from the left edge of the paper. You can change this unit of measurement. The Pos indicator appears in uppercase letters (POS) if the Caps Lock key is activated for typing in uppercase. When the Pos indicator blinks, the Num Lock key is activated so that you can use the numeric keypad to type numbers. When you move the cursor through boldfaced, underlined, or double-underlined text, the Pos indicator number reflects the enhancement of the text.

To Get Acquainted with WordPerfect's Keyboard, Mouse, and Menus

Status line information appears only on-screen; the information does not appear in the printed document.

Note: Through the Setup menu, you can customize many aspects of WordPerfect's screen display. For example, you can change the appearance and color of normal text (if you have a color monitor), specify whether the current file name is displayed on the status line, change the way menu-letter options are displayed on-screen (such as change **E**dit to E**d**it), and specify whether comments are displayed or hidden.

Using the Keyboard

WordPerfect uses the following main areas of the keyboard (see fig. 1.2):

- The function keys, labeled F1 through F12 at the top of the IBM enhanced keyboard.
- The alphanumeric, or "typing," keys, located in the center of the keyboard. (These keys are most familiar to you from your experience with typewriter keyboards.)
- The numeric and cursor-movement keys, found at the right side of the keyboard.

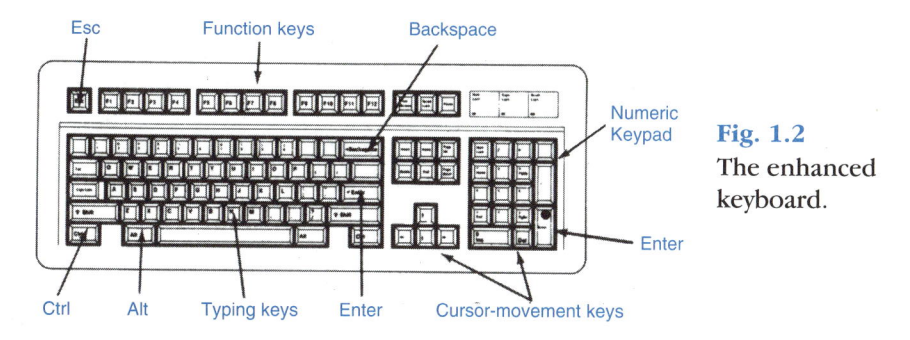

Fig. 1.2
The enhanced keyboard.

Function Keys

The WordPerfect function-key template offers commands at a glance and is located above the function keys of your keyboard. The template illustrates how you can use each function key to carry out four tasks when you use it by itself or in combination with another key. You routinely use the function keys to give instructions, or *commands*, to your computer. To activate a WordPerfect command, you press a function key alone or in combination with the Ctrl, Shift, or Alt key.

11

Getting Started

Note: The IBM enhanced keyboard has 12 function keys. If your keyboard has only 10 function keys, you still can use all of WordPerfect's commands.

Some function keys are *toggle switches*, which you use to turn a feature on and off. To create boldfaced text, for example, first press [F6] (to turn on Bold), and then type the text you want printed in boldface. When you are finished typing the text you want to be boldfaced, you turn off Bold by pressing [F6] again.

When you press some of the function keys, menus appear on-screen. When you press [Ctrl]+[F8], for example, your system displays the Font menu.

Other function keys start a feature that you stop by pressing [↵Enter]. You begin the Center feature, for example, by pressing [⇧Shift]+[F6], and you end centering by pressing [↵Enter].

Notice in figure 1.3 the four commands above each function key. The [F2] key (in this example), alone and in combination with [Ctrl], [Alt], and [⇧Shift], activates four commands. Compare this diagram to your template, and press the key combinations. Some companies place colored dots on each key to correspond to the template, making the functions easier for their employees to remember.

Fig. 1.3
Using a single function key for four commands.

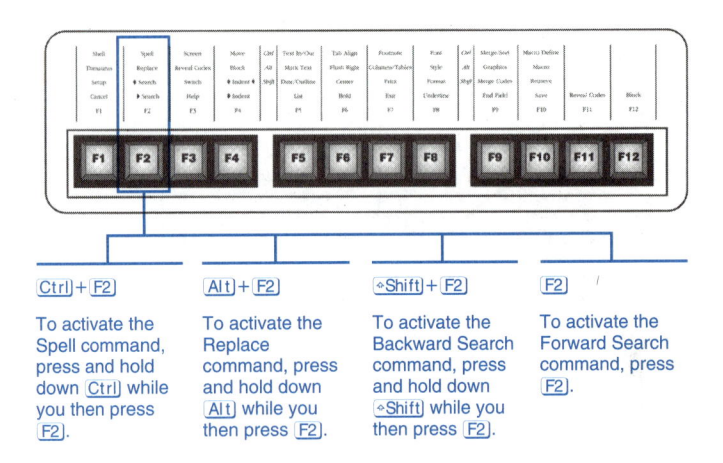

[Ctrl]+[F2]
To activate the Spell command, press and hold down [Ctrl] while you then press [F2].

[Alt]+[F2]
To activate the Replace command, press and hold down [Alt] while you then press [F2].

[⇧Shift]+[F2]
To activate the Backward Search command, press and hold down [⇧Shift] while you then press [F2].

[F2]
To activate the Forward Search command, press [F2].

Note: The commands assigned to the function keys when you first start WordPerfect are the default definitions for those keys. WordPerfect gives you the option of switching to other keyboard definitions so that the keys on your keyboard—the function keys as well as other keys—perform different commands or functions. You also can customize your keyboard by assigning alternative definitions to specified keys. In addition, you can display a map of

To Get Acquainted with WordPerfect's Keyboard, Mouse, and Menus

any user-defined keyboard. To access WordPerfect's feature for alternative keyboard definitions, use the **K**eyboard Layout option on the Se**t**up menu.

Alphanumeric Keys

The alphanumeric keys work similarly to those on a typewriter. Keep in mind a critical but easily overlooked difference between composing with a typewriter and composing with WordPerfect: When you type regular text in WordPerfect, you do not need to press the [⏎Enter] key to end lines at the right margin. When you type text and reach the end of a line, the text "wraps" automatically to the next line (called *word wrap*). You do press [⏎Enter] at the end of a paragraph.

You can use the [⏎Enter] key as a carriage return. You press [⏎Enter] to insert blank lines into your text, such as the lines that separate paragraphs. You also can use [⏎Enter] to initiate some commands in WordPerfect.

Cursor-Movement Keys

The *cursor* is the blinking underline character that marks the location on-screen where the next character you type will appear. In addition, the cursor indicates where codes will be entered (such as those used to create new margin settings).

You use the keys marked with arrows at the far right of the keyboard to control cursor movement. (All keyboards have arrow keys on the numeric keypad, and enhanced keyboards have a separate set of arrow keys between the typing keys and the numeric keypad.) When you press an arrow key, the cursor moves in the direction indicated by the arrow on that key.

If you try to use an arrow key to move the cursor on a blank screen, nothing happens. WordPerfect doesn't permit the cursor to move where nothing exists. The cursor moves only through text, spaces, or codes.

Using the Mouse

WordPerfect 5.1 supports a mouse, but you don't need a mouse to use the program. Even if you have a mouse, you may decide that you don't want to use it with WordPerfect. You use the mouse for two main purposes: to make choices in most menus, including the pull-down menus, and to mark text so that you can perform a block action (such as deleting or moving text) or make a modification (such as underlining or centering text).

Getting Started

The mouse you are using has two or three buttons; you can use either kind of mouse with WordPerfect (see fig. 1.4).

Fig. 1.4
You can use a two-button or a three-button mouse with WordPerfect.

You use mouse buttons in four basic ways:

- You can press and then quickly release a button (*clicking*).
- You can quickly press and release the button twice (*double-clicking*).
- You can press and hold down a button and then move the mouse (*dragging*).
- You can press and hold down one button while you click another button.

Although you can position the mouse pointer (a *block cursor*) in blank areas of the screen, where no text or codes exist, clicking a blank area places the mouse pointer at the last text character or code.

Using Help

WordPerfect has an on-line Help feature that you can access while working on WordPerfect documents. The screens in the Help system can help you learn more about WordPerfect commands and keys. When you press F3, at the edit screen, another screen appears, directing you to other help screens. If you activate a command and then press F3, you get help on the specific command. To return to the document, press the space bar.

Objective 3: To Change the Default Directory

Before typing any document, you should designate the directory where you want to save the document. This step eliminates having to type the drive, directory, and file name each time. Changing the default directory requires that you type only the file name.

Exercise 3.1: Changing the Default Directory

To change the default directory, follow these steps:

1. Press `F5`.
2. Press the equal sign (`=`).
3. Type the new drive and directory and then press `↵Enter`. For example, you can type **a:** or **c:\wp51\data**.
4. Press `↵Enter` twice.
5. Press `F7` to save and exit to the document screen.

Objective 4: To Create a Document

With a word processor, you can get words on-screen as fast as you can type them. In a short time, you will realize that putting words on-screen can be far easier than putting them on paper. WordPerfect doesn't think or plan for you, of course, but it certainly simplifies self-expression.

At any stage of the writing process, you easily can revise your words on-screen. With a word processor, you can freely alter what you write; you can insert new words, delete ones you don't want, and move up and down through a document to see what you have written. Because you can alter text so effortlessly, you can focus first on getting words on-screen; you can edit, revise, and format the text later. You can leave spelling errors for WordPerfect's Speller to catch.

Getting Started

1

Understanding WordPerfect's Built-In Settings

Before you even put fingers to keys and begin typing, WordPerfect has been at work for you. You will recall from your experience with a typewriter that you must do some formatting—for example, set margins, line spacing, and tabs—before you begin composing. With WordPerfect, you don't need to make any formatting decisions before you begin unless the preset values do not suit you.

WordPerfect comes with a number of default settings—for margins, tab settings, base font (basic character style), line spacing, and other features (see fig. 1.5). Note that WordPerfect does not include page numbering as a default, nor does the program automatically use hyphenation. You should be familiar with the basic default settings before you begin writing. Subsequent chapters, especially those devoted to formatting and printing, offer many ways you can alter the look of a document.

Note: Through the Initial Settings option on the Setup menu, you can change a number of WordPerfect's built-in settings. For example, you can change the formatting specifications for all future documents, change the date format, and change the default repeat value (the number of times a character is repeated when you press Esc).

Exercise 4.1: Entering Text

1. Begin typing the document in figure 1.5 in WordPerfect.

    After you type a few words, look at the Pos indicator on the status line. This value increases as you type and as the cursor moves horizontally across the line to the right. WordPerfect doesn't require you to press ↵Enter to end a line, but inserts a soft return at the end of each line and wraps the text to the beginning of the next line. This feature is called *word wrap*.

2. To end a paragraph or to insert blank lines into the text, press ↵Enter . When you come to the end of the last sentence in the first paragraph, press ↵Enter . WordPerfect inserts a hard return.

3. Press ↵Enter again, and WordPerfect inserts another hard return, creating a blank line in the text.

4. Finish typing the document, but don't be concerned with spelling or typing errors at this point.

To Create a Document

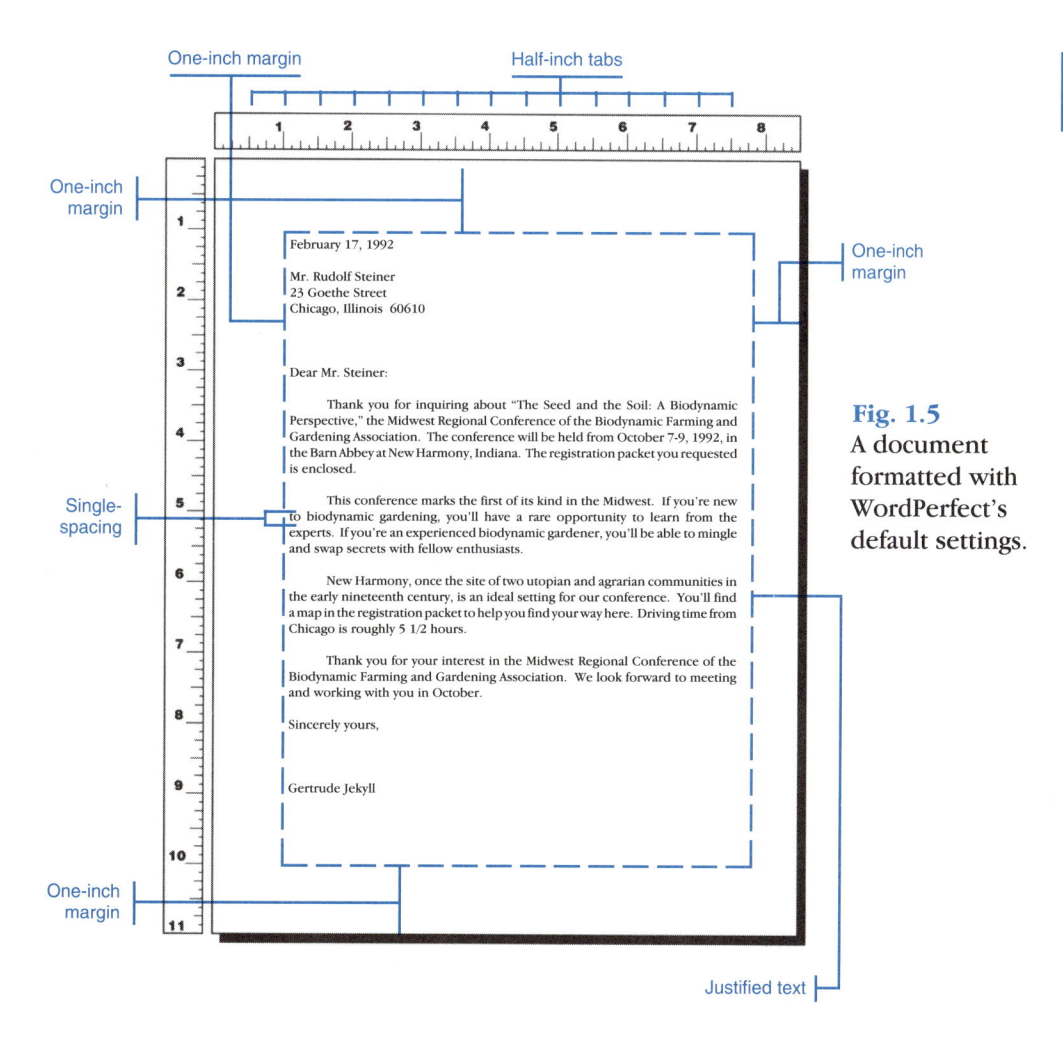

Fig. 1.5
A document formatted with WordPerfect's default settings.

(Figure shows a page with labels: One-inch margin, Half-inch tabs, One-inch margin, Single-spacing, One-inch margin, Justified text. Sample letter contents:)

February 17, 1992

Mr. Rudolf Steiner
23 Goethe Street
Chicago, Illinois 60610

Dear Mr. Steiner:

Thank you for inquiring about "The Seed and the Soil: A Biodynamic Perspective," the Midwest Regional Conference of the Biodynamic Farming and Gardening Association. The conference will be held from October 7-9, 1992, in the Barn Abbey at New Harmony, Indiana. The registration packet you requested is enclosed.

This conference marks the first of its kind in the Midwest. If you're new to biodynamic gardening, you'll have a rare opportunity to learn from the experts. If you're an experienced biodynamic gardener, you'll be able to mingle and swap secrets with fellow enthusiasts.

New Harmony, once the site of two utopian and agrarian communities in the early nineteenth century, is an ideal setting for our conference. You'll find a map in the registration packet to help you find your way here. Driving time from Chicago is roughly 5 1/2 hours.

Thank you for your interest in the Midwest Regional Conference of the Biodynamic Farming and Gardening Association. We look forward to meeting and working with you in October.

Sincerely yours,

Gertrude Jekyll

Moving the Cursor

You move the cursor through text in WordPerfect by using the keyboard or the mouse. Keep in mind that WordPerfect does not allow the cursor to move where nothing exists. The cursor moves only through text, spaces, or codes.

Moving the Cursor with the Keyboard

You can move the cursor through a document with the up- (↑), down- (↓), left- (←), and right-arrow (→) keys; (PgUp), (PgDn); GoTo ((Ctrl)+(Home)); and (Esc)

Getting Started

(the Repeat key). Use the right-arrow key to move across the screen, noticing the `Pos` indicator. You use these keys or special combinations of the keys to move more efficiently through a document.

Using the Arrow Keys

Use the keys marked with arrows to control cursor movement. When you press an arrow key, the cursor moves in the direction indicated by the arrow on that key. Table 1.1 summarizes the actions of the arrow keys.

Table 1.1	The WordPerfect Arrow Keys
Key	*Function*
↑	Moves the cursor up one line
↓	Moves the cursor down one line; when you press this key to move the cursor down through the text, the text is automatically reformatted.
←	Moves the cursor one position to the left
→	Moves the cursor one position to the right
Ctrl+→	Moves the cursor one word to the right
Ctrl+←	Moves the cursor one word to the left
Home, →, or End	Moves the cursor to the right end of the line
Home, ←	Moves the cursor to the left edge of the screen
Home, Home, ↑	Moves the cursor to the top of the document
Home, Home, ↓	Moves the cursor to the bottom of the document
Ctrl+↑	Moves the cursor up one paragraph
Ctrl+↓	Moves the cursor down one paragraph

Exercise 4.2: Moving around in Your Document

WordPerfect provides other keys for moving through a document. Use the document you created in Exercise 3.1, and follow these steps:

1. Press `PgDn` and then `PgUp` to move the cursor to the top of the next page and then to the top of the preceding page. When you press either of these keys, the message `Repositioning` appears on the status line. If no additional page exists, the cursor moves to the bottom of the current page.

2. Press `+` or `Home`, `↓` to move the cursor to the bottom of the screen or to the next screen.

   Note: Be sure to use `-` and `+` on the numeric keypad, not the keys at the top of the keyboard.

3. Press `-` or `Home`, `↑` to move the cursor to the top of the screen or to the preceding screen.

Exercise 4.3: Using the GoTo Key

You use GoTo (`Ctrl`+`Home`) with other keys to move to a specific page or character in a document. You also can use GoTo to move to the top or bottom of the page.

Follow these steps to practice using GoTo:

1. To move to a specific page in the document, press `Ctrl`+`Home`, type a page number, and press `↵Enter`. Type **1** as the page number, and the cursor moves to the top of the page.
2. To move to a specific character in the document, press `Ctrl`+`Home` and then the character (nonnumeric).
3. To move to the top of the page, press `Ctrl`+`Home`, `↑`.
4. To move to the bottom of the page, press `Ctrl`+`Home`, `↓`.
5. To return to the cursor's original position, press `Ctrl`+`Home` twice.

Exercise 4.4: Using the Repeat Key

You use `Esc` (the Repeat key) to repeat an operation a given number of times. You can use `Esc` to move the cursor any number of characters (right or left), any number of words (right or left), any number of lines (up or down), any number of paragraphs (up or down), or any number of pages (forward or backward).

Getting Started

Usually, the number of repeats is eight; that is, WordPerfect repeats eight times. But you can change this repeat value. Follow these steps:

1. Place the cursor at the top of the document. Press `Esc`.
2. Type the number of repetitions, and then press the key you want to repeat. For this exercise, press `Esc`, type **15**, and press `↓`. The cursor moves down 15 lines.
3. To move the cursor *n* characters to the right or left, press `Esc`, enter the number of characters (*n*), and press `→` or `←`. (Note that the default number of characters is eight.)
4. To move the cursor right or left *n* words, press `Esc`, enter the number of words, and press `Ctrl`+`→` or `Ctrl`+`←`.
5. To move the cursor down or up *n* lines, press `Esc`, enter the number of lines, and press `↓` or `↑`.

Some keys on the keyboard automatically repeat when you hold down the key. Many other WordPerfect features can be repeated only with the aid of the `Esc` key.

You can use the following keys or features with the repeat value or by holding down the keys:

- Cursor-movement keys
- `Del`, Delete to End of Line, Delete to End of Page, and Delete Word (explained in Chapter 2)
- `PgUp` and `PgDn`
- Screen Up (`-` on the numeric keypad) and Screen Down (`+` on the numeric keypad)—available with Num Lock turned off
- Word Left and Word Right
- Paragraph Up and Paragraph Down

Moving the Cursor with the Mouse

You can use the mouse to position the cursor anywhere on the screen by placing the mouse pointer at a specific spot and clicking the left button. Dragging the mouse (pressing and holding down the left button while you move the mouse) enables you to scroll the text up, down, left, or right to see more of the text on-screen. You cannot move the cursor through "dead space" (space with no text or codes) beyond where you stopped typing. If you place the mouse pointer in dead space and click the left button, the cursor moves to the nearest text.

Exercise 4.5: Using the Mouse

To practice moving the cursor by using the mouse, follow these steps:

1. To move the cursor one character to the left, place the mouse pointer one space left of the cursor location, and click the left button.
2. To move the cursor one character to the right, place the mouse pointer one space right of the cursor location, and click the left button.
3. To move the cursor to another word, place the mouse pointer anywhere in the word to which you want to move, and click the left button.
4. To move the cursor up or down a line, place the mouse pointer on the line to which you want to move, and click the left button.

You also can scroll line-by-line through a document. Follow these steps:

1. To scroll up, place the mouse pointer anywhere in the top line.
2. Press and hold down the right button, and drag the mouse to move the pointer upward.
3. To scroll down line-by-line through a document, place the mouse pointer at the bottom of the screen.
4. Press and hold down the right button.

Scrolling stops when you reach the top or bottom of the document.

You can scroll left or right to see text not visible on-screen by holding down the right button and dragging the mouse to the left or right edge of the screen. Scrolling stops when you reach the beginning or end of the line.

Making a Menu Selection

WordPerfect uses three types of menus: one-line menus, full-screen menus, and pull-down menus. Many times when you press a function key or function-key combination, a one-line menu appears at the bottom of the screen. Other commands in WordPerfect display full-screen menus. WordPerfect's pull-down menus provide an alternative method of accessing most of the same commands you can activate from the one-line or full-screen menus.

Using the One-Line and Full-Screen Menus

You can make a selection from a one-line or full-screen menu in any of three ways:

Getting Started

- Press the highlighted letter in the name of the menu option.
- Press the number or letter that appears to the left of the menu option.
- Place the mouse pointer on the option, and click the left mouse button.

For example, press ⇧Shift+F8 to display the Format menu (see fig. 1.6). To choose **Line** (**1**), use any of these techniques:

- Press L.
- Press 1.
- Click the **Line** (**1**) selection.

```
Format
    1 - Line
            Hyphenation                 Line Spacing
            Justification               Margins Left/Right
            Line Height                 Tab Set
            Line Numbering              Widow/Orphan Protection

    2 - Page
            Center Page (top to bottom) Page Numbering
            Force Odd/Even Page         Paper Size/Type/Labels
            Headers and Footers         Suppress
            Margins Top/Bottom

    3 - Document
            Display Pitch               Redline Method
            Initial Codes/Font          Summary

    4 - Other
            Advance                     Printer Functions
            Conditional End of Page     Underline Spaces/Tabs
            Decimal Characters          Border Options
            Language                    End Centering/Alignment
            Overstrike
Selection: 0
```

Fig. 1.6
The Format menu.

After you choose **Line** (**1**), the Format: Line menu appears (see fig. 1.7). From this menu, you can choose other options, such as **Margins** (**7**), the option for adjusting the margin settings.

```
Format: Line
    1 - Hyphenation                         No

    2 - Hyphenation Zone - Left             10%
                           Right            4%

    3 - Justification                       Full

    4 - Line Height                         Auto

    5 - Line Numbering                      No

    6 - Line Spacing                        1

    7 - Margins - Left                      1"
                  Right                     1"

    8 - Tab Set                             Rel; -1", every 0.5"

    9 - Widow/Orphan Protection             No


Selection: 0
```

Fig. 1.7
The Format: Line menu.

To Create a Document

If you change your mind and want to back out of a menu selection from a one-line or full-screen menu, press Exit (F7). If you have a mouse, you can back out of a menu by clicking the right mouse button. Pressing Esc in WordPerfect does not exit any menu choice.

Using Pull-Down Menus

Pull-down menus provide an alternative to using the function keys to access WordPerfect menus. The pull-down menus, which group commands according to major categories of functions, make it easier for the occasional or new user to become familiar and productive with WordPerfect. For those who prefer to activate commands with the mouse instead of the keyboard, you can easily access the pull-down menus with the mouse.

The menu bar across the top of the screen offers nine main choices. Each menu choice leads to a pull-down menu. Some of the options on pull-down menus lead to other options, which are displayed in *pop-out menus*. If a menu option leads to a pop-out menu, an arrow appears to the right of the option. If a menu option appears in brackets, it is not available for selection at this time. The **File** pull-down menu, for example, includes the Setup option, which leads to the Setup pop-out menu (see fig. 1.8).

Fig. 1.8
The File pull-down menu and the Setup pop-out menu.

WordPerfect uses pull-down menus as a gateway to the regular menu system. If you want to print a document, for example, you can use the function-key combination for Print (⇧Shift+F7) to access the Print screen, from which you make your printing selection. Alternatively, you can choose **P**rint from the pull-down **F**ile menu to access the same Print screen.

Because you can make so many selections with either the familiar function keys or the pull-down menus, this book includes instructions for both methods. The book's emphasis, however, is on the function-key approach. Each

23

Getting Started

time you see steps describing a procedure, the pull-down alternative, if available, is described after the function-key procedure. Even though you can access the pull-down menus without using a mouse, a mouse icon 🖱 will remind you that the procedure described uses the pull-down menus.

Exercise 4.6: Accessing Pull-Down Menus

You can access the pull-down menus in either of two ways:

- If you have a mouse, click the right button, and the menu bar (if not already permanently visible) appears at the top of the screen.
- If you don't have a mouse (or don't want to use it), press Alt + =.

After you have activated the menu bar, you can make choices with the mouse or the keyboard. To make a selection from a menu when you're using a mouse, follow these steps:

1. Move the mouse pointer to the name of the menu that you want in the menu bar.
2. Click the left mouse button, and the pull-down menu appears.

To make a selection from a menu if you're using the keyboard, follow these steps:

1. Press the highlighted letter for your menu choice.

   As an alternative to pressing the highlighted letter, you can use the arrow keys; the right- and left-arrow keys move across the menu bar, whereas the up- and down-arrow keys highlight the menu selections.

2. After you have highlighted your choice, press ↵Enter to choose it.

If you change your mind, you can back out of the pull-down menus one level at a time by pressing Esc, Cancel (F1), or the space bar. To back out of all the menus at once and to remove the menu bar from the screen, press Exit (F7). If you are using a mouse, you can click the right button to exit; if some of the menus have been pulled down, clicking either button outside a menu also enables you to exit.

Note: One way you can customize the WordPerfect screen display is by making the pull-down menu bar visible at all times. From the Setup menu, you can choose to display the menu bar permanently, as well as display a separating line between the menu bar and the rest of the editing screen.

Accessing the pull-down menus is easier if you use the mouse rather than the keyboard. You can easily choose items from pull-down menus by moving the mouse and clicking the left button. Initially, moving the mouse makes the

To Create a Document

mouse pointer appear on-screen; further movements produce corresponding on-screen movements of the mouse pointer, enabling you to make menu selections and text blocks. Pressing any key makes the mouse pointer disappear.

When the pull-down menu bar is displayed, you can use the left mouse button to perform the following tasks:

- Make visible the menu items for one of the nine menu bar choices by either clicking the choice you want or dragging the mouse pointer across the pull-down menu bar.
- Choose a menu item by clicking it.
- Highlight each choice within a pull-down menu by dragging the mouse pointer down the menu. If you highlight a menu item that has a pop-out menu, the menu pops out. You then can drag down that menu to highlight your choice. Release the mouse button to choose the highlighted option.

From the editing screen, you can use the right mouse button to manage the pull-down menus as follows:

- If you have turned on Assisted Mouse Pointer Movement from the Setup menu and if the menu bar is not permanently visible, clicking the right mouse button makes the menu bar appear and places the mouse pointer on the **File** menu name on the menu bar.

Using the Cancel Command

The Cancel command (F1)—the "oops" key) enables you to perform these tasks:

- Back out of a menu without making a selection
- Restore text you have deleted

When you press Cancel (F1) to back out of a menu, the most recent command is canceled, and you are returned to either the preceding menu or your document. When you press Cancel to restore text, WordPerfect enables you to retrieve the last three items you deleted. An *item* in this case means the characters (letters, numbers, or punctuation) deleted before you moved the cursor. Cancel always acts as an "undelete" key when a menu is not visible.

Pressing more than one button on the mouse has the same effect as pressing Cancel (F1). On a two-button mouse, holding down one button while clicking the other button is the same as pressing Cancel. On a three-button mouse, clicking the middle button is the same as pressing Cancel.

Getting Started

Backing Out of a Menu

With one-line and full-screen menus, WordPerfect disregards your selections if you leave the menu by pressing Cancel (F1). These menus display a message that instructs you to leave the menu by pressing Exit (F7) if you want to save your selections in memory.

You can press Cancel (F1) to return to a preceding one-line or full-screen menu without making a choice from the current menu. When there is no preceding menu to which to return, you are returned to the current document.

Pressing Cancel (F1), Esc, or the space bar enables you to back out of the pull-down menus one level at a time. To back out of all the pull-down menus at once and remove the menu bar from the screen, press Exit (F7). With the mouse, you can click the right button to exit; if some of the menus have been pulled down, clicking either button outside a menu also enables you to exit.

Objective 5: To Preview and Print a Document

After a document is typed, you will want to view and print the document. Use the View Document feature to preview a document before printing it. You save costly printer paper and time by first previewing your document, making changes if needed, and then printing the document when you are certain that it's perfect. You learn more about the View Document feature in Chapter 6.

Exercise 5.1: Previewing a Document

To preview a document, follow these steps:

1. Display on-screen the document you want to preview.
2. Position the cursor anywhere on the page you want to view.
3. Press Shift+F7 to activate the Print command.
    - Alternatively, choose Print on the File menu.
4. From the Print menu that appears, choose View Document (6).

5. Choose 200% (2) to view the document at twice its actual size.
6. Press F7 (Exit) to return to the regular editing screen.

You can press PgUp, PgDn, or GoTo (Ctrl+Home) to view other pages of the document. Note that you cannot edit the previewed version of a document.

Exercise 5.2: Printing a Document

With WordPerfect, you can be flexible about printing. You may not want or need to save every document to disk. If you do not want to save a document, WordPerfect still enables you to print the document without requiring you to save it to disk first. Printing in this manner is called *making a screen print*, because you print what has been created on-screen and then stored in temporary memory (also known as random-access memory, or RAM).

To print the on-screen document, follow these steps:

1. Press ⇧Shift+F7 to activate the Print command.

    Access the File pull-down menu and choose Print.

    The Print menu appears (see fig. 1.9).

```
Print
        1 - Full Document
        2 - Page
        3 - Document on Disk
        4 - Control Printer
        5 - Multiple Pages
        6 - View Document
        7 - Initialize Printer

Options
        S - Select Printer              HP LaserJet III
        B - Binding Offset              0"
        N - Number of Copies            1
        U - Multiple Copies Generated by WordPerfect
        G - Graphics Quality            Medium
        T - Text Quality                High




Selection: 0
```

Fig. 1.9
The Print menu.

2. To print more than one page, choose Full Document (1). To print a single page or less, choose Page (2).

Getting Started

WordPerfect displays a * Please wait * message on the status line as the program prepares to print the text. If the printer is properly configured and hooked up, printing should begin almost immediately.

A document does not have to be on-screen for you to print it. With WordPerfect, you can print any number of documents stored on disk (floppy or hard). You can even have documents in both windows and print a document stored on disk. The various ways of printing and managing print jobs are discussed in Chapter 7, but you know enough now to make a quick print of the text on-screen.

Objective 6: To Save, Exit, and Clear a Document

What you see on-screen is a temporary display; only the documents you transfer to disk storage are secured for future use. Usually, you keep copies on disk of the documents you create. As a rule, you should save your work every 10 or 15 minutes. Use either of two methods to save a document to disk: (1) Save the document with the Save (F10) command and remain in WordPerfect, or (2) save the document with the Exit (F7) command and either clear the screen or exit WordPerfect. Keep in mind that before you can work on a new document or before you can retrieve a document, you must clear the current document from the screen.

When you save a document, you must give it a name. A *file name* consists of a root name of one to eight characters, followed by an optional extension of one to three characters. If you use an extension, you must separate it from the root name by a period (.). When you name a file, you must observe the file-naming guidelines of your operating system (MS-DOS or PC DOS). After you name and save a file, the file name appears on the left side of the status line. You should choose a file name that is descriptive of the file's contents. Table 1.2 shows some valid and invalid file names.

Note: WordPerfect offers two automatic back-up features through the Environment option on the Setup menu: Timed Document Backup and Original Document Backup. With the Timed Document Backup option, at specified intervals WordPerfect automatically saves to disk the document displayed on-screen. With the Original Document Backup option, WordPerfect saves both the original file and the edited version.

To Save, Exit, and Clear a Document

Table 1.2 Naming a File

Valid	Invalid	Reason
FILENAME	FILENAMES	The name has too many characters. WordPerfect will shorten the name to FILENAME.
A	"A"	You cannot use quotation marks in a file name.
1-23-89	1/23/89	/ is not an acceptable character.
december.90	december,90	A comma cannot be used in a file name.
ASSETS.DOC	ASSETS.FILE	The extension is too long. WordPerfect will shorten the name to ASSETS.FIL.
REPORT.NEW	REPORTNEW	The period before the extension is missing. WordPerfect will shorten the name to REPORTNE.
DEC_90	DEC 90	Spaces are not allowed in file names. WordPerfect will shorten the name to DEC.

Exercise 6.1: Saving a Document to Disk and Remaining in WordPerfect

The first time you save a document, WordPerfect prompts you for a file name. Suppose that you have created a document and you now want to save the file. With the document on-screen, follow these steps:

1. Press F10 to activate the Save command.

    Access the File pull-down menu and choose Save.

Getting Started

The following prompt appears on the status line:

```
Document to be saved:
```

2. Type a file name for the document, and press ⏎Enter. Be sure to have a blank formatted disk in drive A or B. For this exercise, to save to a floppy disk, type **a:letter** or **b:letter**, as appropriate for the disk drive you are using, and press ⏎Enter.

   To save to the hard drive in the subdirectory \WP51\DATA, type **c:\wp51\data\letter**.

The document remains on-screen, and you can continue working.

WordPerfect responds a bit differently when you want to save a file that you have saved before. When you press Save (F10) or choose **S**ave from the **F**ile pull-down menu, WordPerfect asks whether you want to replace the file on disk. If you have saved a document called REPORT.TXT, for example, WordPerfect displays a prompt similar to the following:

```
Document to be saved: C:\WP51\BOOK\REPORT.TXT
```

If you want to keep this same file name for the new version of the document, press ⏎Enter. WordPerfect then displays the following prompt:

```
Replace C:\WP51\BOOK\REPORT.TXT? No (Yes)
```

Choose **Y**es to replace the previous version with the new version (press Y if you are using the keyboard). Otherwise, choose **N**o (press N on the keyboard), rename the file, and save it under a different name. If you want to save the document on-screen under a different file name, use the right-arrow key to move the cursor to the previous file name and change it accordingly. You can change any of the information following the `Document to be saved` prompt.

Exercise 6.2: Saving a Document to Disk and Exiting WordPerfect

If you want to save a document to disk and exit WordPerfect, follow these steps:

1. Press F7 to activate the Exit command.

   🖱 Access the **F**ile pull-down menu and choose E**x**it.

   WordPerfect displays the following prompt:

   ```
   Save document? Yes (No)
   ```

2. To begin the saving process, choose **Y**es.

WordPerfect then displays this prompt:

    Document to be saved:

A:letter or B:letter should appear.

3. Press `⏎Enter`.

4. If the document already exists, WordPerfect presents the following prompt:

    Replace A:letter or B:letter? No (Yes)

   Choose **Y**es to save the document with the old name. If you don't want to save it with the old name, choose **N**o, type a new file name, and press `⏎Enter`. The document is stored to disk under the name you select.

   The following message appears:

    Exit WP? No (Yes)

5. Choose **N**o to return to the WordPerfect editing screen, or choose **Y**es to exit WordPerfect and return to DOS.

Exercise 6.3: Clearing the Screen

You must clear the current document from the screen before you start work on a new document or retrieve a document. To clear the screen without saving the current document, you can press Exit (`F7`) or choose the Exit option from the File pull-down menu. Clearing the screen without saving your document is handy when you decide to discard what you have written. If you do not clear the current document before starting a new document or before retrieving a document from memory, the old and the new documents merge to form a continuous (and confusing) document.

If you don't want to save the document you have created, or if you have saved the document previously but you want to clear the screen, follow these steps:

1. Press `F7` to activate the Exit command.

   🖱 Access the File pull-down menu and choose Exit.

2. At the prompt Save Document? Yes (No), choose **N**o.

   The following prompt then appears:

    Exit WP? No (Yes)

3. In response to the prompt, choose **N**o or press `⏎Enter` to clear the screen and stay in WordPerfect. If you press `F1` (Cancel) instead, you are returned to the document displayed on-screen.

Getting Started

Chapter Summary

In this chapter, you received an introduction to the word processing features available in WordPerfect. The program's basic features are convenient and efficient for creating, editing, formatting, and printing documents. WordPerfect's specialized features, addressed in other chapters, give you a full range of tools for further supplementing your documents with elements such as spell checking and graphics.

You also learned how to start the program on a hard disk system and on a dual floppy-disk system. You became familiar with the editing screen, from which you perform most of your work in WordPerfect. You learned how to use the keyboard and mouse, access the Help feature, type text, move the cursor, and make a menu selection. You also learned about WordPerfect's built-in settings that help you begin to create documents quickly. Finally, you learned how to print and save your work, and how to exit the document and the program.

In the next chapter, you examine WordPerfect's features for editing a document. You learn, for example, how to retrieve files you have saved to disk, to insert and delete text in those files, and to restore the deleted text.

Testing Your Knowledge

True/False Questions

1. The status line on the editing screen describes the cursor's status.
2. Each function key can accomplish at least three tasks.
3. Pressing `Enter` at the end of each line of text typed is designated by a hard return code.
4. Pop-up menus are available through pull-down menus in WordPerfect.
5. Viewing a document prints the document to disk.

Multiple Choice Questions

1. LN on the status line indicates
    A. the horizontal position of the cursor.
    B. the vertical position in inches from the top edge of the paper.
    C. the page number.
    D. the document number.
2. When you press [Ctrl]+[F2] on the keyboard,
    A. you activate the Format menu.
    B. you activate the Spell Check menu.
    C. you activate the Cancel command.
    D. you activate the Setup menu.
3. Default settings for each document are
    A. one-inch left and right margins.
    B. single-spacing.
    C. one-inch top and bottom margins.
    D. all of the above.
4. Previewing a document does *not* enable you to
    A. save costly printer paper and time.
    B. edit the document.
    C. view the document at twice its actual size.
    D. view other pages of the document.
5. An acceptable file name is
    A. PRICES.NEW.
    B. DETAILS.FIRST.
    C. JAN 93.
    D. DESCRIPTION.

Fill-in-the-Blank Questions

1. The number of the page where the cursor is currently located is designated by_____ in the cursor line.
2. To activate a WordPerfect command, you press a_____ key alone or in combination with the [Ctrl], [Shift], or [Alt] keys.

Getting Started

3. When typing text in WordPerfect, the _____ feature enables text to move to the next line automatically.

4. If you press ⇧Shift + F7 and then press V, you will _____ a document.

5. To save and exit WordPerfect, press _____.

Review: Short Projects

1. Type and Print Text

   Start WordPerfect, and type your name, street address, city, state, and ZIP code.

   Print the document.

   Clear the screen without saving the text.

2. Work with the Editing Screen

   Type **Harry Truman**, beginning in horizontal position 3.24 inches and line position 3.14.

   Type **Abraham Lincoln**, beginning in horizontal position 2.03 inches and line position 5.27.

   Print the document, and exit without saving.

3. Preview, Print, Save, and Exit

   Type the following text:

   > The Setup menu enables you to customize many aspects of WordPerfect. You can change the appearance and color of normal text, change cursor speed, choose the mouse option, and display the menu bar. You can change the Setup menu at any time, according to your needs.

   Save the document as SETUP, and exit WordPerfect.

Review: Long Projects

1. Type, Save, and Print a Document

   Type the following document, save it as MEMO, and print it.

Testing Your Knowledge

>   January 28, 1993
>   To: Meredith Becker
>   Training Coordinator
>   From: Allan Townes
>   Application Software Instructor
>   Re: Computer Training Update
>
>   It has been six months since the last training session, and I would like to arrange a meeting to discuss future dates for training. At this time, we should be thinking of group training sessions and then follow-up sessions for individual needs.
>
>   I have organized and implemented computer training sessions for all departments. I have been available to work with both small and large groups to increase the use of computers and software in all departments. Many departments have expressed interest in more advanced training.
>
>   Please contact me at your earliest convenience at EXT 4055.

2. Type, Preview, Print, and Save a Document

   Type the following document, preview and print it, and save it as KEYTERMS.

   >   Key Terms in This Chapter
   >
   >   Defaults
   >
   >   Standard WordPerfect settings that are in effect each time you start the program.
   >
   >   Status Line
   >
   >   The bottom line on the WordPerfect editing screen is the status line. The status line indicates the disk drive, file name, and position of the cursor on-screen. From time to time, the WordPerfect status line displays system messages and prompts.
   >
   >   Cursor
   >
   >   An on-screen marker that indicates where a character will appear if you type. The cursor also marks the location where a hidden formatting code will be entered.

Getting Started

Word Wrap

> A WordPerfect feature that eliminates the need to press the Enter (Return) key each time you reach the right margin. With word wrap, you need to press Enter only when you come to the end of a paragraph, short line, or command.

Soft Return

> The code inserted at the end of each line when the text reaches the right margin and is automatically wrapped to the next line.

Hard Return

> The code for a carriage return, inserted when you press the Enter key at the end of a line.

File name

> A descriptive title that you assign to a file before storing it in system memory.

Editing

2

Revising a draft is an important part of polishing any document. Revision can consist of changing, adding, or deleting material; correcting grammar and punctuation; and making any other changes to your document. WordPerfect enables you to revise text easily with a number of built-in editing tools. This chapter focuses on the basic editing changes you can make with WordPerfect.

Objectives

1. To Retrieve Files
2. To Use the List Files Screen
3. To Insert Text
4. To Delete Text
5. To Display and Delete Hidden Codes

Editing

2

Key Terms in This Chapter	
Insert mode	The alternative to WordPerfect's Typeover mode. When you type in Insert mode (WordPerfect's default), new characters are inserted, and existing text moves forward.
Typeover mode	The alternative to WordPerfect's Insert mode. When you type in Typeover mode, the characters you type replace the original text.
Reveal Codes	The WordPerfect command that displays the hidden codes inserted into the text when you press certain keys. Hidden codes tell WordPerfect when to execute tabs, margin settings, hard returns, and so on.

Objective 1: To Retrieve Files

You can retrieve documents stored on disk in either of two ways:

- You can issue the Retrieve command and type the file name. You can use this method only if you know the exact name of the file.
- You can display the List Files screen and choose the file name from the list. This method is handy for locating any file, regardless of whether you remember the exact file name.

Before you retrieve a file with either method, be sure to clear the screen by pressing Exit (F7). If you do not clear the screen first, WordPerfect inserts the retrieved file into the document displayed on-screen.

Exercise 1.1: Using the Retrieve Command

To retrieve a file with the Retrieve command, follow these steps:

1. Press ⇧Shift + F10 to activate the Retrieve command.

    🖱 Access the File pull-down menu, and choose Retrieve (see fig. 2.1).

    WordPerfect displays the following prompt:

    ```
    Document to be retrieved:
    ```

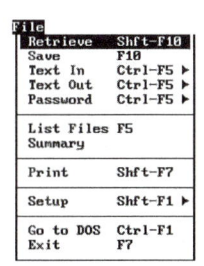

Fig. 2.1
The Retrieve command on the File menu.

2. Type **letter**, which is the name of the document, and press ⏎Enter. The left side of the status screen displays the drive, the path, and the name of the file.

If the message `ERROR: File not found` appears, either you have typed the name incorrectly, or the file doesn't exist in the directory. Type the name again, making sure to use the correct drive and subdirectory. If you cannot remember the name of the document you want to retrieve, use the List Files screen.

Suppose that after you press Retrieve (⇧Shift + F10), you decide not to retrieve a file. You can press Cancel (F1) to cancel the command.

Objective 2: To Use the List Files Screen

Using the List Files feature, you can accomplish—from within WordPerfect—much of the file and directory management you ordinarily perform in DOS.

Exercise 2.1: Getting to the List Files Screen

To get to the List Files screen, follow these steps:

1. Press F5 to activate the List command.

    🖱 Access the File pull-down menu, and choose List Files.

    WordPerfect displays the message `Dir` in the lower left corner, followed by a file specification for all files in the default directory, such as the following:

    `Dir C:\WP51\BOOK\*.*`

    The message says that WordPerfect is ready to give you a list of all files in the default directory.

Editing

2. If this directory is the one you want, press ⏎Enter. If it is not the directory you want, change the specification and then press ⏎Enter.

    🖰 Double-clicking the left mouse button is the same as pressing ⏎Enter. For example, after choosing List Files from the File pull-down menu, you can double-click `Dir C:\WP51\BOOK\*.*` to accept the default file specification.

If you type a new file specification, it replaces the original specification. You can also edit the file specification, just as you edit regular text—by using keys such as Del and ⬅Backspace.

After you accept the current file specification or enter a new one, the List Files screen appears. The three areas on this screen are the heading, the file list, and the menu.

The Heading

The first line of the two-line heading on the List Files screen displays the date, the time, and the directory being listed. The second line shows the size of the document currently being edited, the amount of free space left on the disk, the amount of disk space taken up by files in the current directory, and the number of files shown in the list.

The File List

The two-column file list on the List Files screen displays the names and directories in alphabetical order across the screen. (Files with names starting with numbers are listed first.) This list shows the complete file name, file size, and the date and time the file was created or last modified. You can print this list, along with most of the information in the heading, by pressing Print (⇧Shift + F7) or by accessing the **File** pull-down menu and choosing **P**rint.

Notice that the top line of the file list contains the following information:

    . Current <Dir> .. Parent <Dir>

`<Dir>` indicates that the items are directories. Other directories in the list are similarly labeled. The entry labeled `Current` refers to the currently listed directory. The other entry, labeled `Parent`, refers to the parent directory of the listed directory. The parent directory is one level higher than the current directory.

A highlight bar also appears on the top left entry. You can move this bar with the cursor keys to highlight any name in the list. If you want to display files from a different directory, you can highlight the name of that directory and press ⏎Enter twice.

Note: With the Location of Files option on the Setup menu, you can specify that certain types of files be stored automatically in separate directories. For example, you can designate separate directories for dictionaries, back-up files, and macros.

From the List Files menu at the bottom of the screen, you can choose from 10 menu items (see fig. 2.2). Each operation, when chosen, acts on the highlighted file or directory. After you make a menu selection, WordPerfect often asks for confirmation. For example, if you choose **D**elete (**2**) to delete the file ELECTION.TXT, WordPerfect displays the following prompt:

```
Delete C:\WP51\BOOK\ELECTION.TXT? No (Yes)
```

```
02-18-92  01:34p            Directory C:\WP51\BOOK\*.*
Document size:          0  Free:  9,902,080 Used:    578,897     Files:      25

 .    Current      <Dir>                      |  ..    Parent      <Dir>
 ALIGN    .TXT       835  02-17-92 04:31p  | BIBLIO   .TXT       594  02-17-92 04:28p
 BRAIN    .TXT     1,849  02-18-92 01:03p  | CENTER   .TXT       493  02-18-92 11:00a
 CHAP01   .ZIP    62,728  02-17-92 11:12a  | CHAP02   .ZIP    64,844  02-17-92 02:30p
 CHAP03   .ZIP   131,211  02-17-92 02:29p  | CHAP04   .ZIP    97,745  02-17-92 04:59p
 CHAP05   .ZIP   108,018  02-18-92 11:40a  | CHAP06   .ZIP    94,068  02-18-92 01:29p
 CLINIC   .          718  02-17-92 04:45p  | DESCRIBE.TXT       819  02-17-92 11:01a
 ELECTION.TXT        902  02-18-92 11:19a  | EXERCISE.TXT       459  02-17-92 12:18p
 HARMONY  .LTR     1,720  02-18-92 11:09a  | INDENT   .TXT     1,006  02-17-92 04:23p
 JUSTIFY  .TXT     1,189  02-17-92 04:39p  | NOTES    .          650  02-17-92 12:11p
 PARK     .LTR       853  02-17-92 10:44a  | REDLINE  .TXT       716  02-18-92 11:23a
 SPELL    .TXT       926  02-18-92 01:13p  | STEINER  .LTR     1,531  02-17-92 10:59a
 TABLE    .BLK       996  02-17-92 02:20p  | TABS     .TXT     3,091  02-17-92 04:16p
 TRAVEL   .LTR       936  02-17-92 12:08p

1 Retrieve; 2 Delete; 3 Move/Rename; 4 Print; 5 Short/Long Display;
6 Look; 7 Other Directory; 8 Copy; 9 Find; N Name Search: 6
```

Fig. 2.2
The List Files screen and menu.

Although WordPerfect displays the **N**o response, you can choose **Y**es to delete the file, or you can choose **N**o or press Enter to cancel the command.

List Files Menu

You can use the options on the List Files menu to manage your files without leaving WordPerfect and going to DOS. The first step you perform for any operation is to highlight the name of the file or directory with which you want to work. You can use the cursor keys to move to the entry, or you can use the **N**ame Search option.

Exercise 2.2: Doing a Name Search

Using the **N**ame Search (**N**) option on the List Files menu, you can move the highlight bar to a file name as you type the name. Follow these steps:

Editing

1. Press **N** and then type the first letter of the file name (for example, BUSINESS.LTR) for which you want to search. If you type **b**, for example, the highlight bar jumps to the first file name starting with that letter.

2. Press the second letter of the name, and the highlight bar jumps to the first file name that starts with these two letters. If you still don't find the file, type the third letter—in this case, **s**—and the highlight bar jumps to the first file name starting with these three letters.

3. If you make a mistake or change your mind, you can press [◆Backspace]; the last letter you typed is deleted, and the highlight bar jumps to its previous position.

4. When the file name you want is highlighted, turn off Name Search by pressing Cancel ([F1]), [⏎Enter], or one of the arrow keys. Then you can perform on that file any of the List Files operations described in this chapter.

You can use Name Search to search for a directory name as well as a file name. Just type a backslash (\) before the first character of the directory name. For example, to find the LEARN directory, type **\learn**.

Retrieve

The **Retrieve** (**1**) option works like Retrieve ([◆Shift]+[F10]) from the editing screen and like **Retrieve** from the **File** pull-down menu: The retrieve operation brings a file into WordPerfect for editing. Like Retrieve ([◆Shift]+[F10]), this option inserts the retrieved file at the cursor position.

Exercise 2.3: Retrieving a Document

To retrieve a document, follow these steps:

1. With the List Files screen displayed, highlight the file with the arrow keys.

2. Press **1** to retrieve the file.

   If you already have a file on-screen, choosing **Retrieve** (**1**) from the List Files menu inserts the retrieved file into that document at the cursor position. Whenever you choose this option with a file already on-screen, WordPerfect displays the following prompt to prevent you from accidentally combining files:

   ```
   Retrieve into current document? No (Yes)
   ```

To Use the List Files Screen

Choose **Y**es if you want to combine the new file with the file on-screen. In this case, choose **N**o if you don't want to combine the files.

WordPerfect tries to protect you from retrieving any improper files. It does not retrieve program files, nor does it retrieve any temporary or permanent WordPerfect system files.

You now should be back at the document screen.

The Retrieve option retrieves and automatically converts to WordPerfect 5.1 format any DOS text file or any file created with an earlier version of WordPerfect. WordPerfect also automatically converts spreadsheet files created by PlanPerfect; Lotus 1-2-3 (Releases 1.0, 2.1, and 2.2); Microsoft Excel; Quattro; or Quattro Pro, for use in WordPerfect. In addition, you can perform many conversion operations through the Text In/Text Out (Ctrl+F5) feature.

Delete

The **Delete** (**2**) option on the List Files menu deletes files or directories. If the highlight bar is on a file name, that file is deleted. If the bar is on a directory name, the directory is deleted (as long as it does not contain any files). If the directory contains files, WordPerfect displays an error message. Whether you are deleting files or directories, WordPerfect displays a prompt similar to the following:

```
Delete C:\WP51\BOOK\CHAP2? No (Yes)
```

Choose **Y**es to confirm the deletion, or choose **N**o to cancel the deletion.

Copy

Like the DOS COPY command, the **Copy** (**8**) option on the List Files menu copies the file.

Exercise 2.4: Copying a File

To copy a file, follow these instructions:

1. On the List Files screen, highlight the name of the file you want to copy.
2. Choose **C**opy (**8**).

   WordPerfect displays the following prompt:

   ```
   Copy this file to:
   ```

Editing

3. To copy the file to another disk or directory, type the drive or directory and press [⏎Enter]. To make a copy of the file in the current directory, type a new file name and press [⏎Enter].

Print

The **Print** (**4**) option on the List Files menu prints the highlighted file on the currently selected printer. Unlike many other programs, WordPerfect can print while you continue to edit another document. You can even tell the program to print more than one file. For a detailed discussion of WordPerfect's Print options, see Chapter 7, "Printing."

Look

The **Look** (**6**) option on the List Files menu displays the highlighted file without retrieving it to the editing screen. Note that this option is the default menu choice. You don't have to choose **Look** (**6**) to display a file (although you can if you want); you can just press [⏎Enter]. Use Look to examine a number of files quickly—for example, if you forget which file you need to edit.

🖱 Using the left mouse button to double-click a file name in the List Files screen causes the file to be displayed as if you had highlighted the file and chosen **Look** (**6**).

The file name appears at the top of the screen. If you have created a document summary for the file, that information also appears on-screen.

You can use the up- and down-arrow keys to move the cursor through the file. You cannot edit the file. The Look option also continuously displays or scrolls through each succeeding line of the document if you press S. Pressing S a second time stops the scrolling. Press Exit ([F7]) or [⏎Enter] to cancel the Look option.

When you choose **Look** (**6**) for a file that doesn't have a document summary, WordPerfect displays the Look menu at the bottom of the screen.

Choosing **Next Doc** (**1**) or pressing [PgDn] moves the cursor to the first page of the next file in the file list. Choosing **Prev Doc** (**2**) or pressing [PgUp] moves the cursor to the first page of the preceding file in the list. Use these options to scan quickly the document summaries and first pages of a list of files.

Exercise 2.5: Using Other Directory

Use the **O**ther Directory (**7**) option on the List Files menu to change the default directory. Follow these steps:

1. Choose **O**ther Directory (**7**) from the List Files menu.

    WordPerfect displays in the lower left corner of the screen the message `New directory =`, followed by the name of either the default directory or any directory you highlighted before starting this operation.

2. Type the name of the directory you want to make the default, or press `⏎Enter` to use the currently listed directory as the default.

    WordPerfect displays `Dir` with the file specification for all the files in the selected directory—for example, `Dir C:\WP51\LEARN\*.*`.

If you decide that you don't want to change directories, press Cancel (`F1`) before pressing `⏎Enter` the second time.

You can edit both the `New directory =` and `Dir` messages. You thereby can change directly to any directory on your hard disk.

In addition, you can create a new directory by choosing **O**ther Directory (**7**) and entering a unique name. For example, if you enter **c:\wp51\essays**, WordPerfect displays the prompt `Create c:\wp51\essays? No (Yes)`. Choose **Y**es to create a new subdirectory called ESSAYS, or choose **N**o if that isn't what you want.

Objective 3: To Insert Text

Inserting text is a basic part of the editing process. This section shows how easily you can improve what you have written, by using Insert mode to insert additional text or by using Typeover mode to type over and replace the existing text with new text. The basic difference between Typeover mode and Insert mode is that Typeover mode replaces your original text; Insert mode adds new text to existing text. For this objective, be sure that LETTER is your current document (see fig. 2.3).

Exercise 3.1: Adding Text with Insert Mode

WordPerfect usually operates in Insert mode. As you type, the new characters are inserted on-screen; existing text moves forward and is automatically formatted. You may notice that sentences often push beyond the right margin

Editing

and do not immediately wrap to the next line. Don't worry. The lines adjust as you continue to type. If you want, you can press the down-arrow key to reformat the text immediately.

Fig. 2.3
The LETTER document.

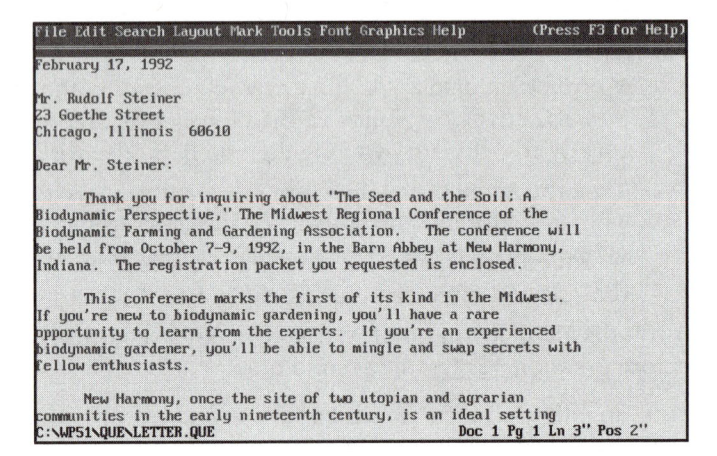

```
File Edit Search Layout Mark Tools Font Graphics Help      (Press F3 for Help)
February 17, 1992

Mr. Rudolf Steiner
23 Goethe Street
Chicago, Illinois  60610

Dear Mr. Steiner:

        Thank you for inquiring about "The Seed and the Soil: A
Biodynamic Perspective," The Midwest Regional Conference of the
Biodynamic Farming and Gardening Association.  The conference will
be held from October 7-9, 1992, in the Barn Abbey at New Harmony,
Indiana.  The registration packet you requested is enclosed.

        This conference marks the first of its kind in the Midwest.
If you're new to biodynamic gardening, you'll have a rare
opportunity to learn from the experts.  If you're an experienced
biodynamic gardener, you'll be able to mingle and swap secrets with
fellow enthusiasts.

        New Harmony, once the site of two utopian and agrarian
communities in the early nineteenth century, is an ideal setting
C:\WP51\QUE\LETTER.QUE                         Doc 1 Pg 1 Ln 3" Pos 2"
```

To add text in Insert mode, place the cursor where you want to insert new text. Type the new text.

Place the cursor on the *r* in *registration*, type **new**, and press the space bar. Move to the next *registration* and do the same.

Exercise 3.2: Typing over Existing Text

You generally use Typeover mode if you have typed text incorrectly. For example, you probably will choose Typeover mode to replace text if you mistakenly typed *February* for *December* in the document LETTER.

To type over existing text, follow these steps:

1. Place the cursor on the *F* in *February*.
2. Press [Ins] to turn off Insert mode and to turn on Typeover mode. The Typeover mode indicator appears in the lower left portion of the screen.
3. Type **December**.
4. Press [Ins] again to return to Insert mode.

Inserting Spaces

In either Insert or Typeover mode, you can create blank character spaces by pressing the space bar. In Insert mode, you add blank spaces by pressing the space bar. In Typeover mode, however, if you press the space bar while the cursor is under a character, a blank space replaces the character. Remember that Typeover mode is always destructive to the text on-screen.

Exercise 3.3: Inserting Blank Lines

In either Insert or Typeover mode, you can insert blank lines by pressing [↵Enter] once for each blank line you want to insert. Inserting blank lines causes existing lines of text to move down the page.

Insert another blank line between each pair of paragraphs of the document.

Objective 4: To Delete Text

With WordPerfect, you can delete unwanted text of various lengths. For example, you can delete single characters, a word, a line, several lines, or part of a page. WordPerfect also has special options for deleting a sentence, paragraph, or page.

Exercise 4.1: Deleting Single Characters

To delete a character at the cursor position, press [Del]. The text to the right of the deleted character moves in to fill the gap.

To delete a character to the left of the cursor, press [←Backspace] if the cursor is one character to the right of the character you want to delete. (On some keyboards, the [←Backspace] key is marked with a single left arrow at the top of the keyboard. Don't confuse this key with the left-arrow key on the numeric keypad or in the group of cursor-movement keys.) When you use press [←Backspace], any text to the right moves one character position to the left.

Keep in mind that both the [Del] and [←Backspace] keys are repeat keys. If you hold down either key (rather than press it once), you delete multiple characters. Be careful not to hold down the key too long.

Editing

With WordPerfect in Insert mode, make a change in your document by following these steps:

1. Move the cursor to the *O* in *October*.
2. Press `Ins`.
3. Type **March**.
4. Press `Del` twice.
5. Press `Ins`. You return to Insert mode. The typeover indicator at the bottom left corner of your screen should disappear.

Exercise 4.2: Deleting Words

To delete a word at the cursor position, do the following:

1. Move the cursor to any position within the word *Sincerely*.
2. Press Delete Word (`Ctrl`+`Backspace`) if the cursor is anywhere in the word to be deleted. Note that, for WordPerfect, a "word" is the text of the word and the space following the text.
3. Retype **Sincerely**.

To delete a word to the left of the cursor, follow these steps:

1. Place the cursor in the blank space to the right of the word *Sincerely*, or under the first character of the word following the word *Sincerely*.
2. Press Delete Word (`Ctrl`+`Backspace`); or press `Home` and then press `Backspace`.
3. Retype **Sincerely**.

To delete a word to the right of the cursor, follow these steps:

1. Place the cursor under the first character of the word *Sincerely*.
2. Press `Home` and then press `Del`.
3. Retype **Sincerely**.

Alternatively, you can do the following to delete characters to the left of the cursor:

1. Place the cursor on the line beginning with *Sincerely yours*.
2. Move the right-arrow key to the end of the line (positioned on the comma).
3. Press `Backspace` six times.

Deleting Lines

To delete a single line of text or a portion of a line, position the cursor under the first character on the line, or on the first character in the portion you want to delete. Then press Delete to End of Line (Ctrl+End).

To delete several lines at a time, follow these steps:

1. Position the cursor under the first character on the first line of the last paragraph of text.
2. Count the number of lines you want to erase (including the line where the cursor is located).
3. Press Esc (the Repeat key).

   The message n=8 appears on the status line. The default repeat value is 8, but you can change that number to reflect the number of lines you want to delete.
4. If the number of lines to be deleted is not 8, type the number you want. For this exercise, type *3*.
5. Press Ctrl+End to activate Delete to End of Line.

To delete a blank line, move the cursor to the left margin at the beginning of the blank line. Then press Del.

Deleting to the End of the Page

To delete text from the cursor position to the end of the page, follow these steps:

1. Position the cursor under the first character in the last paragraph of text.
2. Press Ctrl+PgDn to activate Delete to End of Page.

   WordPerfect prompts you to confirm that you want to delete the rest of the page:

   ```
   Delete Remainder of page? No (Yes)
   ```
3. Choose **Y**es to delete the text or **N**o if you have changed your mind.

To delete several pages at once, press Esc, and enter the number of pages you want to delete. Then press Ctrl+PgDn.

Editing

Exercise 4.3: Deleting a Sentence, Paragraph, or Page

To delete a sentence, paragraph, or page, follow these steps:

1. Position the cursor anywhere within the text that you want to delete. In this example, a sentence is deleted.

2. Press Ctrl + F4 to activate the Move command.

    Access the Edit pull-down menu, and choose Select (see fig. 2.4).

    Fig. 2.4
    The Select pop-out menu.

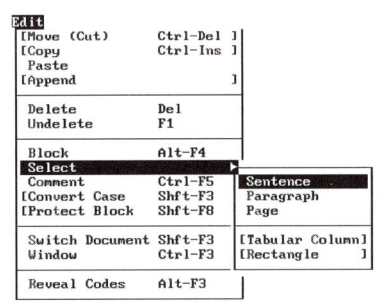

3. Choose **S**entence (**1**), **P**aragraph (**2**), or P**a**ge (**3**). For this example, choose **S**entence (**1**).

    The sentence, paragraph, or page to be deleted is highlighted (see fig. 2.5).

    Fig. 2.5
    Deleting a highlighted sentence.

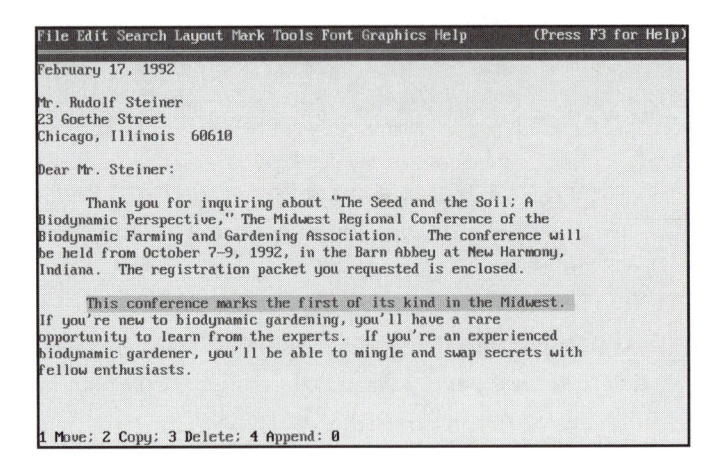

To Delete Text

4. Choose **D**elete (**3**).

The highlighted sentence, paragraph, or page is deleted. Press ↓ to reformat the text.

Exercise 4.4: Deleting Text with the Mouse

You can mark blocks of text for deletion more quickly with the mouse than with the Block command (explained in Chapter 3). And using the mouse instead of the **E**dit menu's **S**elect command is not only faster but also more powerful.

To delete text with the mouse, follow these steps:

1. Start to define the block by positioning the mouse pointer at the beginning or end of the block (character, word, sentence, or paragraph) you want to delete.
2. Drag to the opposite end of the block you are defining (the area is highlighted as you move the mouse).
3. Press `Del` or `◆Backspace`.

    🖱 Access the **E**dit pull-down menu, and choose **D**elete.
4. At the prompt `Delete Block? No (Yes)`, choose **Y**es.

Exercise 4.5: Restoring Deleted Text

To restore deleted text to its original location or to another location, follow these steps:

1. Move the cursor to the place where you want to restore the deleted text.
2. Press `F1` to activate the Cancel command.

    🖱 Access the **E**dit pull-down menu, and choose **U**ndelete.

    A block of highlighted text—the most recently deleted text—appears at the cursor position. WordPerfect displays the Undelete menu at the bottom of the screen (see fig. 2.6).
3. Choose **R**estore (**1**) if the highlighted text is what you want to restore.

    Choose **P**revious Deletion (**2**) if you want to undelete previously deleted text. When the appropriate text appears on-screen, choose **R**estore (**1**).

Editing

Fig. 2.6
The Undelete menu.

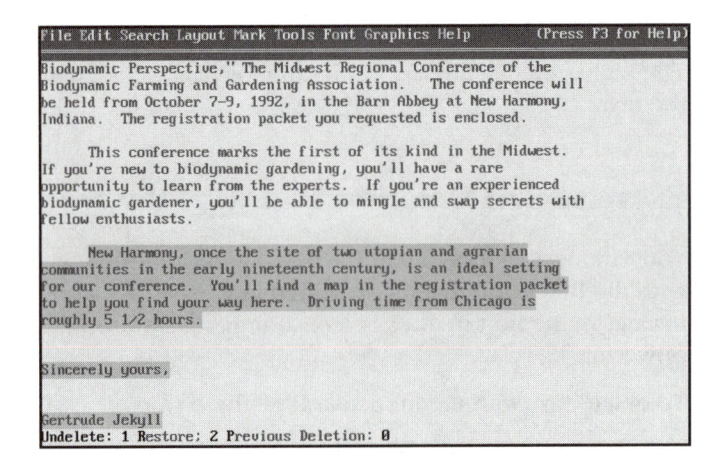

Remember, however, that WordPerfect stores only the last three deletions. When you make a fourth deletion, the oldest of the three preceding deletions is erased from memory.

Adjusting the Screen after Editing

After you insert or delete text, you may need to adjust the alignment of the text. Press ↓ to *reformat* the text. As you move the cursor down, notice how WordPerfect adjusts the arrangement of the words. You may need to press ↓ more than once to reformat the text.

Objective 5: To Display and Delete Hidden Codes

Often when you press a key in WordPerfect, a hidden code is inserted into the text. The term *hidden* is appropriate, because you cannot see the code on-screen. By hiding the codes, WordPerfect keeps the editing screen uncluttered.

These hidden codes, which you can view with WordPerfect's Reveal Codes command, tell the program when to execute tabs, margin settings, hard returns, indents, and so on. Some codes—such as the codes for math and columns—turn features on or off. Other codes—such as the codes for boldface, underline, and italic—work in pairs. The first code in a pair acts as a

To Display and Delete Hidden Codes

toggle switch to turn on the feature; the second code serves to turn off the feature. When you press Reveal Codes (Alt+F3, or F11 on an enhanced keyboard) the hidden codes appear on-screen. When you press Alt+F3 or F11 again, the hidden codes disappear from the screen.

Note: In the Reveal Codes screen, clicking the left mouse button or dragging the mouse is impossible.

Exercise 5.1: Displaying Hidden Codes

To display the hidden codes, follow these steps:

1. Turn on the Reveal Codes feature by pressing Alt+F3 or F11.

    🖱 Access the Edit pull-down menu, and choose Reveal Codes.

    The screen splits into two windows (see fig. 2.7).

    The same text appears in both windows, but the text in the bottom window includes the hidden codes; the codes are highlighted and appear in brackets. The ruler line between the windows displays the tab and margin settings for the line where the cursor is located.

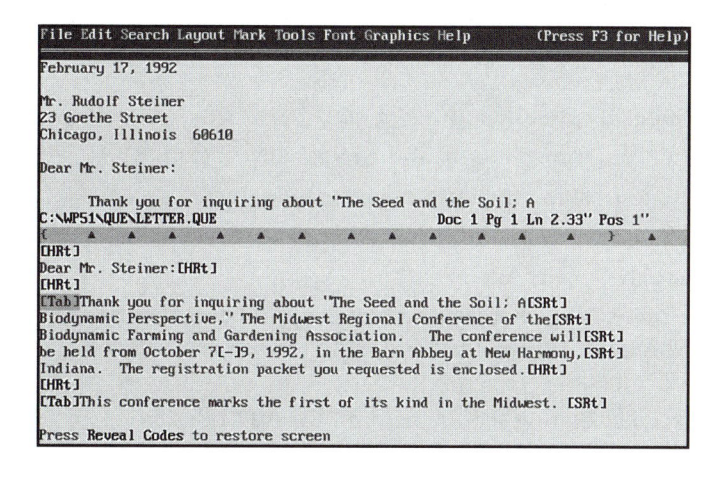

Fig. 2.7
The split document screen.

2. To restore the regular editing screen, turn off Reveal Codes by pressing Alt+F3 or F11 again.

    🖱 Access the Edit pull-down menu, and choose Reveal Codes.

53

Editing

Editing in Reveal Codes

Editing in Reveal Codes is a little different from editing in the regular editing screen. The cursor in the upper window looks the same, but the cursor in the lower window is displayed as a highlight bar.

When the cursor comes to a hidden code (in the lower window), the cursor expands to cover the entire code (refer to fig. 2.7).

Exercise 5.2: Deleting Hidden Codes

You can delete hidden codes in the regular editing screen or in the Reveal Codes screen. Because you can see the codes in the Reveal Codes screen, deleting them there is easier.

As you delete hidden codes from the Reveal Codes screen, notice that the upper window reflects your changes. With Reveal Codes turned on, you can enter commands and text and immediately observe the position of any new hidden codes.

To delete a hidden code, follow these steps:

1. Move the cursor to the place in the document where the code is likely to be located.
2. Turn on Reveal Codes by pressing Alt + F3 or F11 .

    Access the Edit pull-down menu, and choose Reveal Codes.
3. Use the arrow keys to position the cursor on the hidden code.

    In this example, the cursor is on the [TAB] code (refer to fig. 2.7).
4. Press Del to delete the hidden code.

    Your text reflects any editing changes you make in the Reveal Codes screen. Because you deleted the [TAB] code, the text moves back to the left margin (see fig. 2.8).
5. To return to the regular editing screen, turn off Reveal Codes by pressing Alt + F3 or F11 .

    Access the Edit pull-down menu, and choose Reveal Codes.

Be sure to exit and save the document as LETTER1 before beginning the exercises at the end of the chapter.

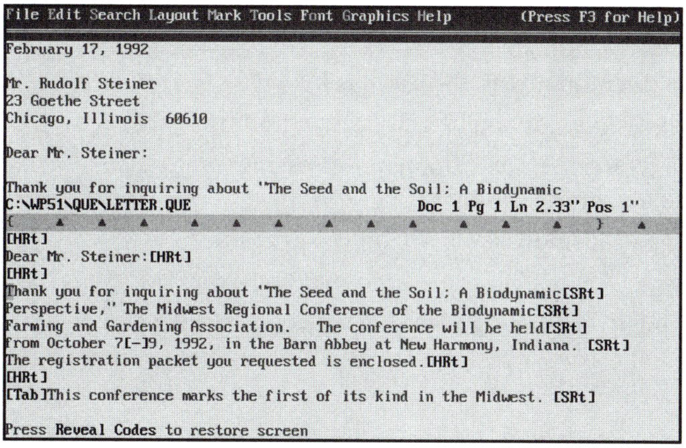

Fig. 2.8
Text after the code has been deleted.

Chapter Summary

This chapter introduces WordPerfect's editing tools for revising your documents. You have learned to retrieve files already saved to disk, and you learned to insert text, delete text, and restore deleted text in those files. You then learned to display and delete WordPerfect's hidden codes.

In the next chapter, you examine another of WordPerfect's editing tools: the Block feature.

Testing Your Knowledge

True/False Questions

1. Retrieving a document places the document in computer memory to be edited.
2. The basic difference between Typeover and Insert mode is that Typeover mode adds new text to existing text.
3. To insert a blank line, press ⏎Enter.
4. If you press ⬅Backspace, you delete text to the left of the cursor.
5. The Reveal Codes screen displays all hidden codes in the document.

Editing

Multiple Choice Questions

1. You can retrieve a document stored on a disk by
   A. pressing `Shift`+`F10`, typing the file name, and pressing `Enter`.
   B. pressing `F5` to activate List Command, pressing `Enter`, choosing the file, and pressing **1**.
   C. pressing `F5` to activate List command, and pressing `Enter`.
   D. A and B only.

2. When you are typing over existing text, the status line displays
   A. `Ins Mode`.
   B. `Ins`.
   C. `Typeover`.
   D. `Type`.

3. To delete a single character or word at the cursor position, press
   A. `Backspace`.
   B. `←`.
   C. `Del`.
   D. `Shift`+`Tab`.

4. Position the cursor in the text and press `F1`;
   A. then choose **1** to restore if the highlighted text is what you want to restore.
   B. then choose **2** to restore the previous deletion.
   C. then press the **space bar** to restore deleted text.
   D. and the Help Screen will appear.

5. The Reveal Codes screen enables you to
   A. display hidden codes.
   B. edit hidden codes.
   C. delete hidden codes.
   D. all of the above.

Fill-in-the-Blank Questions

1. When you press _____ , you change from Insert to Typeover mode. By pressing _____ again, you return to Insert mode.

Testing Your Knowledge

2. Del and ⬅Backspace are _____ keys.
3. WordPerfect has special options for deleting a _____, paragraph, or page.
4. Often when you press a key in WordPerfect, a _____ code is inserted into the text.
5. To display the hidden codes, also known as the _____ code screen, press _____ or _____.

Review: Short Projects

1. Retrieve a File

   Retrieve the file SETUP from your disk. Save the file by using the Replace option.

2. Insert and Delete Text

   A. Retrieve the document SETUP from your disk.

   B. Add the following paragraph to the text.

   Through the Initial Settings Option on the Setup menu, you can change a number of WordPerfect's built-in settings. For instance, you can change the formatting for all future documents, change the date format, and change the default repeat value (the number of times a character is repeated when you press Esc).

   C. Change the *For instance* to *For example* in the text you typed.

   D. Delete the text in parentheses.

   E. Save the document as SETUP, using the Replace option.

3. Display and Delete Hidden Codes

   A. Retrieve the document LETTER1.

   B. Display the hidden codes.

   C. Delete one of the hard returns between paragraphs.

   D. Save the document and exit WordPerfect.

Review: Long Projects

1. Retrieve, Insert, and Delete Text

   A. Retrieve the document MEMO.

   B. Change the date of the memo to *February 4, 1993*.

   C. Change *Meredith Becker* to *All Management*.

   D. Delete *Training Coordinator*.

Editing

E. Change *Computer* to *WordPerfect*, and delete *Update*.

F. Delete the first and third paragraphs of the memo.

G. Type the following as the second paragraph:

On Monday, February 15, 1993, there will be a meeting for all managers to coordinate the WordPerfect training schedule. Be sure to bring your calendars for setting the dates and times. We will meet in Building D, Room 204, at 9:00 A.M. A list of employees eligible for training will be distributed.

H. Add the following text to the last paragraph:

If you are unable to attend the meeting, please contact Mary Hand at Ext 5251.

I. Save the document as MEMO2 and exit WordPerfect.

2. Retrieve the Document KEYTERMS

A. Add the following text to the document.

Insert mode

The alternative to WordPerfect's Typeover mode is Insert mode. When you type in Insert mode (WordPerfect's default), new characters are inserted, and existing text moves forward.

Typeover mode

The alternative to WordPerfect's Insert mode is Typeover mode. When you type in Typeover mode, the characters you type replace the original text.

Reveal Codes

This WordPerfect command displays the hidden formatting and other codes inserted into the text when you press certain keys. Hidden codes tell WordPerfect when to execute tabs, margin settings, hard returns, and so on.

B. Print the document.

C. Display the hidden codes. Use Print Screen to print the document.

D. Save the document as KEYTERMS, using the Replace option, and exit WordPerfect.

Working with Blocks

3

The most powerful and flexible command in WordPerfect is the Block command. You use this command with other WordPerfect features to mark, or *block*, a segment of text so that only the blocked text is affected by the selected feature.

A block of text can be as short as a single letter or as long as an entire document. Flexibility is the Block command's strength. You define the size and shape of the block, and then you specify what to do with that selected text.

Objectives

1. To Define a Block of Text
2. To Move, Copy, and Delete Text
3. To Save, Print, and Append a Block of Text
4. To Boldface, Underline, and Center a Block of Text

Working with Blocks

Key Terms in This Chapter	
Block	A portion of text marked (highlighted) so that only it is affected by a WordPerfect command you choose. A block can be a single character, a single word, a phrase, a sentence, a paragraph, a page, a column, or an entire document.
Move	An operation that moves a block of text from one location to another. The text appears only in the new location.
Copy	An operation that duplicates a block of text. The text appears in both the original location and the location to which you copy the text.

Objective 1: To Define a Block of Text

First, you must tell WordPerfect exactly what portion of the text you want to affect. To define the text, you can use the keyboard or the mouse. With the keyboard, you position the cursor at the beginning of the block of text, turn on the Block feature, and move the cursor to the end of the block. The block of text is highlighted. Alternatively, you can move the mouse pointer to the beginning of the block and drag the mouse to the end of the block. When you begin dragging the mouse, the Block feature is turned on automatically, and the block becomes highlighted (see fig. 3.1).

Fig. 3.1
A highlighted block of text.

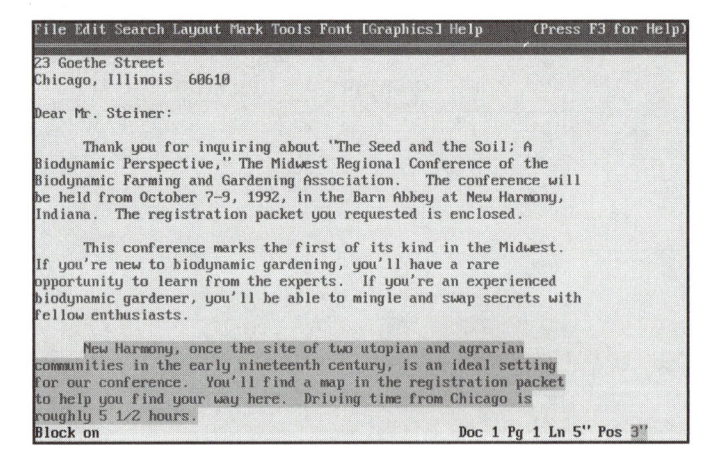

To Define a Block of Text

Highlighting text is the first step in any block operation. After you highlight a block of text, you can go on to perform any number of operations on the highlighted block. For example, you can move or copy the block of text to another location, change the text to boldface, underline the text, or delete it.

Exercise 1.1: Highlighting a Block with the Keyboard

To highlight a block of text with the keyboard, follow these steps:

1. Retrieve the document LETTER from your disk.
2. Move the cursor to the character that begins the block of text to be highlighted (refer to fig. 3.1).
3. Activate the Block command by pressing `Alt`+`F4` or `F12` (on an enhanced keyboard).

    The Block on message flashes in the lower left corner of the screen.
4. Try each of the ways to highlight text:
    - A. To highlight an entire line, press `End`.
    - B. To highlight text from the cursor position to the bottom of the current screen, press Screen Down (`+` on the numeric keypad).
    - C. To highlight multiple pages, press GoTo (`Ctrl`+`Home`), and type the number of the last page you want to highlight.
    - D. Use the arrow keys to move the cursor until the last character in the block is highlighted.
5. Press `Alt`+`F4` or `F12` to turn off the Block feature.

You also can use some shortcuts in highlighting text with the keyboard. To highlight a sentence, for example, you can turn on the Block feature at the beginning of the sentence and then press the period (.) key. The highlighting extends to the period at the end of the sentence. To highlight a paragraph, turn on Block and press `Enter`. The highlighting extends to the next hard return in the text.

Exercise 1.2: Highlighting a Block with the Mouse

One of the most valuable uses of the mouse in WordPerfect is highlighting a block of text. In the editing screen, dragging the mouse turns on Block automatically—as if you had pressed Block (`Alt`+`F4` or `F12`).

Working with Blocks

To highlight a block of text with the mouse, follow these steps:

1. Place the mouse pointer on the character that begins the text you want to highlight (refer to fig. 3.1).
2. Press and hold down the left mouse button as you drag the mouse over the block of text to be highlighted.
3. When you reach the end of the block, release the left mouse button.

If you drag the mouse beyond the top or bottom edge of the screen display, the text scrolls. You can increase or decrease the amount of text highlighted after you release the left mouse button by using the arrow keys to reposition the cursor at the end of the block.

Exercise 1.3: Rehighlighting a Block

Block highlighting disappears automatically as soon as the task (such as move, copy, or bold) is completed. If you want to use the same block with another feature, or if you accidentally turn off the Block feature, you easily can rehighlight the block.

To restore highlighting with the keyboard, follow these steps:

1. Activate the Block command by pressing [Alt]+[F4] or [F12].
2. Press [Ctrl]+[Home] to activate the GoTo command.
3. Press [Ctrl]+[Home] again to return to the beginning of the block.

If you have a mouse, you may prefer to rehighlight the block by dragging.

Exercise 1.4: Backing Out of a Block Operation

To back out of the operation while a block is highlighted, do one of the following:

- Using the keyboard, press Cancel ([F1]) or Block ([Alt]+[F4] or [F12]) to turn off the Block command.
- 🖱 To turn off the Block command with the mouse, click the left mouse button; if you have a three-button mouse, click the middle mouse button.

The Block on message disappears, and the text no longer appears highlighted. The cursor remains at the end of the block (where the cursor was located when you finished highlighting).

Objective 2: To Move, Copy, and Delete Text

After you highlight a block of text, you press the key or key combination that invokes the feature you want to use on the block of text. The feature you choose is executed only on the highlighted block. If the feature doesn't work with the Block command, WordPerfect signals you with a beep. (Although the Block feature is flexible, it cannot be used with all WordPerfect features.)

Some features, such as Move, Copy, or Block Delete, require confirmation. If a confirmation prompt, such as `Delete Block? No (Yes)`, appears in the lower left portion of the screen, choose **Yes** or **No**. After a block of text is highlighted, you can perform a specific task, such as move, copy, or delete, to improve the organization and structure of the document. These specific operations increase the flexibility you have in editing the document.

Moving and Copying

Moving a block of text is a "cut and paste" operation—except that you don't fuss with scissors, paper, paste, and tape. With WordPerfect, you highlight the block, cut it from its current location, and paste it to a new location in the document. The block is erased from its original location and appears in the new location (see fig. 3.2). The new location can even be in another document.

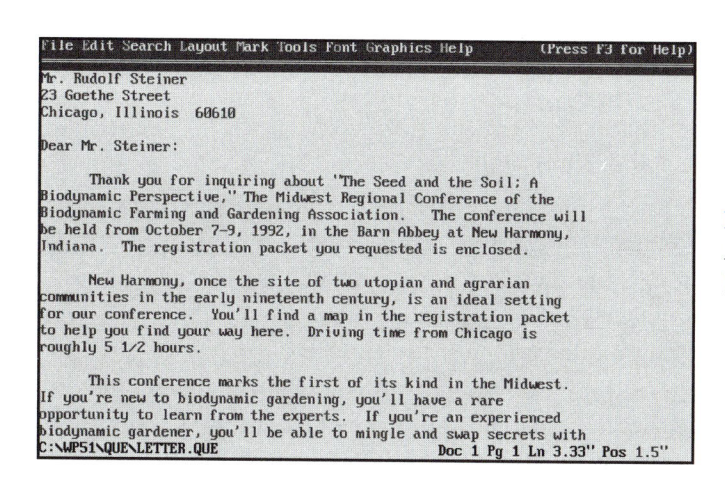

Fig. 3.2
A block of text that has been moved.

Working with Blocks

When you copy a block of text, WordPerfect places into memory a duplicate of the text you have highlighted. You then can retrieve this block from memory and insert the block at another location in the same document or in another document. If you copy a block, the text appears in both the original location and the new location.

Exercise 2.1: Moving a Block

To move a block of text, follow these steps:

1. Highlight the block by pressing `Alt`+`F4` or `F12` to activate the Block command, or by dragging the mouse.

2. Press `Ctrl`+`F4` to activate the Move command, choose **B**lock (**1**), and choose **M**ove (**1**). Alternatively, press `Ctrl`+`Del`.

   Alternatively, access the Edit pull-down menu and choose Move (Cut).

   WordPerfect cuts the highlighted block, and it disappears from the screen. Don't worry; the block is stored in temporary memory.

   WordPerfect displays the following message:

   ```
   Move cursor; press Enter to retrieve.
   ```

3. Move the cursor to the location in the document where you want the cut block to appear.

4. Press `Enter` to insert the block at the new location (refer to fig. 3.2).

Exercise 2.2: Copying a Block

To copy a block of text, follow these steps:

1. Highlight the block by using `Alt`+`F4` or `F12` to activate the Block command, or by dragging the mouse.

2. Press `Ctrl`+`F4` to activate the Move command, choose **B**lock (**1**), and choose **C**opy (**2**). Alternatively, press `Ctrl`+`Ins`.

   Access the Edit pull-down menu, and choose Copy.

3. Move the cursor to the location in the document where you want the duplicate text to appear.

4. Press `Enter`, and WordPerfect makes the change.

You can retrieve the copied block as many times as you want. Generally, you use the Copy feature to repeat (without retyping) standard blocks of text in long documents, such as legal, technical, or sales documents.

To Move, Copy, and Delete Text

To retrieve the same block of text again, follow these steps:

1. Move the cursor to the location in the document where you want the block of text to appear.

2. Press [Ctrl]+[F4] to activate the Move command, choose **R**etrieve (**4**), and choose **B**lock (**1**).

    🖱 Access the Edit pull-down menu, choose Paste, and choose Block (1).

Exercise 2.3: Moving or Copying a Sentence, Paragraph, or Page

If the block you want to move or copy is a sentence, paragraph, or page, WordPerfect can highlight the block for you. Instead of using the Block command, follow these steps:

1. Place the cursor anywhere within the sentence, paragraph, or page to be moved or copied.

2. Press [Ctrl]+[F4] to activate the Move command. Then choose **S**entence (**1**), **P**aragraph (**2**), or P**a**ge (**3**).

    🖱 Access the Edit pull-down menu, choose Select, and then choose Sentence, Paragraph, or Page.

3. Choose **M**ove (**1**) or **C**opy (**2**).

4. Move the cursor to the location where you want the highlighted block of text to appear.

5. Press [↵Enter].

Exercise 2.4: Deleting a Block

In a few keystrokes, you can delete a sentence or several pages of text. To delete a block of text, follow these steps:

1. Highlight the block shown in figure 3.3 by using [Alt]+[F4] or [F12] to activate the Block command, or by dragging the mouse. Then press [Del] or [←Backspace].

    WordPerfect displays a confirmation prompt at the bottom of the screen.

2. To confirm the deletion, choose **Y**es. (If you choose **N**o, you are returned to the highlighted text.)

    WordPerfect deletes the block from the document.

Working with Blocks

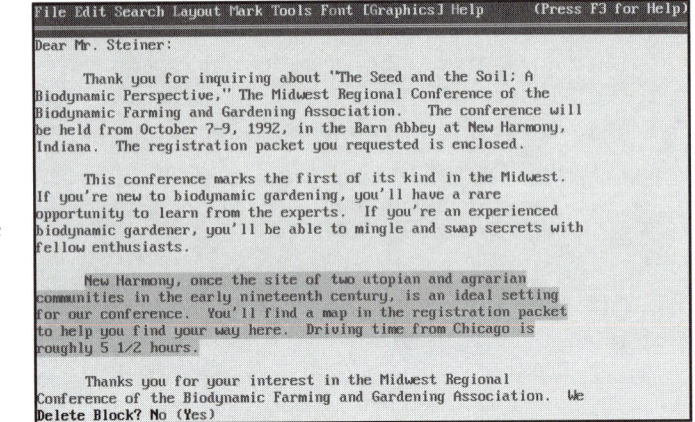

Fig. 3.3
Confirming that you want to delete a block of text.

You can delete as many as three blocks and restore all of them by pressing Cancel (F1).

To restore deleted text, follow these steps:

1. Press Cancel (F1) to display the most recently deleted text.

    Hold down either button of a two-button mouse, and click the other button; click the middle button of a three-button mouse.

    The most recently deleted text reappears at the cursor position, and the Undelete menu appears at the bottom of the screen.

2. To restore the text you deleted most recently, choose **R**estore (**1**).

    To restore a previous deletion, choose **P**revious Deletion (**2**). Then choose **R**estore (**1**) to restore that text.

    Choose **P**revious Deletion (**2**) to see the third deletion. Then choose **R**estore (**1**) to restore that text. Be sure to restore the text in the document.

Objective 3: To Save, Print, and Append a Block of Text

After highlighting a block of text, you may want to save, print or append the block. Saving a block of text enables you to use the block of text in other documents. Sometimes you may need to print a certain part of the document for further reference, using the Print block command. *Appending* a block enables you to append the block to the end of a file. The feature you choose executes only on the highlighted block.

To Save, Print, and Append a Block of Text

Saving a Block

When you need to type the same block of text in one document several times, WordPerfect's Block Save feature helps reduce the amount of work. With Block Save, you first highlight the block of text you plan to use frequently, and then save the block as a separate file. Block Save enables you to build a time-saving library of frequently used blocks of text. You can even build an entire document from these files.

Exercise 3.1: Saving a Block of Text

To practice saving a block of text, follow these steps:

1. Again highlight the block shown in figure 3.3 by using Alt + F4 or F12 to activate the Block command, or by dragging the mouse.
2. Press F10 to activate the Save command.

    Access the File pull-down menu, and choose Save (see fig. 3.4).

    WordPerfect displays the following prompt:

    Block name:

3. Type the name of the file in which you want to save the block; type **a:***place* or **b:***place* (where *place* is the file name) or the subdirectory and file name, and then press ↵Enter.

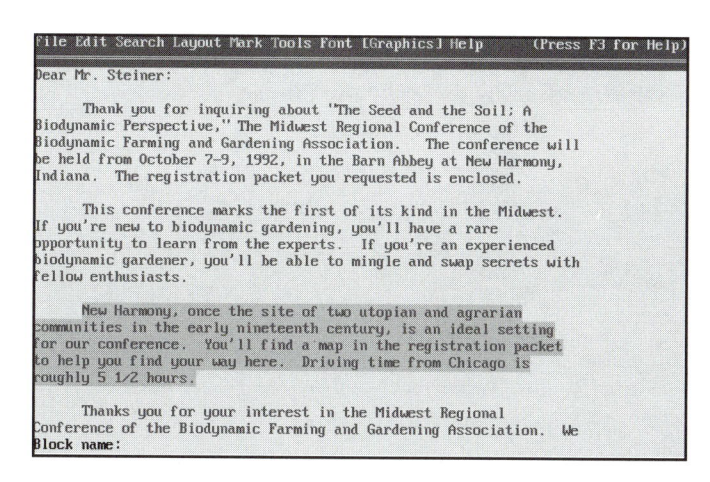

Fig. 3.4
The Save command on the File menu.

Use a file name that clearly identifies the block you are saving. Be sure to include a drive letter and path name before the file name if you want to save the block to a directory other than the current directory.

67

Working with Blocks

Exercise 3.2: Printing a Block

Sometimes you may want to print from a document just a single block of text—perhaps a page that lists sales quotas or a list of new personnel. You can use the Block Print feature to print just a part of the document.

To print a block of text, follow these steps:

1. Highlight the block shown in figure 3.3 by using [Alt]+[F4] or [F12] to activate the Block command, or by dragging the mouse.
2. Press [Shift]+[F7] to activate the Print command.

   Be sure the printer is turned on and on-line.

   🖱 Access the File pull-down menu, and choose Print.

   WordPerfect displays this prompt:

   `Print block? No (Yes)`

3. Choose **Y**es.

Exercise 3.3: Appending a Block

WordPerfect provides a simple way to add text to one document while you are working on another. With the Block Append feature, you can copy a block of text from the document on-screen to the end of another file on disk.

To append a block of text, follow these steps:

1. Highlight the block shown in figure 3.3 by using [Alt]+[F4] or [F12] to activate the Block command, or by dragging the mouse.
2. Press [Ctrl]+[F4] to activate the Move command, choose **B**lock (**1**), and choose **A**ppend (**4**).

   🖱 Access the Edit pull-down menu, choose Append, and choose To File (see fig. 3.5).

   WordPerfect displays the following prompt:

   `Append to:`

3. Enter the file name of the document to which you want the block appended. For example, type **a:memo** or **b:memo** or the subdirectory and file name where you want to append the block.

The block remains in the current document and is appended (as a duplicate) to the end of the document in the specified file.

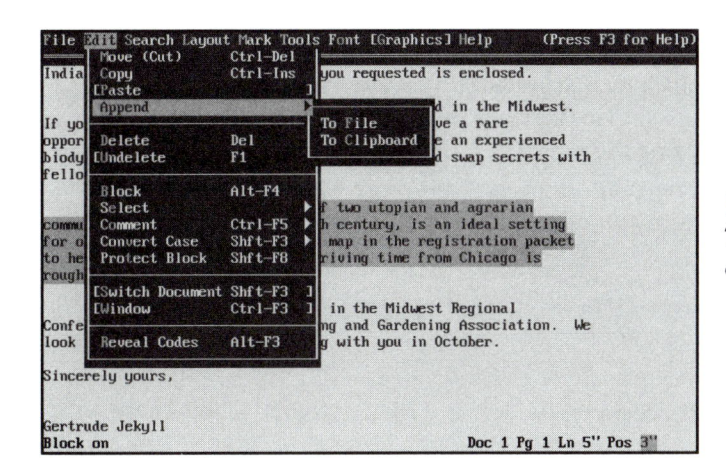

Fig. 3.5
The Append command options.

Objective 4: To Boldface, Underline, and Center a Block of Text

WordPerfect offers a number of ways to add visual impact to your text. You can call attention to a section of text by centering, boldfacing, or underlining it.

Exercise 4.1: Boldfacing or Underlining a Block

The appearance of your text on-screen depends on the type of monitor you are using. A color monitor can show boldfaced and underlined text in colors different from the color of regular text. You can change the way WordPerfect displays these enhancements on your monitor by customizing the program through the Display option on the Setup menu.

When you print the text, you can clearly distinguish the enhancements.

To boldface or underline a block of text you already have typed, follow these steps:

1. Again highlight the block shown in figure 3.3 by using [Alt]+[F4] or [F12] to activate the Block command, or by dragging the mouse.
2. Press [F6] to turn on the Bold feature, or press [F8] to turn on the Underline feature.

69

Working with Blocks

If you want the block to be both boldfaced and underlined, follow these steps:

1. Rehighlight the block by first pressing Alt + F4 or F12 and then pressing Ctrl + Home (GoTo) twice. Alternatively, you can rehighlight the block by dragging the mouse.
2. Press F6 to turn on Bold, or press F8 to turn on Underline (depending on which feature you used the first time).

Exercise 4.2: Centering a Block between the Left and Right Margins

To center a block of text between the left and right margins, follow these steps:

1. Highlight the block containing the date by pressing Alt + F4 or F12 to activate the Block command, or by dragging the mouse.
2. Press Shift + F6 to activate the Center command.
3. Choose **Y**es to confirm that you want to center the block.

   🖱 Access the Layout pull-down menu, choose Align, and choose Center (see fig. 3.6).

   WordPerfect centers the highlighted block between the left and right margins (see fig. 3.7).

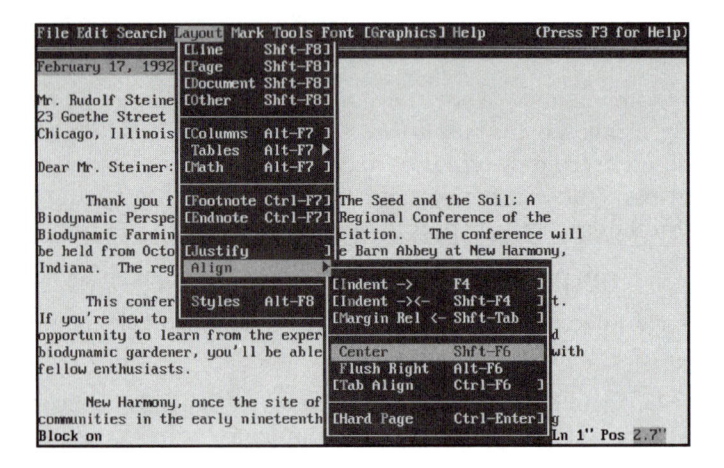

Fig. 3.6
The Center command.

If the block contains full lines in paragraph form, not much blank space is left for centering between the margins. As a result, the effect of centering may not be readily apparent. To correct this problem, shorten the individual lines by ending each one with a hard return (by pressing `Enter`), and then center the text. Exit the document without saving.

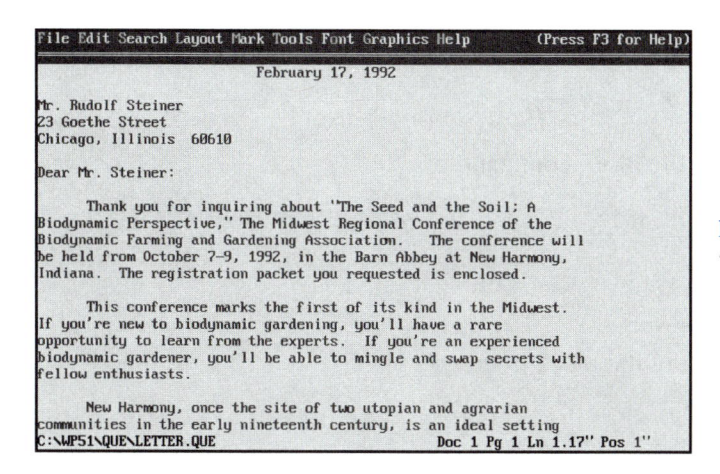

Fig. 3.7
The centered date.

Chapter Summary

Knowing how to use WordPerfect's Block feature gives you great versatility in editing documents. This chapter has shown you how to define a block of text by highlighting the block. You learned how to move or copy the highlighted block, delete the block, save it, print it, and even append it to another file. You learned several ways to enhance your text by using the Block feature.

In the next chapter, you learn how to format lines, paragraphs, and pages of text so that you can perform tasks such as changing the left and right margins, setting tabs, indenting text, and centering a line of text.

Testing Your Knowledge

True/False Questions

1. You can activate the Block command by pressing `Alt` + `F4` or `F12`.
2. To highlight a block of text, the cursor can be on any character in the block of text.
3. Moving a block of text places into memory a duplicate of the text highlighted.

Working with Blocks

4. You can delete as many as three blocks and restore all of them by pressing Cancel (F1).
5. You can boldface highlighted text by pressing F6 .

Multiple Choice Questions

1. You can activate the Block command by
    A. pressing Alt + F4 .
    B. pressing F12 .
    C. dragging the mouse.
    D. all of the above.
2. You can back out of the Block operation by
    A. pressing the **space bar**.
    B. pressing Alt + F4 , F1 , or F12 .
    C. pressing ↵Enter .
    D. pressing F8 .
3. You pressed Ctrl + F4 . Then you pressed 1 , pressed 1 again, moved the cursor to a new location, and pressed ↵Enter . By performing those steps, you
    A. moved a paragraph.
    B. copied a paragraph.
    C. moved a sentence.
    D. moved a page.
4. You can underline highlighted text by
    A. pressing F6 .
    B. pressing F8 .
    C. pressing Alt + F4 .
    D. pressing Alt + F4 , and then pressing F6 .
5. You highlighted a block of text, activated the Layout menu, and want to center the text. Next, you
    A. choose Align, and then press ↵Enter .
    B. choose Align, and then choose Center.
    C. choose Page.
    D. none of the above.

Testing Your Knowledge

Fill-in-the-Blank Questions

1. You can activate the Block command by pressing _____ or by _____ the mouse.
2. To back out of the operation while the block is highlighted, you press _____ or _____ to turn off the Block operation.
3. When you move a block of text, you _____ it from its previous location and _____ it to a new location.
4. You may copy an entire paragraph by placing the cursor on any character within the paragraph, pressing _____ to activate the Move command, pressing _____ to choose Paragraph, pressing _____ to choose Copy, moving the cursor to the new location, and pressing _____ to complete the operation.
5. Centering, boldfacing, and underlining are ways to _____ a block of text.

Review: Short Projects

1. Define a Block of Text

   Retrieve the MEMO2 document. Use the Block command to highlight the third paragraph, back out of highlighting, and rehighlight the block of text.

2. Manipulate a Block of Text

   With MEMO2 as your current document, move the second paragraph to the first paragraph's location. Save the document as MEMO2.

3. Enhance a Block of Text

   Retrieve the SETUP document as your current document. Type the title *SETUP FEATURES*; boldface, center, and capitalize the title. Underline the word *SETUP* throughout the document. Print the document. Save the document as SETUP, using the Replace option.

Review: Long Projects

1. Move and Copy

   Retrieve the KEYTERMS document.

   A. Move the necessary paragraphs so that the key terms are alphabetized.

   B. Type *KEYTERMS* as the title and then center it.

Working with Blocks

    C. Copy the first term and its definition to the end of the document.

    D. Save the document as KEYTERMS, using the Replace option, and do not exit WordPerfect.

2. Move, Copy, and Enhance

    Retrieve the KEYTERMS document.

    A. Add the following text:

    Block

    A portion of text marked (highlighted) so that only it is affected by a WordPerfect feature you choose. A block can be a single character, a single word, a phrase, a sentence, a paragraph, a page, a column, or an entire document.

    Move

    An operation that moves a block of text from one location to another. The text appears only in the new location.

    Copy

    An operation that duplicates a block of text. The text appears in both the original location and the location where the text is copied.

    B. Put the paragraphs in alphabetical order.

    C. Delete the duplicate paragraph.

    D. Boldface and capitalize the title.

    E. Underline each term before the definition.

    F. Insert a blank line before each term.

    G. Save the document as KEYTERMS, using the Replace option, and exit WordPerfect.

Formatting Lines and Paragraphs

4

WordPerfect presets all initial or default settings for margins, tabs, and other basic features. If these settings do not fit your needs, you can change the settings for only the document on which you are working, or you can change the settings permanently through the Setup menu. Generally, this chapter tells you how to change the settings for the current document only.

This chapter discusses the formatting techniques that apply to lines and paragraphs. The next chapter covers the formatting of pages.

Objectives

1. To Change Left and Right Margins
2. To Change Line Spacing
3. To Set Tab Stops
4. To Indent Text
5. To Use Justification
6. To Enhance Text

Formatting Lines and Paragraphs

Key Terms in This Chapter	
Initial font	The font in which text is normally printed, also called the default base font or current font. Other font sizes and appearances are usually variations of the initial font.

Objective 1: To Change Left and Right Margins

WordPerfect's default margins are one inch for the left and one inch for the right—appropriate margins for 8 1/2-by-11-inch paper. WordPerfect measures margins from the left and right edges of the paper or from the perforation on pin-feed paper. You can change the margins for just the current document or permanently for all future documents. In addition, you can change the unit that WordPerfect uses to measure settings such as margins. If you want to change the margins, simply measure your stationery or paper and decide how many inches of white space you want as margins.

Changing Left and Right Margins for the Current Document Only

You can change the settings for left and right margins for only the current document by using either of two methods. The first method is to insert margin setting codes at the location in the document where you want those codes to take effect. If you insert the codes at the beginning of the document, they affect the entire document. If you insert the codes elsewhere, they affect only the portion from the codes to the end of the document or to the next codes.

The second method is to insert the codes in the Document Initial Codes screen. You can access this screen from anywhere in a document, and the settings you specify affect the entire document. In addition, if you specify settings this way, you cannot easily delete them inadvertently, as you can if you use the first method. You may find that using this second method is advantageous for establishing many WordPerfect settings in addition to those for left and right margins.

To Change Left and Right Margins

Exercise 1.1: Changing the Margin Settings within the Document

You first place the cursor at the left margin of the line where you want the new margin settings to begin. If you want to change the margins for the entire document, move the cursor to the beginning of the document before setting the margins (or use the second method). After you position the cursor, follow these steps to change the left and right margins for either a portion of the document or the entire document:

1. Place the cursor on the first character in the first paragraph of text.
2. Press `Shift`+`F8` to activate the Format command. From the Format menu, choose **L**ine (**1**). Figure 4.1 shows the Format menu.

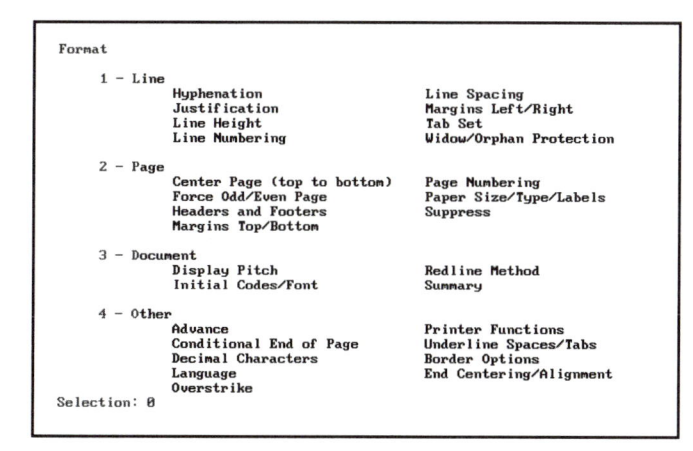

```
Format
    1 - Line
            Hyphenation                 Line Spacing
            Justification               Margins Left/Right
            Line Height                 Tab Set
            Line Numbering              Widow/Orphan Protection

    2 - Page
            Center Page (top to bottom) Page Numbering
            Force Odd/Even Page         Paper Size/Type/Labels
            Headers and Footers         Suppress
            Margins Top/Bottom

    3 - Document
            Display Pitch               Redline Method
            Initial Codes/Font          Summary

    4 - Other
            Advance                     Printer Functions
            Conditional End of Page     Underline Spaces/Tabs
            Decimal Characters          Border Options
            Language                    End Centering/Alignment
            Overstrike
Selection: 0
```

Fig. 4.1
The Format menu.

   Access the Layout pull-down menu, and click Line.

   Many of WordPerfect's formatting tasks begin at the Format menu or the Layout pull-down menu.

   After you choose **L**ine (**1**), the Format: Line menu appears.

3. Choose **M**argins Left/Right (**7**).
4. Type a value of **.75** for the left margin and press `Enter`.
5. Type a value of **.75** for the right margin and press `Enter` (see fig. 4.2).
6. Press `F7` (Exit) to return to the document.

These margin settings take effect from this point in the document until they are changed again.

Formatting Lines and Paragraphs

```
Format: Line

    1 - Hyphenation                          No

    2 - Hyphenation Zone - Left              10%
                          Right              4%

    3 - Justification                        Full

    4 - Line Height                          Auto

    5 - Line Numbering                       No

    6 - Line Spacing                         1

    7 - Margins - Left                       0.75"
                  Right                      0.75

    8 - Tab Set                              Rel; -1", every 0.5"

    9 - Widow/Orphan Protection              No


Selection: 7
```

Fig. 4.2
The new margin settings.

If you change your mind about the new margin settings, pressing Cancel (F1) doesn't cancel the new settings. You can use Reveal Codes (Alt + F3, or F1 on an enhanced keyboard) to display the [L/R Mar:] code and then delete it.

Exercise 1.2: Changing the Margin Settings in the Document Initial Codes Screen

To change left and right margin settings by using the second method, which affects the entire document, follow these steps:

1. Press ⇧Shift + F8 to activate the Format command. From the Format menu, choose **D**ocument (3).

    ▭ Access the Layout pull-down menu and choose Document.

    The Format: Document menu appears (see fig. 4.3).

```
Format: Document

    1 - Display Pitch - Automatic    Yes
                        Width        0.1"

    2 - Initial Codes

    3 - Initial Base Font            Courier 10cpi

    4 - Redline Method               Printer Dependent

    5 - Summary




Selection: 0
```

Fig. 4.3
The Format: Document menu.

To Change Left and Right Margins

2. Choose Initial Codes (2).

   The Document Initial Codes screen appears. From this screen, you can change any settings you want to settings that govern the entire document.

3. Press Format (Shift+F8) and choose Line (1).

   ▭ Access the Layout pull-down menu and choose Line.

4. From the Format: Line menu, choose Margins Left/Right (7).
5. Type a value for the left margin and press Enter.
6. Type a value for the right margin and press Enter.
7. Press Exit (F7), and you see a Document Initial Codes screen similar to the one shown in figure 4.4.

```
Initial Codes:  Press Exit when done                    Ln 1" Pos 1.5"
[L/R Mar:1.5",1.5"]
```

Fig. 4.4
The Document Initial Codes screen with new margin settings.

The margins in this example have been changed to 1.5".

8. Press Exit (F7) two more times to return to the document.

Changing Left and Right Margins Permanently

If you only occasionally produce a document with different margins (or other formatting options), you can change the settings for individual documents. You may, however, always use a specific setting—.75" margins, for example. In this case, you can permanently change the margins, or other initial settings, through the Setup menu.

Exercise 1.3: Changing the Margins Permanently

To change the margins permanently for all future documents, follow these steps:

1. Press Shift+F1 to activate the Setup command. The Setup menu is shown in figure 4.5.

   ▭ Access the File pull-down menu and choose Setup.

2. From the Setup menu, choose Initial Settings (4) to display the Setup: Initial Settings menu (see fig. 4.6).

Formatting Lines and Paragraphs

3. Choose **I**nitial Codes (**5**) to display the Setup Initial Codes screen shown in figure 4.7.

   From this point, you follow the same steps that you use for changing the margins for the current document only.

4. Press Format (⇧Shift + F8) and choose **L**ine (**1**).

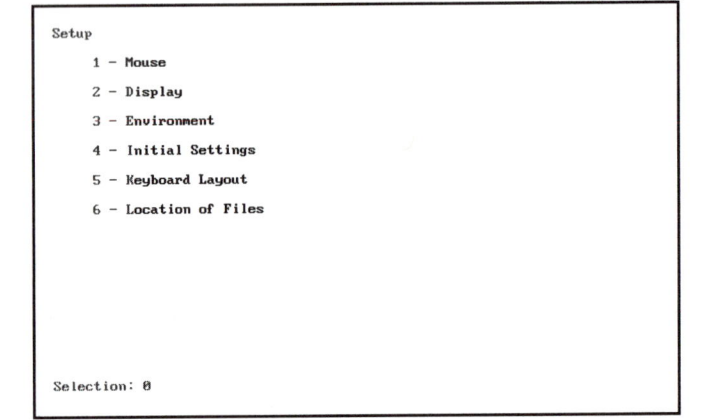

Fig. 4.5
The Setup menu.

```
Setup
    1 - Mouse
    2 - Display
    3 - Environment
    4 - Initial Settings
    5 - Keyboard Layout
    6 - Location of Files




Selection: 0
```

Fig. 4.6
The Setup: Initial Settings menu.

```
Setup: Initial Settings
    1 - Merge
    2 - Date Format                          3 1, 4
                                             March 10, 1992
    3 - Equations
    4 - Format Retrieved Documents           Yes
        for Default Printer
    5 - Initial Codes
    6 - Repeat Value                         8
    7 - Table of Authorities
    8 - Print Options



Selection: 0
```

Fig. 4.7
The Setup Initial Codes screen.

```
Initial Codes:  Press Exit when done                              Ln 1" Pos 1"
```

80

⌨ Access the Layout pull-down menu and choose Line.

5. From the Format: Line menu, choose **M**argins Left/Right (**7**).
6. Type a value for the left margin and press ⏎Enter.
7. Type a value for the right margin and press ⏎Enter.
8. Press Exit (F7) three times to return to the document.

Any document you create in WordPerfect will have this margin code placed in its Document Initial Codes screen.

Objective 2: To Change Line Spacing

To format your text, you can change the line spacing. *Line spacing* controls the blank lines between lines of text; for example, double-spacing leaves one blank line between the lines of text.

Line Spacing

WordPerfect's line spacing default is single spacing. To double-space or triple-space a document, you can change the line spacing default rather than enter hard returns as you type. You can make line spacing changes permanently or for the current document only. To change the line spacing for the entire current document, either move the cursor to the beginning of the document, or go to the Document Initial Codes screen before you complete the following steps. If the cursor is within the body of the document, the new setting affects only the portion of the document that follows the cursor position. Although you can enter any number for the line spacing setting, you don't see changes in line spacing on-screen unless you enter a line height of 1.5 or larger.

Exercise 2.1: Changing Line Spacing for the Current Document

To change line spacing for the current document only, follow these steps:

1. Place the cursor within the first paragraph of the text.
2. Press ⇧Shift + F8 to activate the Format command, and choose **L**ine (**1**).

   ⌨ Access the Layout pull-down menu and choose Line.

3. Choose **L**ine **S**pacing (**6**).

Formatting Lines and Paragraphs

4. Type a number for the amount of line spacing you want (with up to two decimal places). Then press ⏎Enter.

   For example, to double-space the lines, type **2** and press ⏎Enter.

   For one-and-one-half spacing, you would type **1.5** and press ⏎Enter.

   Note that if you reduce the space between the lines too much, words may print on top of one another.

5. Press Exit (F7) to return to the document.

The document is double-spaced. If the document does not appear to be double-spaced, press ↓ to reposition the text.

Objective 3: To Set Tab Stops

WordPerfect comes with tab stops predefined at half-inch intervals. Four basic types of tabs are available: left, center, right, and decimal. In addition, each type of tab can have a dot leader (a series of periods before the tab). You can establish tab stops in relation to the left margin or the left edge of the physical page.

Exercise 3.1: Displaying the Tab Ruler

To view current tab settings, you use the Window feature to display the tab ruler at the bottom of the screen. To display the tab ruler, follow these steps:

1. Press Ctrl+F3 to activate the Screen command, and choose **W**indow (**1**).

   🖱 Access the Edit pull-down menu and choose Window.

   WordPerfect displays the following prompt along with a number after the colon:

   `Number of lines in this window:`

2. Enter a number that is 1 less than the number displayed in the prompt. For example, if the prompt displays 24, type **23**, and press ⏎Enter.

In figure 4.8, the tab ruler at the bottom of the screen indicates the left and right margins with curly braces—{ and }. Tab stops are marked with triangles.

Fig. 4.8
The tab ruler.

Instead of displaying curly braces, the tab ruler may display square brackets—
[and]. *Braces* indicate margins and tabs at the same position; *brackets*
indicate margins alone.

Hiding the Tab Ruler

To hide the tab ruler, you use almost the same procedure as for displaying the
tab ruler. The only difference is that you type a number that is one greater
than the number displayed in the prompt.

Changing Tab Settings

You can change tab settings for all documents or for only the document in
which you are working. When you change the settings for just the current
document, the settings affect the text only from that point forward.

You can set tab stops one at a time, or you can specify the increment and set
several tab stops at once. Similarly, you can delete one tab stop, all tab stops,
or only the tab stops to the right of the cursor. You can set multiple tab stops
across 8 1/2 inches of a page. If you print on wider paper, you can extend tab
stops from 8 1/2 inches to 54 1/2 inches, but you must set the tab stops at the
far right individually. You can set a maximum of 40 tab stops.

Table 4.1 shows the various types of tabs available in WordPerfect.

Exercise 3.2: Changing Tab Settings

To change tab settings, follow these steps:

1. Press ⇧Shift + F8 to activate the Format command, and choose
   Line (**1**).

   Access the Layout pull-down menu and choose Line.

2. From the Format: Line menu, choose **T**ab Set (**8**).

The bottom of the screen, as shown in figure 4.9, displays a graphical
representation of the current tab stops.

```
L....L....L....L....L....L....L....L....L....L....L....L....L....L....L....L...
!    ^    !    ^    !    ^    !    ^    !    ^    !    ^    !    ^    !
0"        +1"       +2"       +3"       +4"       +5"       +6"       +7"
Delete EOL (clear tabs); Enter Number (set tab); Del (clear tab);
Type; Left; Center; Right; Decimal; .= Dot Leader; Press Exit when done.
```

Fig. 4.9

A graphical representation of tab stops.

Formatting Lines and Paragraphs

After displaying the tab ruler, you can delete or add single or multiple tab stops. After you have changed the tab stops, press Exit (F7) twice to return to the document.

Table 4.1 Types of Tabs Available in WordPerfect	
Tab Type	*Operation*
Left (L)	Text is indented to the tab stop; then text continues to the right. A left tab (the default) is the most commonly used tab stop.
Center	Text is centered at the tab stop. A center tab works much the same as Center (Shift+F6), except that a center tab can force centering anywhere on the line, not just the center between margins. Use center tabs to create column headings.
Right (R)	After a right tab stop, text continues to the left. A right tab works much the same as Flush Right (Alt+F6), except that a right tab can be placed anywhere on the line, not just at the right margin. Use right tabs to create headings over columns of numbers and dates.
Decimal	After a decimal tab stop, text continues to the left until the alignment character is typed; then text continues to the right. Decimal tab stops work much the same as Tab Align (Alt+F6), except that you preset the alignment character as a tab stop. The default alignment character is a period (.), but you can change it to any character (for example, : or $). Use decimal tabs to line up columns of numbers.
Dot Leaders (.)	Any of the four tab types can be preceded by a dot leader (a series of periods). Use dot leaders for long lists that require scanning from left to right (phone lists, for example).

Exercise 3.3: Deleting Tab Stops

To delete single tab stops, all tab stops, or tab stops to the right of the cursor, use one of the following methods.

To delete a single tab stop, do the following:

1. Use the cursor keys to move to the tab stop you want to delete.
2. Press `Del` or `*Backspace` to delete the tab stop.

To delete all tab stops, follow these steps:

1. Move the cursor to the left margin by pressing `Home`, `Home`, `←`.
2. Press `Ctrl`+`End`.

To delete tab stops to the right of the cursor, do the following:

1. Type the number (in inches) of the first tab stop you want to delete, and press `Enter`.
2. Press `Ctrl`+`End`.

Exercise 3.4: Adding Tab Stops

To add a single tab stop, follow these steps:

1. Use the cursor keys or mouse to move to the place where you want to add a tab stop.
2. Press the letter for the appropriate tab type: **L** to add a left tab, **C** to add a center tab, **R** to add a right tab, or **D** to add a decimal tab. To add a dot leader, press the period (**.**) key.

Alternatively, type the position for the first tab and press `Enter`. For example, type **3 1/8** and press `Enter` to place a tab at 3 1/8 inches. Note that Word-Perfect automatically changes the number to its decimal equivalent of 3.125.

Exercise 3.5: Adding Multiple Left Tab Stops

To add multiple left tab stops, follow these steps:

1. Delete the existing tabs.
2. Type the number of inches that marks the location where the tabs are to begin.
3. Type a comma (**,**).
4. Type the spacing increment.
5. Press `Enter`.

For example, to space tabs one-half inch apart, beginning at one inch, you type **1,.5** and then press `Enter`.

Exercise 3.6: Adding Multiple Center, Right, or Decimal Tab Stops and Dot Leaders

To add multiple center, right, or decimal tab stops and dot leaders, do the following:

1. Use the cursor keys to move the cursor to the place where you want the tab stops to begin. Alternatively, type the position for the first tab and press ⏎Enter.
2. Press **C** (Center), **R** (Right), or **D** (Decimal), according to what you want to insert. If you want a dot leader, press the period (**.**) key.
3. Type the number of inches that marks the location where the tab stops are to begin.
4. Type a comma (**,**).
5. Type the spacing increment.
6. Press ⏎Enter.

For example, to space right-aligned tab stops one-half inch apart, beginning at one inch, position the cursor at one inch, press **R**, type **1,.5**, and then press ⏎Enter.

When adding multiple tab stops that start at a position less than one inch, enter the number for the starting position as a decimal with a leading zero. For example, if the tab stops start at one-half inch and are spaced at half-inch intervals, type **0.5,.5**.

Creating Tables

For creating tabular material, you will find WordPerfect's Table feature easier to use than inserting tab stops. The Table feature combines the best aspects of columns, math functions, and spreadsheets.

WordPerfect's tables are easy to create—even for a first-time user. You can create a table on a blank screen or in an existing document. You can create a table of any size and locate it anywhere in the document.

With the Table feature, you can create parallel columns, create merge templates that function as fill-in forms, create mathematical formulas and perform math functions, sort data, import spreadsheet information into a table, place a table in a graphics box, and place a graphics box in a table. You can also retrieve into a document a spreadsheet as a table.

Creating Tables

When you create a table, a group of empty boxes, called cells, forms a grid on-screen. The grid is composed of columns and rows. Columns are named from left to right with letters of the alphabet beginning with A. Rows are named from top to bottom with numbers beginning with 1. A cell is the intersection of a column and a row. The cell takes its name from the column and row. For example, the cell at the intersection of column A and row 1 is called cell A1.

Within a cell, you can format text by using all WordPerfect's font attributes for size and appearance. Text-editing keys and cursor-movement keys, with a few exceptions, function as they do in the main document. The WordPerfect table editor enables you to define and change a table's structure and cell format.

With WordPerfect's Table feature, creating a basic table is reduced to a few simple steps. You don't need to bother setting tab stops or defining columns. Instead, you use the Table feature to create a column and row structure. Then you can move the cursor within that structure, enter text, and edit it. Follow these steps:

1. Move the cursor to the left margin.
2. Press Alt + F7 to activate the Columns/Table command, and select Tables (2).

    Access the Layout pull-down menu, and select Tables.

    WordPerfect displays a new menu:

    Table: 1 Create; 2 Edit; 0

3. Select Create (1).

    WordPefect displays the prompt Number of Columns: 3.

4. Type a value from 1 to 32, and press Enter.

    WordPerfect displays the prompt Number of Rows: 1.

5. Type a value from 1 to 32,765, and press Enter.

Wordperfect creates a blank table and displays the table editor menu. The status line at the bottom of the screen indicates the cell location of the cursor.

The table editor enables you to define or modify the structure or format of a table. The table structure is the physical layout of the rows and columns, the size, and the type of grid lines. The table format is the appearance of the text in the rows, columns, and cells. You can use the table editor whenever you edit a document containing a table. Keep in mind, however, that text cannot be entered or edited while the table editor is active.

As you edit the table structure, you can perform the following tasks:

- Insert and delete columns or rows
- Join or split cells

Formatting Lines and Paragraphs

- Change the grid lines
- Add shading to rows
- Adjust the width of columns
- Change the attributes for a single cell, a highlighted block of cells, or a column
- Align text within cells or columns

You enter, format, or edit text in a cell within a table in the same way that you accomplish these tasks in the main document. As you enter text in a cell, the cell expands downward as necessary. As you delete text, the cell contracts to the smallest height required by the largest cell in the row.

Objective 4: To Indent Text

Although WordPerfect's Tab and Indent features are similar, each has specific uses.

In figure 4.10, the first line of text is indented with [Tab]. An entire paragraph is indented from the left margin with [F4] (Indent). An entire paragraph is indented from both the left and right margins with [Shift]+[F4] (Left-Right Indent).

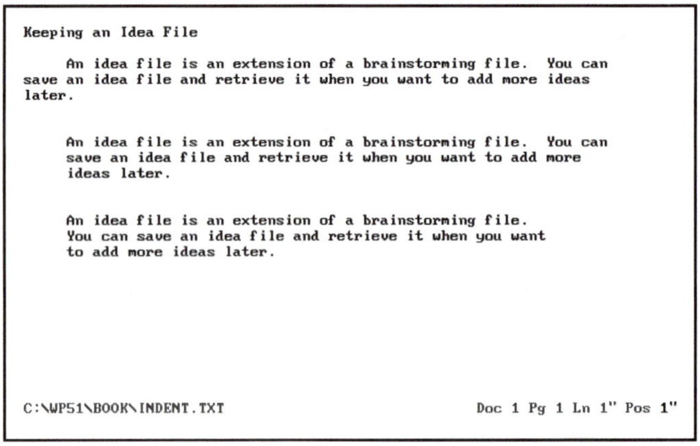

Fig. 4.10
Three types of indents.

```
Keeping an Idea File
        An idea file is an extension of a brainstorming file.  You can
save an idea file and retrieve it when you want to add more ideas
later.

        An idea file is an extension of a brainstorming file.  You can
        save an idea file and retrieve it when you want to add more
        ideas later.

        An idea file is an extension of a brainstorming file.
        You can save an idea file and retrieve it when you want
        to add more ideas later.




C:\WP51\BOOK\INDENT.TXT                              Doc 1 Pg 1 Ln 1" Pos 1"
```

Never use the space bar for indenting or tabbing. If your printer supports proportional spacing, text will not align properly at the left indent or tab stop. Use instead the [Tab] key or the Indent key ([F4]).

To Indent Text

Exercise 4.1: Using the Tab Key

Use the Tab key to indent only the first line of a paragraph from the left margin. The Tab key, represented by left and right arrows at the left side of the keyboard, works like the Tab key on a typewriter. Each time you press Tab in WordPerfect, the cursor moves across the screen to the next tab stop. Practice using the Tab key by doing the following:

1. Position the cursor at the beginning of a paragraph of text.
2. Press Tab. Notice that only the first line of the paragraph has been indented.

Exercise 4.2: Using the Indent Key

Now try indenting an entire paragraph from the left margin by using either the keyboard or the mouse.

Using the keyboard, follow these steps:

1. Position the cursor at the beginning of a paragraph of text.
2. Press Indent (F4) to indent an entire paragraph from the left margin.

 Using the mouse, access the **Layout** pull-down menu, choose **Align**, and then choose **Indent** →.

The cursor moves one tab stop to the right, and the left margin is reset temporarily. Everything you type, until you press Enter, is indented one tab stop. To indent more than one tab stop, press Indent (F4) until the cursor is located where you want to begin.

Exercise 4.3: Using the Left-Right Indent Key

Try indenting a paragraph from both the left and right margins by using either the keyboard or the mouse.

Using the keyboard, follow these steps:

1. Position the cursor at the beginning of a paragraph of text.
2. Press Left-Right Indent (Shift + F4) to indent a paragraph from both the left and right margins.

 Using the mouse, access the **Layout** pull-down menu, choose **Align**, and choose **Indent** →← .

Formatting Lines and Paragraphs

The cursor moves to the right one tab stop and temporarily resets both the left and right margins. Everything you type, until you press [⏎Enter], is indented one tab stop from the left margin and indented the same distance from the right margin. To indent more than one tab stop from both margins, press Left-Right Indent ([Ctrl]+[⇧Shift]) more than once.

Exercise 4.4: Indenting an Existing Paragraph

You can use Indent ([F4]) or Left-Right Indent ([⇧Shift]+[F4]) to indent an existing paragraph. Follow these steps:

1. Move the cursor to the first character of the text you want to indent (or to the left of a tab indent at the beginning of a paragraph).

2. Press [F4] (Indent) or [⇧Shift]+[F4] (Left-Right Indent).

    ⌨ Access the Layout pull-down menu, choose Align, and choose either Indent → or Indent →←.

3. Press [↓] to reformat the screen so that the entire paragraph is indented.

Figure 4.11 shows the paragraph indented from both the left and right margins.

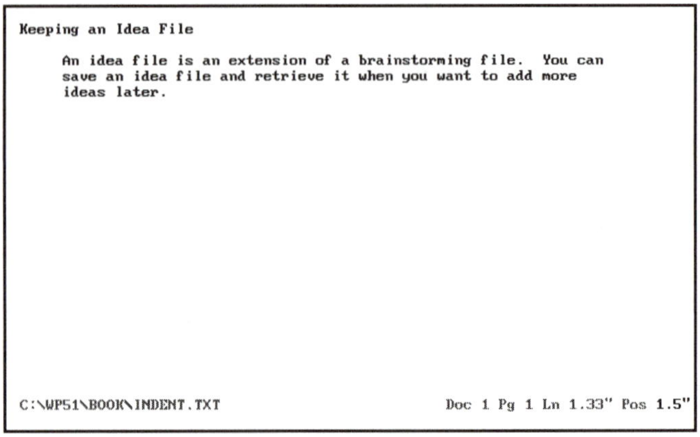

Fig. 4.11
The indented paragraph.

```
Keeping an Idea File
        An idea file is an extension of a brainstorming file.  You can
        save an idea file and retrieve it when you want to add more
        ideas later.




















C:\WP51\BOOK\INDENT.TXT                          Doc 1 Pg 1 Ln 1.33" Pos 1.5"
```

Exercise 4.5: Creating a Hanging Indent

A *hanging indent* is one in which the first line of the paragraph is flush with the left margin, and the rest of the paragraph is indented to the first tab stop.

Hanging indents are useful in report formats such as bibliographies (see fig. 4.12).

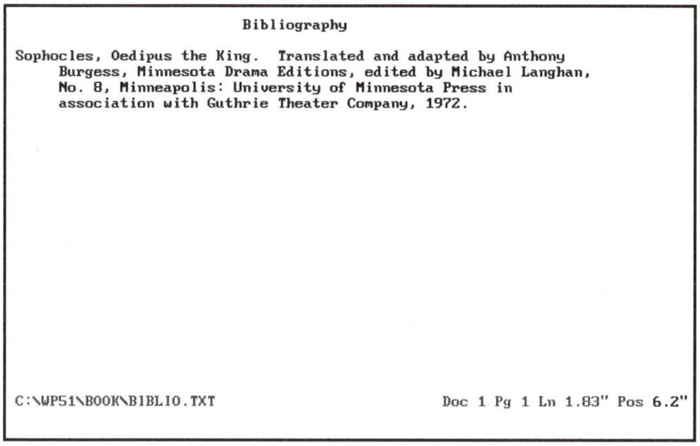

Fig. 4.12
A hanging indent.

To create a hanging indent, follow these steps:

1. Position the cursor at the left margin.
2. Press F4 (Indent) to move the cursor to the first tab stop.

   Access the Layout pull-down menu, choose Align, and choose Indent →.

3. Press Shift+Tab (Margin Release) to move the cursor back to its original position, at the left margin.

   Access the Layout pull-down menu, choose Align, and choose Margin Rel ←.

4. Type your text.
5. To end the hanging indent, press Enter.

Objective 5: To Use Justification

WordPerfect offers the following four types of justification:

- *Full Justification* aligns the text on the printed page along both the right and left margins. Use Full Justification (the default setting) when you have a printer capable of proportional spacing and you want a formal look.
- *Left Justification* leaves a ragged right margin.
- *Center Justification* centers all text.
- *Right Justification* aligns all text on the right margin, leaving the left margin ragged.

Formatting Lines and Paragraphs

The four types of justification are used in the sample document displayed in figure 4.13. Notice that you cannot see on-screen the impact of Full Justification. The screen appears with a ragged-edge margin, but you can verify justification through the Reveal Codes screen.

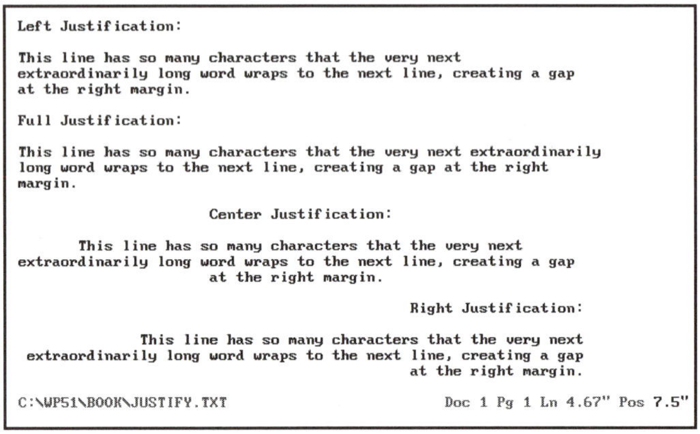

Fig. 4.13
The four types of justification.

```
Left Justification:
This line has so many characters that the very next
extraordinarily long word wraps to the next line, creating a gap
at the right margin.

Full Justification:
This line has so many characters that the very next extraordinarily
long word wraps to the next line, creating a gap at the right
margin.
                        Center Justification:
           This line has so many characters that the very next
extraordinarily long word wraps to the next line, creating a gap
                         at the right margin.
                                              Right Justification:
                    This line has so many characters that the very next
 extraordinarily long word wraps to the next line, creating a gap
                                               at the right margin.

C:\WP51\BOOK\JUSTIFY.TXT                        Doc 1 Pg 1 Ln 4.67" Pos 7.5"
```

Because Full Justification is not visible on-screen in figure 4.13, you either must use View Document or print the page to see the full effect. Because text is justified by the addition of spaces between words and letters, the attractiveness of justified text depends on the capabilities of your printer. Figure 4.14 shows a printout that does justice to Full Justification.

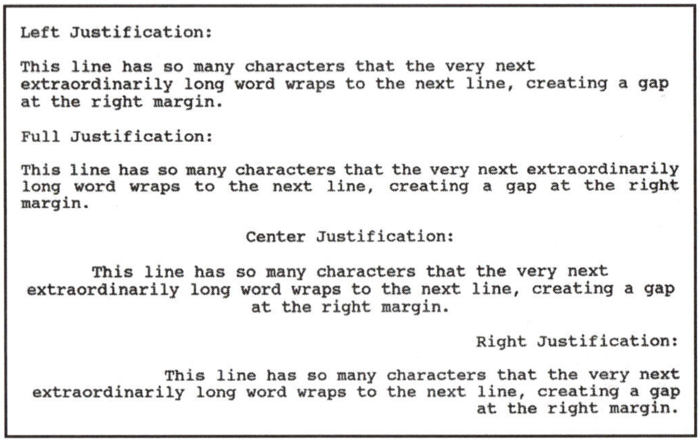

Fig. 4.14
A printout that shows the impact of Full Justification.

```
Left Justification:
This line has so many characters that the very next
extraordinarily long word wraps to the next line, creating a gap
at the right margin.

Full Justification:
This line has so many characters that the very next extraordinarily
long  word  wraps  to  the  next  line,  creating  a  gap  at the right
margin.
                        Center Justification:
           This line has so many characters that the very next
extraordinarily long word wraps to the next line, creating a gap
                         at the right margin.
                                              Right Justification:
                    This line has so many characters that the very next
 extraordinarily long word wraps to the next line, creating a gap
                                               at the right margin.
```

You can change the justification setting through the Format menu. If the cursor is within the body of the document, the new setting affects only the portion of the document that follows the cursor position. If you want to change the justification setting for the entire document, either move the cursor to the beginning of the document, or go to the Document Initial Codes screen before you complete the following steps.

Exercise 5.1: Changing the Justification Setting with the Format Menu

To change the justification setting with the Format menu, follow these steps:

1. Press ⇧Shift + F8 to activate the Format command, and choose **L**ine (**1**).

    🖱 Access the Layout pull-down menu and choose Line.

2. From the Format: Line menu, choose **J**ustification (**3**).
3. Choose **L**eft (**1**), **C**enter (**2**), **R**ight (**3**), or **F**ull (**4**).
4. Press Exit (F7) to return to the document.

If you are not sure whether justification is on or off, complete steps 1 and 2 to check the setting. Then press Exit (F7) to return to the document.

Centering a Line

WordPerfect enables you to center text instantly, without laboriously counting characters. You can center a line of text between the left and right margins as you type the line or after you type it. You also can center text on a specific point.

Figure 4.15 illustrates centering, as well as other types of text alignment.

Exercise 5.2: Centering Text You Are about To Type

To center text you are about to type, follow these steps:

1. Move the cursor to the left margin of the blank line on which you want to center text.
2. Press ⇧Shift + F6 to activate the Center command.

    🖱 Access the Layout pull-down menu, choose Align, and choose Center.

    The cursor is centered between the left and right margins.

Formatting Lines and Paragraphs

Fig. 4.15
Centering and other types of text alignment.

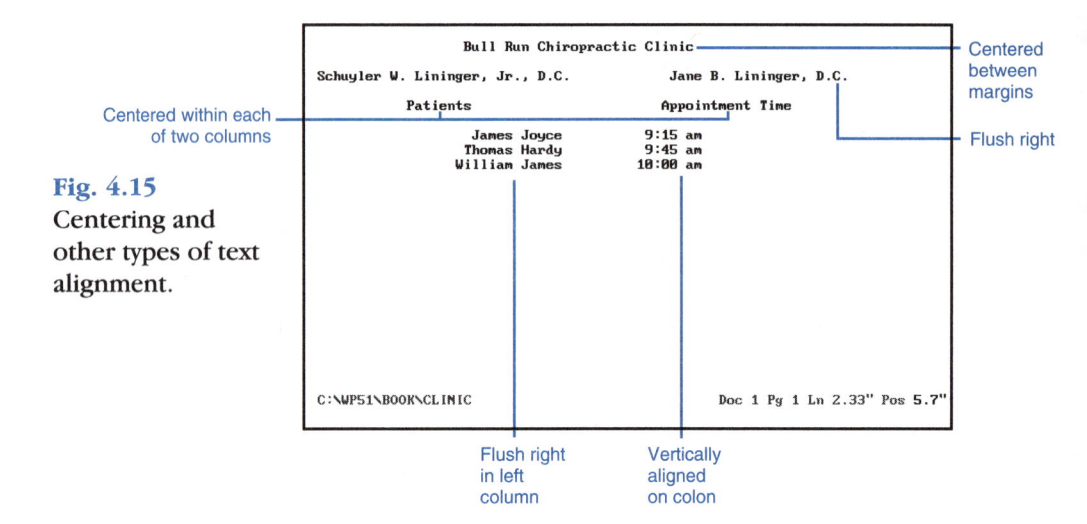

[Screen illustration with labels: "Centered between margins", "Flush right", "Centered within each of two columns", "Flush right in left column", "Vertically aligned on colon" — showing a Bull Run Chiropractic Clinic appointment list with Schuyler W. Lininger, Jr., D.C. and Jane B. Lininger, D.C.; Patients / Appointment Time; James Joyce 9:15 am, Thomas Hardy 9:45 am, William James 10:00 am.]

3. Type your text.

   As you type, the text adjusts to the left and to the right, remaining centered.

4. Press ⏎Enter to end centering.

If you type more characters than can fit between the left and right margins, the rest of the text moves to the next line. Only the first line is centered. To center several lines, highlight the lines as a block, as described in Chapter 3, or change the justification, as described earlier in this chapter.

Exercise 5.3: Centering an Existing Line of Text

To center an existing line of text, follow these steps:

1. Press Alt+F8 or F11 to turn on Reveal Codes.

   ▭ Access the Edit pull-down menu and choose Reveal Codes.

   Check to be sure that the line ends with a hard return code ([HRt]).

2. Press Alt+F3 or F11 to turn off Reveal Codes.

   ▭ Access the Edit pull-down menu and choose Reveal Codes.

3. Place the cursor at the left margin of the line of text to be centered.

4. Press ⇧Shift+F6 to activate the Center command.

   The text moves to the center of the screen.

5. Press ↓ to reformat the screen.

To Use Justification

Exercise 5.4: Centering on a Specific Point

To center text on a specific point, follow these steps:

1. Use the **space bar** or press `Tab` to move the cursor to the specific point on which you want to center the text.
2. Press `Shift`+`F6` to activate the Center command.
3. Type your text.
4. Press `Enter`.

The text is centered on the position of the cursor. You cannot center previously typed text on a specific point.

Exercise 5.5: Aligning Text Flush Right

Use the Flush Right feature to align text with the right margin. This feature aligns the right edge of all headings, columns, and lines of text *flush* (even) with the right margin.

You can align text flush right either before or after you type the text (see fig. 4.16).

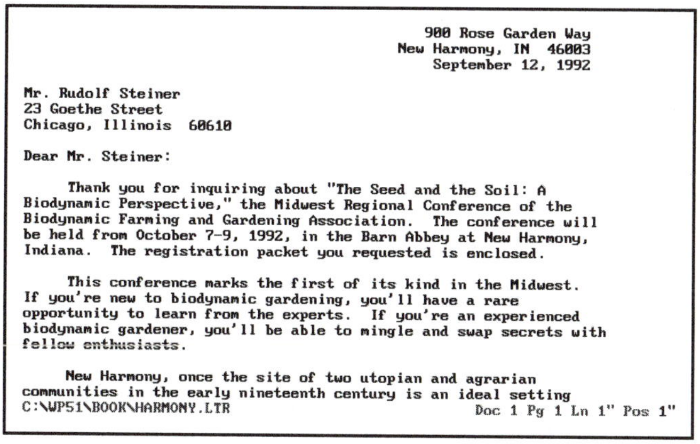

Fig. 4.16
Flush-right text in the return address.

Exercise 5.6: Creating Flush-Right Text as You Type

To create flush-right text as you type, follow these steps:

1. Move the cursor to a blank line.
2. Press `Alt`+`F6` to activate the Flush Right command.

Formatting Lines and Paragraphs

⌨ Access the Layout pull-down menu, choose Align, and choose Flush Right.

The cursor jumps to the right margin.

3. Type your text.

   As you type, the cursor stays at the right margin, and the text moves to the left.

4. Press `Alt` to stop aligning text with the right margin.

Exercise 5.7: Aligning Existing Text with the Right Margin

To align existing text with the right margin, follow these steps:

1. Place the cursor at the left margin.
2. Press `Alt` + `F6` to activate the Flush Right command.

   ⌨ Access the Layout pull-down menu, choose Align, and choose Flush Right.

   The line of text jumps past the right margin.

3. Press ↓ to reformat the screen.

When you use the Flush Right feature, some of the text may disappear past the right edge of the screen. Pressing ↓ adjusts the screen display.

You can use the Block feature to right-align several lines at once. First highlight the block, using one of the methods described in Chapter 3, "Working with Blocks." Then follow the preceding steps to align the block of text flush right. An alternative is to use the Justification feature, as described earlier in this chapter.

Using Hyphenation

When a line of text becomes too long to fit within the margins, the last word in the line wraps to the next line. With short words, wrapping does not present a problem. With long words, however, the following problems can occur:

- If Justification is set to Left, a large gap can occur at the right margin, making the margin appear too ragged.
- If Justification is set to Full, large spaces between words become visually distracting.

To Use Justification

Hyphenating a long word at the end of a line solves the problem and creates a visually attractive printed document. When you use WordPerfect's Hyphenation feature, the program fits as much of the word as possible on one line before hyphenating, and wraps the balance of the word to the next line.

Exercise 5.8: Using Hyphenation Settings

To turn on the Hyphenation feature for the entire document, follow these steps:

1. Press `Shift`+`F8` to activate the Format command, choose **D**ocument (**3**), and choose Initial **C**odes (**2**).

    Access the Layout pull-down menu, choose Document, and choose Initial Codes (2).

    WordPerfect displays the Document Initial Codes screen.

2. Press Format (`F7`+`F8`) and choose **L**ine (**1**).

    Access the Layout pull-down menu and choose Line.

    The Format: Line menu appears.

3. From the Format: Line menu, choose H**y**phenation (**1**).
4. Choose **Y**es to turn on hyphenation.
5. Press Exit (`F7`) three times to return to the document.

    A [Hyph On] code is inserted into the document.

Hyphenation remains on until you turn off the feature. To turn it off, repeat the preceding steps, but choose **N**o instead of **Y**es in step 4.

When hyphenation is on, as you type or scroll the document, WordPerfect may hyphenate some words. At other times, WordPerfect may prompt you to make a decision regarding the hyphenation of a particular word.

When WordPerfect reaches a word, such as *justification*, the program beeps and displays a message similar to the one shown at the bottom of the screen in figure 4.17.

At this point, you have three options:

- You can press `Esc` to hyphenate the word as displayed.
- You can use the cursor keys to move the hyphen to another hyphenation point, and then press `Esc` to hyphenate the word.
- You can press Cancel (`F1`) to avoid hyphenating the word and wrap it to the next line. If you choose this option, a cancel-hyphenation

Formatting Lines and Paragraphs

code ([/]) is inserted before the word; you must delete this code manually if you later decide to hyphenate the word.

```
     When you are planning your printed document, consider the
appearance you want to present.  With ragged text, you have an
uneven right margin and a less formal look. With right-justification




















Position hyphen; Press ESC justifica-tion
```

Fig. 4.17
Confirming hyphenation.

If you want to turn off hyphenation temporarily (for example, while scrolling a document or checking spelling), press Exit (F7). When WordPerfect finishes scrolling or checking spelling, hyphenation is automatically turned on again.

Note: To control hyphenation in the ways you prefer, you can customize WordPerfect with the Environment option on the Setup menu. You can choose to turn on hyphenation permanently, and you can choose the type of hyphenation you want. In addition, if you don't want WordPerfect to beep every time you are prompted for hyphenation, you can turn off the Beep option for hyphenation. The Environment option on the Setup menu also enables you to choose whether WordPerfect should beep when you make an error or when a search string cannot be found.

Controlling Hyphenation

WordPerfect provides many features that enable you to control hyphenation of the text at the right margin. Among these features are a variety of hyphens, returns, and hard spaces.

Understanding the Types of Hyphens

At first glance, a hyphen simply looks like a hyphen, but WordPerfect uses—and enables you to use—several kinds of hyphens, including hard hyphens, hyphen characters, and soft hyphens.

A *hard* hyphen is part of the spelling of a word, as in *father-in-law* and *jack-of-all-trades*. A hard hyphen is displayed and printed at all times. The hard hyphen code appears on the Reveal Codes screen as [-]. If a hard hyphen appears in a word that needs to be hyphenated, WordPerfect uses the hard hyphen as the breaking point instead of prompting you for a hyphenation decision. To enter a hard hyphen, you press the hyphen key (located on the same key as the underline character).

The *hyphen character* appears on-screen the same as a hard hyphen, but WordPerfect treats the hyphen character as if it were a character. A word containing a hyphen character is not necessarily split at the hyphen. You may be prompted for hyphenation. In Reveal Codes, the hyphen appears as an unhighlighted -. To enter a hyphen character, you press (Home) and then press the hyphen key. Be sure to use the hyphen key in the row of numeric keys, not the minus sign on the numeric keypad. (The minus sign is used in formulas.)

A *soft hyphen* is inserted between syllables during hyphenation. A soft hyphen is visible and prints only when it appears as the last character in a line; otherwise, a soft hyphen remains hidden. The soft hyphen appears in Reveal Codes as a highlighted -. You can insert soft hyphens at points where you want hyphenation to occur by pressing (Ctrl)-hyphen.

To insert a *dash* in the text, use a combination of two kinds of hyphens. For the first hyphen, you press (Home) and then press the hyphen key for the hyphen character. For the second hyphen, you press the hyphen key for a hard hyphen. WordPerfect does not separate the two hyphens at the end of a line.

If your printer is capable, you also can use the Compose feature to print an actual dash (printers call this an *em dash*). To print an em dash (—), you place the cursor where you want the dash to appear, press (Ctrl)+(V), and press the hyphen key twice.

Understanding Line Breaks

Another way you can control the text at the right margin is by specifying what kind of line break you want. In WordPerfect, a line can end with a soft return, a hard return, or an invisible soft return.

WordPerfect inserts a soft return code ([SRt]) at the end of each line when the text reaches the right margin and is wrapped to the next line.

Formatting Lines and Paragraphs

The program inserts a hard return code ([HRt]) when you press `↵Enter` to end a line. You can insert a hard return when you don't want a line to wrap to the next line or when you want to insert a blank line.

WordPerfect inserts an invisible soft return code ([ISRt]) when you press `Home` and then press `↵Enter`. This feature is handy for dividing words without inserting a hyphen—for example, dividing words such as *and/or* or *either/or* after the slash, or dividing words connected with an ellipsis (…).

WordPerfect inserts a deletable soft return code ([DSRt]) if hyphenation is off and a line doesn't fit between the left and right margins.

Keeping Words Together

If you want to keep two words together on a line, you can insert a hard space between them by pressing `Home`, space bar. For example, you can keep the words *San Francisco* on one line by first pressing `Home` and then the Space bar after you type **San**. A hard space signals WordPerfect to treat the two words as a single unit. WordPerfect does not divide the words when they fall at the end of a line but moves both words to the following line. A hard space appears as [ ] in Reveal Codes.

Objective 6: To Enhance Text

You can enhance a document by changing the size and appearance of the text. You accomplish some formatting tasks as you enter text simply by pressing the appropriate key, typing the text, and pressing the key again. For example, from anywhere within the document, you can boldface or underline text as you type. You can apply other text enhancements by choosing them through the Font menu. To make text italic, for example, you choose that type style from the menu.

Enhancing Text from within a Document

A common text enhancement that you can make from within a document is to boldface or underline a portion of text. Although you can make either of these enhancements through the Font menu (as described in the next section), the simplest way to boldface or underline text that you are about to type is to press Bold (`F6`) or Underline (`F8`).

Exercise 6.1: Boldfacing a Portion of Text You Are about To Type

To boldface a portion of text you are about to type, follow these steps:

1. Press F6 to turn on the Bold feature.
2. Type the text you want to boldface.

   The text that you type appears brighter (or in a different color) on-screen. The Pos number in the status line also changes in brightness or color.
3. Press F6 again to turn off the Bold feature.

Exercise 6.2: Underlining Text

To underline text, follow these steps:

1. Press F8 to turn on the Underline feature.
2. Type the text you want to underline.
3. Press F8 again to turn off the Underline feature.

Bold (F6) and Underline (F8) work as on/off *toggle switches*. You press the key once to turn on the feature; you press the key again to turn off the feature. If you press either Bold or Underline twice without entering text, the text you enter does not reflect bold or underline enhancements.

To enhance text that you already have typed, use the Block command as described in Chapter 3, "Working with Blocks." You first highlight the block of text with the Block command or the mouse. You then press either Bold (F6) or Underline (F8) once to enhance the highlighted block of text.

Enhancing Text with the Font Feature

With WordPerfect's Font feature, you can choose from the fonts (typefaces) available for use with your printer. The Font feature also controls size, color, and other variations of printed text, such as outline and shadow printing, subscripts, and superscripts.

When your computer's printer was installed, an *initial font*, also called the *default base font*, or the *current font*, was installed. The base font is the font in which text is normally printed. Other font sizes and appearance options are usually variations of the base font. For example, if 10-point Helvetica is the base font, boldfaced text is printed in 10-point Helvetica Bold, and italic text is printed in 10-point Helvetica Italic.

Changing Font Attributes

Font attributes refer to the variations in a font's size and appearance that are available with your printer for a given base font. *Size attributes* include superscript and subscript, fine, small, large, very large, and extra large. *Appearance attributes* include boldface, underline, double-underline, italic, outline, shadow, small caps, redline, and strikeout. Remember that not all printers can print all attributes.

You can choose the font attributes by pressing Font (Ctrl+F8) or by accessing the Font pull-down menu. When you press Font (Ctrl+F8), WordPerfect displays the following menu:

    1 Size; **2** Appearance; **3** Normal; **4** Base Font; **5** Print Color: **0**

Slightly different options are displayed on the Font pull-down menu.

Changing the Font Size

WordPerfect offers a variety of font sizes through the Font menu. All the sizes are determined by the base font. For example, if your base font is 10-point Helvetica, the large font may be 12-point Helvetica, the very large font may be 14-point Helvetica, and so on. Note that you may not be able to distinguish the different sizes on-screen. How the various sizes appear in print depends on your printer.

Exercise 6.3: Changing the Size of the Font

To change the size of the font, use the following procedure:

1. Press Ctrl+F8 to activate the Font command. From the Font menu, choose **S**ize (**1**). WordPerfect then displays the following attribute menu:

    1 Suprscpt; **2** Subscpt; **3** Fine; **4** Small; **5** Large; **6** Vry Large; **7** Ext Large: **0**

        Access the Font pull-down menu.

2. Choose any one of the attributes to change the size of the font.

When you choose font size options such as Fine, Large, Very Large, and Extra Large, WordPerfect chooses the correct line spacing (so that a large font doesn't overprint the preceding line, and fine print doesn't print with too much line spacing). If you later decide to print the same document with another printer or set of fonts, WordPerfect performs any required adjustments and sets the correct font, pitch, and line height automatically.

You can change a font attribute of existing text by first blocking the text with the Block command or the mouse, and then choosing the new font attribute with the procedure just described.

Changing the Font Appearance

WordPerfect offers a variety of font attributes for appearance through the Font menu. Note that you may not be able to distinguish the different appearance attributes on-screen. How the various attributes for appearance are printed depends on your printer.

Exercise 6.4: Changing the Appearance of the Font

To change the appearance of the font, follow these steps:

1. Press Ctrl+F8 to activate the Font command. From the Font menu, choose Appearance (2).

    WordPerfect displays the following attribute menu:

    1 Bold 2 Undrln 3 Dbl Und 4 Italc 5 Outln 6 Shadw 7 Sm Cap 8 Redln 9 Stkout: 0

    🖱 Access the Font pull-down menu and choose Appearance.

2. Choose any one of the attributes to change the appearance of the font.

Exercise 6.5: Restoring Font Size and Appearance to Normal

To restore a single attribute for font size or appearance to normal after typing the text, press the right-arrow key one time to move the cursor past the attribute-off code. If more than one attribute is turned on, press the right-arrow key one time for each attribute you want to turn off.

Alternatively, after you have made several font attribute changes, you can restore the font size and appearance to normal by doing the following:

1. Press Font (Ctrl+F8).
2. Choose Normal (3).

Formatting Lines and Paragraphs

Alternatively, you can access the **Font** pull-down menu and choose **Normal**. Either method pushes the cursor beyond all attribute-off codes and ends all size and appearance attributes at that point in the document.

Changing the Base Font

In addition to changing font attributes, you can change the base font that the printer uses—permanently (for all future documents), for the entire current document, or for a portion of the current document. To change the base font permanently, you use the Print menu. To change the base font for the entire current document, you change the Initial Base Font setting on the Format: Document menu. To change the base font for a portion of the current document, you use the Font menu.

Exercise 6.6: Changing the Base Font for the Entire Current Document

To change the base font for the entire current document, follow these steps:

1. Press `Shift`+`F8` to activate the Format command, and choose **D**ocument (*3*).

    Access the Layout pull-down menu and choose Document.

2. Choose Initial Base **F**ont (*3*) from the Format: Document menu.
3. Highlight the font you want; then press `Enter` or choose **S**elect (*1*).

The screen display adjusts to reflect for the new base font the number of characters that can be printed in a line with the current margin settings. If, for example, you choose a 6-pitch font, the on-screen lines are shorter than if you choose a 10-pitch font. (*Pitch* indicates the number of characters per inch.)

Exercise 6.7: Changing the Base Font for a Portion of the Current Document

To change the base font for a portion of the current document, follow these steps:

1. Move the cursor to the place in the document where you want to change the base font.
2. Press `Ctrl`+`F8` to activate the Font command, and choose Base **F**ont (*4*).

🖰 Access the Font pull-down menu and choose Base Font.

WordPerfect displays a list of the fonts available for use with your printer. The fonts listed are the printer's built-in fonts, plus any fonts you have chosen with the Cartridges and Fonts feature.

3. Choose **N**ame Search and type the first letters of the font you want to choose. When the name of the font is highlighted, press ⏎Enter or choose **S**elect (**1**).

🖰 Use the mouse pointer to highlight the font you want. Choose Select (1) or double-click the font to choose it.

Chapter Summary

This chapter has presented many formatting options you can use to determine the format for the lines and paragraphs of your documents. You learned how to change the settings for the left and right margins, and how to enhance your text with boldfacing and underlining. You also learned how to enhance text by changing the font attributes and the base font. And you learned ways to indent text, align text, and use hyphenation. In the next chapter, you examine formatting techniques that apply to pages as well as to the entire document.

Testing Your Knowledge

True/False Questions

1. You can change the margins for just the current document or permanently for all future documents.
2. Pressing ⇧Shift + F8 and choosing **1** accesses the Format: Line menu.
3. A right tab is the most commonly used tab stop.
4. With the keyboard, press ⇧Shift + F4 to indent an entire paragraph from the left margin.
5. The Font feature controls the size and appearance of text.

Formatting Lines and Paragraphs

Multiple Choice Questions

1. To change the left and right margins for the current document, you
   A. press **Shift**+**F8**, press **L**ine (**1**), choose **M**argins (**7**), type the values, and then press **F7** to exit.
   B. press **Shift**+**F8** and then choose **M**argins (**7**).
   C. access the **L**ayout pull-down menu, choose **L**ine, choose **M**argins (**7**), type the values, and press **F7** to exit.
   D. press **Shift**+**F1**.
   E. can do both A and C.

2. Type of tabs available in WordPerfect are
   A. left, center, right, and decimal.
   B. left justified.
   C. centered.
   D. table.
   E. left and right.

3. To indent an existing paragraph from both the left and the right margins, you
   A. press **F4**.
   B. press **Shift**+**F4**.
   C. press **Ctrl**+**F4**.
   D. press **Alt**+**F4**.
   E. do none of the above.

4. If you press **Shift**+**F8**, choose **1**, choose **6**, and type **2**, you have
   A. set the line spacing to triple-space.
   B. set the line spacing to double-space.
   C. set the line spacing to single-space.
   D. set the line spacing for all documents.
   E. set the line spacing to double-space for all paragraphs above the cursor.

5. Enhancing text with the Font feature enables you to
   A. control line spacing.
   B. control the length of the document.
   C. control the size and appearance of text.
   D. create your own font size.
   E. do none of the above.

Testing Your Knowledge

Fill-in-the-Blank Questions

1. Many of WordPerfect's formatting tasks begin at the _____ menu or the _____ pull-down menu.

2. To change left and right margins, press _____ and choose _____; then choose _____ and type the values.

3. To boldface a portion of text you are about to type, press _____; then type the text and press _____.

4. The _____ font is the font in which text is normally printed.

5. Using the _____ key indents only the first line of a paragraph, but the _____ key indents every line of a paragraph.

Review: Short Projects

1. Changing Margins and Spacing

   Retrieve the MEMO document and change the margins to 2" left and right and the line spacing to double-spacing.

   Print the document and save without replacing.

2. Setting Tabs

   Type the following and set tabs at 1" L, 2.5" L, and 5" D.

Name	Social Security Number	Price
Jack Frost	000-90-8331	$55.25

   Add two more names and print the file.

   Save the file as TABS.

3. Changing Fonts and Indent

   A. Change the font to Large Size, and type

       TEST FONTS

   B. Change the font to normal size and type

       This is a test.

   C. Change the font to Italics and type

       This is test two.

   Save the file as FONT.

Formatting Lines and Paragraphs

Review: Long Projects

1. Changing Margins, Tabs, and Spacing

    Type the following, with the left margin = 2" and the right margin = 1.5, spacing = 2, and tabs = .5", 3", 5". Save the file as MESSAGE.

    For your convenience, we now providing voice mail to service your message needs. This service was activated upon your check-in to the hotel. Please press the message button to retrieve your voice mail messages. In some cases, the message light may be dim. We suggest you check for your messages frequently. If you have any questions, please

Contact the Operator	Press 0	Press 22

    Other Services Provided are as follows:

Message	Press 5	Press 35
Front Desk	Press 15	Press 88
Health Spa	Press 02	Press 66

2. Using Indent and Fonts

    Retrieve the KEYTERMS document. Add the following text:

    Initial Font

    > The font in which text is normally printed, also called the default base font, or current font. Often, font sizes and appearances are variations of the initial font.

    Instructions:

    A. Change the headers (the word being defined) of each definition in the document to double underline and the size to very large.

    B. Indent the paragraphs from the left once.

    C. Italicize the words shown.

    D. Save the file as KEYTERMS.

Formatting Pages

Designing a document means making formatting choices at several levels. In the preceding chapter, you learned to format lines and paragraphs. In this chapter, you learn to format an entire document, or just a page or group of pages.

Formatting pages involves decisions such as changing the top and bottom margins, centering pages top to bottom, designing headers and footers, numbering pages, and controlling page breaks.

Objectives

1. To Choose Paper Size and Type
2. To Change Top and Bottom Margins
3. To Design Headers and Footers
4. To Number Pages
5. To Control Page Breaks

Formatting Pages

Key Terms in This Chapter	
Header	Information that prints automatically at the top margin of every page.
Footer	Information that prints automatically at the bottom margin of every page.
Soft page break	A page break that occurs automatically. A soft page break appears on-screen as a dashed line.
Hard page break	A page break you insert to force a break at a certain spot. A hard page break appears on-screen as a line of equal signs.
Widow	In WordPerfect, a paragraph's first line at the bottom of a page.
Orphan	In WordPerfect, a paragraph's last line at the top of a page.
Superscript	A number or letter written immediately above, or above and to the right or left of, another character.
Subscript	A number or letter written immediately below, or below and to the right or left of, another character.

Objective 1: To Choose Paper Size and Type

In WordPerfect, a *form definition* includes the paper size and type, the location of the paper in the printer, and whether the orientation of the printing is portrait (vertical) or landscape (horizontal). When you first start WordPerfect, several forms—such as those for standard paper, legal paper, and business envelopes—already are defined for you.

Exercise 1.1: Defining a New Page Size and Type

If you need to define a new form, however, follow these steps:

To Choose Paper Size and Type

1. Press ⇧Shift + F8 to activate the Format command, and choose **Page** (**2**).

   ⌨ Access the Layout pull-down menu and choose Page.

   WordPerfect displays the Format: Page menu shown in figure 5.1, offering a number of page formatting options.

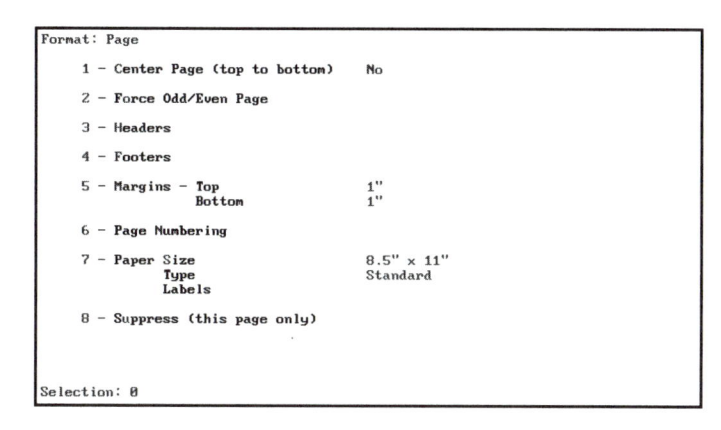

   ```
   Format: Page
       1 - Center Page (top to bottom)    No
       2 - Force Odd/Even Page
       3 - Headers
       4 - Footers
       5 - Margins - Top                  1"
                     Bottom               1"
       6 - Page Numbering
       7 - Paper Size                     8.5" x 11"
                Type                      Standard
                Labels
       8 - Suppress (this page only)



   Selection: 0
   ```

   Fig. 5.1
   The Format: Page menu.

2. Choose Paper **S**ize/Type (**7**).

   WordPerfect displays the Format: Paper Size/Type menu (see fig. 5.2). This menu lists information about some standard forms already defined by WordPerfect and ready to use. At the bottom of the screen is a menu from which you can choose to select, add, copy, delete, or edit a form.

   ```
   Format: Paper Size/Type
                                                    Font   Double
   Paper type and Orientation  Paper Size  Prompt Loc  Type Sided Labels

   Envelope - Wide             9.5" x 4"    No   Manual Land No
   Legal                       8.5" x 14"   No   Contin Port No
   Legal - Wide                14" x 8.5"   No   Contin Land No
   Standard                    8.5" x 11"   No   Contin Port No
   Standard - Wide             11" x 8.5"   No   Contin Land No
   [ALL OTHERS]                Width ≤ 8.5" Yes  Manual      No








   1 Select; 2 Add (Create); 3 Copy; 4 Delete; 5 Edit; N Name Search: 1
   ```

   Fig. 5.2
   The Format: Paper Size/Type menu.

111

Formatting Pages

3. Choose **A**dd (Create) (**2**).

   WordPerfect displays the Format: Paper Type menu (see fig. 5.3). The *paper type* is the name you choose for the form. When you choose any of the first seven options from the Paper Type menu, you are choosing that option's name as the paper type on the Format: Edit Paper Definition menu (see step 4).

   Choosing [**A**LL OTHERS] (**8**) stops the form-definition process and returns you to the Format: Paper Size/Type menu. Choosing **O**ther (**9**) causes WordPerfect to prompt you to enter a name for some other form type. The name that you type becomes the form's paper type.

Fig. 5.3
The Format: Paper Type menu.

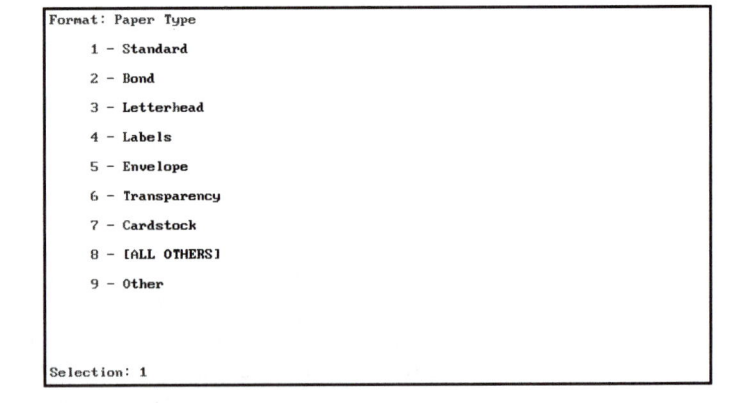

```
Format: Paper Type

      1 - Standard
      2 - Bond
      3 - Letterhead
      4 - Labels
      5 - Envelope
      6 - Transparency
      7 - Cardstock
      8 - [ALL OTHERS]
      9 - Other




Selection: 1
```

4. Choose **S**tandard (**1**).

   WordPerfect displays the Format: Edit Paper Definition menu (see fig. 5.4). On your screen, the `FILENAME` portion of `FILENAME.PRS` will be the name of WordPerfect's definition for your printer.

Fig. 5.4
The Format: Edit Paper Definition menu.

```
Format: Edit Paper Definition
          Filename                    HPLASIII.PRS
      1 - Paper Size                  8.5" x 11"
      2 - Paper Type                  Standard
      3 - Font Type                   Portrait
      4 - Prompt to Load              No
      5 - Location                    Continuous
      6 - Double Sided Printing       No
      7 - Binding Edge                Left
      8 - Labels                      No
      9 - Text Adjustment - Top       0"
                           Side       0"

Selection: 0
```

To Choose Paper Size and Type

5. Choose Paper Size (1) from the Format: Edit Paper Definition menu.

    WordPerfect displays the Format: Paper Size menu (see fig. 5.5). The *paper size* is the actual dimensions of the sheet on which WordPerfect will print the document. These dimensions can be a standard size, such as 8 1/2 by 11 inches, or a unique size, such as 4 by 9 inches.

    If you choose any of the first nine options, WordPerfect uses the predefined dimensions listed for the option you choose. If you choose Other, WordPerfect prompts you to define the width and height for the form.

```
Format: Paper Size           Width   Height
     1 - Standard            (8.5" x 11")
     2 - Standard Landscape  (11" x 8.5")
     3 - Legal               (8.5" x 14")
     4 - Legal Landscape     (14" x 8.5")
     5 - Envelope            (9.5" x 4")
     6 - Half Sheet          (5.5" x 8.5")
     7 - US Government       (8" x 11")
     8 - A4                  (210mm x 297mm)
     9 - A4 Landscape        (297mm x 210mm)
     o - Other

Selection: 0
```

Fig. 5.5
The Format:
Paper Size menu.

6. For this exercise, choose Standard Landscape (2) to choose a form 11 inches wide and 8 1/2 inches high.

    WordPerfect displays the Format: Edit Paper Definition menu (see fig. 5.6). The paper size now appears as 11" × 8.5". The paper type has changed to Standard – Wide.

```
Format: Edit Paper Definition
         Filename                HPLASIII.PRS
     1 - Paper Size              11" x 8.5"
     2 - Paper Type              Standard - Wide
     3 - Font Type               Landscape
     4 - Prompt to Load          No
     5 - Location                Continuous
     6 - Double Sided Printing   No
     7 - Binding Edge            Left
     8 - Labels                  No
     9 - Text Adjustment - Top   0"
                          Side   0"

Selection: 0
```

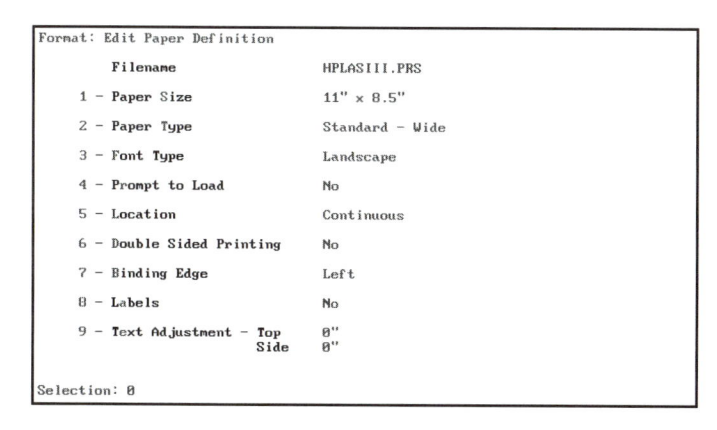

Fig. 5.6
A new paper size on the Format: Edit Paper Definition menu.

Formatting Pages

7. To define another form, choose Paper Type (**2**).

   WordPerfect again displays the Format: Paper Type menu.

8. This time, choose Other (**9**).

   WordPerfect displays the prompt `Other paper type:`. You can choose your own unique name for the form.

9. For this exercise, type **TEST** (in uppercase letters) and press ⏎Enter.

   WordPerfect displays the Format: Edit Paper Definition menu. The paper type is now listed as `TEST - Wide`.

10. Choose Font Type (**3**).

    The *font type* tells WordPerfect whether you want to print with characters in portrait (vertical) or landscape (horizontal) orientation, relative to the paper's insertion edge. This setting is meaningful only if you are using a laser printer. If you don't use a laser printer, you can omit this option when you define the form.

    WordPerfect displays the following menu at the bottom of the screen:

    Orientation: 1 Portrait; **2** Landscape: **0**

11. Regardless of whether you use a laser printer, choose Landscape (**2**).

    On the Format: Edit Paper Definition menu, the font type is now Landscape.

12. Choose Prompt to Load (**4**).

    WordPerfect displays the `No (Yes)` prompt. Choose Yes only if you want to hand-feed sheets into your printer. For this exercise, assume that you do not hand-feed sheets into the printer. Choose No or press F1 (Cancel).

13. Choose Location (**5**).

    The *location* indicates how the paper is inserted into the printer. WordPerfect displays the following menu at the bottom of the screen:

    Location: 1 Continuous; **2** Bin Number; **3** Manual: **0**

    The default setting is Continuous (**1**). Note that the following options are available:

Continuous (**1**)	Choose this option if the printer uses continuous-form paper inserted by a tractor feed or if the printer is a Hewlett-Packard LaserJet with a paper tray.
Bin Number (**2**)	Choose this option if the sheets are inserted individually by a feeder from one or more cassettes. WordPerfect displays a `Bin number:` prompt.

To Choose Paper Size and Type

   Manual (3)   Choose this option if the sheets are inserted by hand.

For this exercise, assume that you have a sheet feeder and that the paper is being drawn from bin (cassette) number 1.

14. Choose **B**in Number (**2**), type **1**, and press ⏎Enter.

    On the Format: Edit Paper Definition menu shown in figure 5.7, the location has changed to Bin 1.

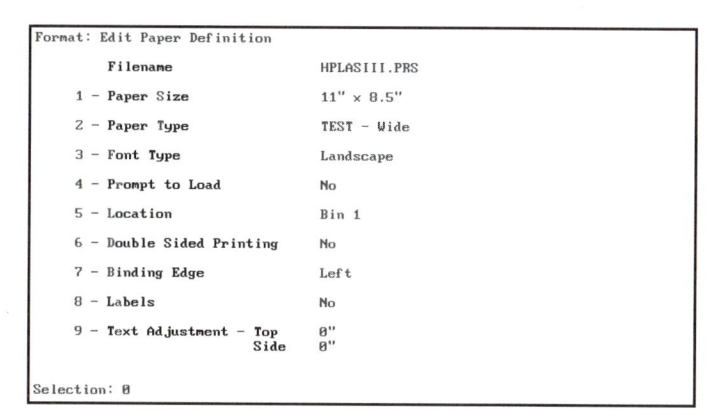

```
Format: Edit Paper Definition
        Filename              HPLASIII.PRS
    1 - Paper Size            11" x 8.5"
    2 - Paper Type            TEST - Wide
    3 - Font Type             Landscape
    4 - Prompt to Load        No
    5 - Location              Bin 1
    6 - Double Sided Printing No
    7 - Binding Edge          Left
    8 - Labels                No
    9 - Text Adjustment - Top 0"
                       Side   0"

Selection: 0
```

Fig. 5.7
The location is now Bin 1.

15. Choose **D**ouble Sided Printing (**6**).

    WordPerfect displays the No (Yes) prompt. Choose **Y**es if you have a laser printer capable of printing on both sides of the sheet (a process called *duplex printing*). If you don't use a duplex laser printer, you can omit this option when you define the form.

    For this exercise, assume that your printer does not print on both sides of the sheet. Choose **N**o or press F1 (Cancel).

16. Choose **B**inding Edge (**7**).

    WordPerfect displays the following menu at the bottom of the screen:

    Binding Edge: 1 Top; **2** Left: 0

    The default selection is **L**eft (**2**). If you have a laser printer capable of duplex printing, this option controls the way the document prints on each side of the sheet.

    You choose **T**op (**1**) to print the document with the second side upside-down so that the document can be bound on the top. You choose **L**eft (**2**) to print the document in the same manner on both sides of the sheet so that the document can be bound on the side. Again, if you do not use a duplex laser printer, you can omit this option when you define the form.

Formatting Pages

For this exercise, assume that your printer does not print on both sides of the sheet. Press F1 (Cancel).

17. Choose Labels (8).

    At the No (Yes) prompt, choose Yes.

    WordPerfect displays the Format: Labels menu, which you use to enter specifications for printing labels (see fig. 5.8). Choose the Labels option only if you want to print a document in a label format. You learn more about labels in Chapter 8, "Merging Documents." Press F1 to cancel this menu.

```
Format: Labels
     1 - Label Size
                Width              11"
                Height             8.5"

     2 - Number of Labels
                Columns            1
                Rows               1

     3 - Top Left Corner
                Top                0"
                Left               0"

     4 - Distance Between Labels
                Column             0"
                Row                0"

     5 - Label Margins
                Left               0.22"
                Right              0.25"
                Top                0.29"
                Bottom             0.25"

Selection: 0                              (Press F3 for Help)
```

Fig. 5.8
The Format: Labels menu.

18. Choose Text Adjustment (9) if you need to move the printed image horizontally or vertically on the sheet.

    With this option, you can make minor changes (less than .25 inch) to fine-tune the placement of the printed image on the sheet. If major changes (.25 inch or more) are necessary, adjust the settings for the printer, according to the printer's manual, rather than use this option.

    WordPerfect displays the following menu:

    Adjust Text: 1 Up; **2** Down; **3** Left; **4** Right: **0**

    If you choose any of these options, WordPerfect displays the prompt Text Adjustment Distance: 0". You then enter (in decimal inches or as a fraction) the amount of adjustment that you want to make, such as **0.1**, and press ↵Enter. Press F1 to cancel the selection.

19. Press F7 (Exit).

WordPerfect displays the Format: Paper Size/Type menu shown in figure 5.9. The form definition has been added to the list of forms.

To Change Top and Bottom Margins

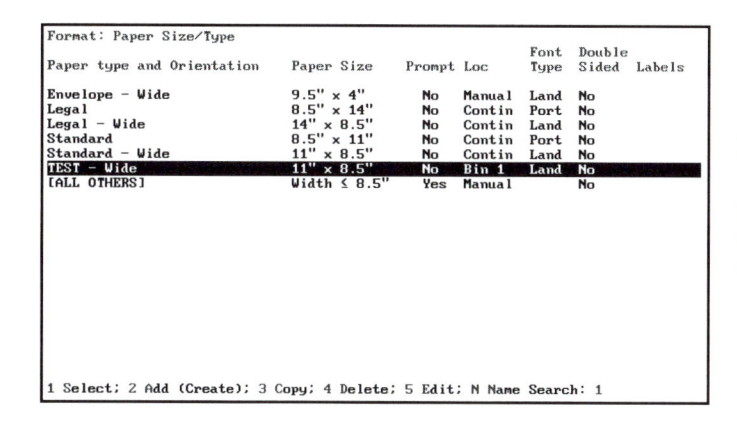

```
Format: Paper Size/Type
                                              Font  Double
Paper type and Orientation   Paper Size   Prompt Loc  Type  Sided  Labels

Envelope - Wide              9.5" x 4"    No   Manual  Land  No
Legal                        8.5" x 14"   No   Contin  Port  No
Legal - Wide                 14" x 8.5"   No   Contin  Land  No
Standard                     8.5" x 11"   No   Contin  Port  No
Standard - Wide              11" x 8.5"   No   Contin  Land  No
TEST - Wide                  11" x 8.5"   No   Bin 1   Land  No
[ALL OTHERS]                 Width ≤ 8.5" Yes  Manual        No




1 Select; 2 Add (Create); 3 Copy; 4 Delete; 5 Edit; N Name Search: 1
```

Fig. 5.9
The new definition added to the Format: Paper Size/Type menu.

Note: Press F1 (Cancel) or Esc three times to cancel all the settings you have entered and to return to the editing screen. To save your changes, press F7 (Exit) twice.

To use one of the defined forms, follow these steps:

1. Press Shift + F8 to activate the Format command, and choose **P**age (**2**).

    Access the Layout pull-down menu and choose Page.

2. Choose Paper **S**ize/Type (**7**).

    WordPerfect displays the Format: Paper Size/Type menu.

3. Use the arrow keys to move the highlight bar to the form you want to use.

4. Choose **S**elect (**1**) to accept the form definition, and press F7 (Exit) to return to the editing screen.

    Note: Press F1 (Cancel) or Esc three times to exit the Format: Paper Size/Type menu and to return to the editing screen without choosing a form definition.

Objective 2: To Change Top and Bottom Margins

WordPerfect is preset to leave one-inch margins at the top and bottom of the page. Page numbers, headers, footers, and footnotes are placed within the allotted text area.

117

Formatting Pages

WordPerfect's default measurement is the inch; therefore, margins are measured in inches. The top margin is the distance between the top edge of the paper and the first line of text. The bottom margin is calculated from the bottom edge of the paper to the last line of text. A margin setting governs the placement of all text that follows the margin code—until a different setting changes the margins.

Exercise 2.1: Changing the Top and Bottom Margins

To change the top and bottom margins, follow these steps:

1. Move the cursor to the place in the document where you want to set margins. If you want to change the margins for the entire document, move the cursor to the top of the document.

2. Press ⇧Shift + F8 to activate the Format command, and choose Page (**2**).

    ▣ Access the Layout pull-down menu and choose Page.

3. From the Format: Page menu, choose **M**argins Top/Bottom (**5**).

4. Type a new top margin, such as **1.5**, and press ⏎Enter. Then type a new bottom margin, such as **1.5**, and press ⏎Enter. Figure 5.10 shows the new margin settings on the Format: Page menu.

Fig. 5.10
New top and bottom margin settings on the Format: Page menu.

```
Format: Page

     1 - Center Page (top to bottom)      No

     2 - Force Odd/Even Page

     3 - Headers

     4 - Footers

     5 - Margins - Top                    1.5"
                   Bottom                 1.5"

     6 - Page Numbering

     7 - Paper Size                       8.5" x 11"
                 Type                     Standard
                 Labels

     8 - Suppress (this page only)


Selection: 0
```

5. Press F7 (Exit) to return to the document.

118

To Change Top and Bottom Margins

Centering Pages Top to Bottom

When you center a page between the top and bottom margins, the setting applies to just one page—the page where you make the setting. For example, you may want to center the title page of a sales report. The end of a centered page can be defined by either a soft page break or a hard page break. Ending the centered page with a hard page break ensures that the page never merges accidentally with the next page.

Before you insert the code to center a page, be sure that the cursor is located at the beginning of the page, before any other formatting codes or text. You can press Reveal Codes (Alt+F3, or F11 on an enhanced keyboard) to verify the cursor position.

Exercise 2.2: Centering a Page Top to Bottom

To center a page top to bottom, follow these steps:

1. Press Shift+F8 to activate the Format command, and choose **P**age (**2**).

    Access the Layout pull-down menu and choose Page.

2. Choose **C**enter Page (top to bottom) (**1**).
3. Choose **Y**es.
4. Press F7 (Exit) to return to the document.

    WordPerfect inserts a [Center Pg] code.

Although the page doesn't appear centered on-screen as shown in figure 5.11, it will be centered when you print the document. If you change your mind about centering the page, delete the [Center Pg] code.

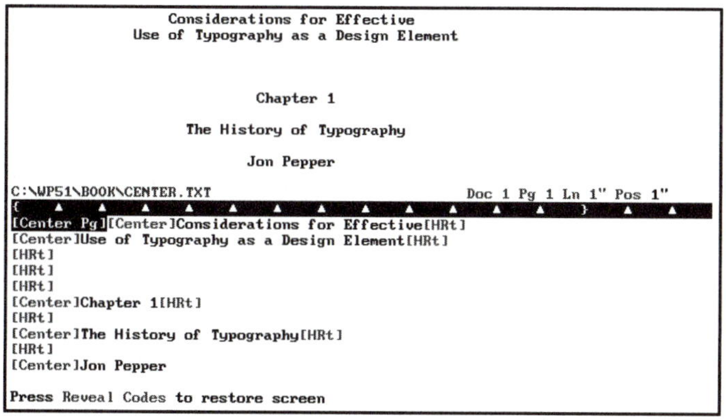

Fig. 5.11

The [Center Pg] code inserted into a document.

Formatting Pages

Note that the text is centered between the top and bottom margins of the page, not between the top and bottom edges of the paper. To adjust the centered text on the page, you can change the top and bottom margins, as described earlier in this chapter.

Objective 3: To Design Headers and Footers

A *header* is information (text, numbers, or graphics) that prints automatically at the top margin of every page. A *footer* is information that prints automatically at the bottom margin of every page. Typical header and footer information may include chapter titles and page numbers, or revision numbers and dates.

You cannot see headers or footers on the editing screen; you can use either of two methods to see them. First, you can press ⇧Shift+F7 (Print) and choose View Document (6); or you can access the File pull-down menu, choose **Print**, and then choose View Document (6). Second, you can press Reveal Codes (Alt+F3 or F11) to view header and footer text; alternatively, you can access the **E**dit pull-down menu and choose **R**eveal Codes.

Exercise 3.1: Creating a Header or Footer

To create a header or footer, follow these steps:

1. Press ⇧Shift+F8 to activate the Format command, and choose **P**age (**2**).

   ▱ Access the Layout pull-down menu and choose Page.

2. Choose **H**eaders (**3**) or **F**ooters (**4**).

   You can create two headers (A and B) and two footers (A and B).

3. Choose Header **A** (**1**) or Header **B** (**2**); or choose Footer **A** (**1**) or Footer **B** (**2**).

4. From the menu at the bottom of the screen, choose one of three specifications (see fig. 5.12).

   Choose Every **P**age (**2**) if you want the header or footer to appear on every page.

   Choose **O**dd Pages (**3**) if you want the header or footer to appear on odd pages only.

To Design Headers and Footers

Choose E**v**en Pages (**4**) if you want the header or footer to appear on even pages only.

```
Format: Page

    1 - Center Page (top to bottom)      No

    2 - Force Odd/Even Page

    3 - Headers

    4 - Footers

    5 - Margins - Top                    1"
                  Bottom                 1"

    6 - Page Numbering

    7 - Paper Size                       8.5" x 11"
            Type                         Standard
            Labels

    8 - Suppress (this page only)


1 Discontinue; 2 Every Page; 3 Odd Pages; 4 Even Pages; 5 Edit: 0
```

Fig. 5.12
Choosing the pages to have the header or footer.

5. Type the header or footer text, using any of WordPerfect's formatting features.
6. Press [F7] (Exit) twice to return to the document.

WordPerfect automatically skips one line between the header or footer and the first line (for headers) or last line (for footers) of text. If you want to insert more blank lines between the header or footer and the text, include blank lines when you define the header or footer.

Exercise 3.2: Editing a Header or Footer

You can make changes to a header or footer from anywhere in a document. For example, you can change the text or the appearance of the text in the header or footer.

To edit a header or footer, follow these steps:

1. Press [⇧Shift]+[F8] to activate the Format command, and choose Page (**2**).

    🖱 Access the Layout pull-down menu and choose Page.

2. Choose **H**eaders (**3**) or **F**ooters (**4**).
3. Choose Header **A** (**1**) or Header **B** (**2**); or choose Footer **A** (**1**) or Footer **B** (**2**).
4. Choose **E**dit (**5**).

    An editing screen appears, showing the header or footer text.

Formatting Pages

5. Edit the header or footer.
6. Press [F7] (Exit) twice to return to the document.

Including Automatic Page Numbering in a Header or Footer

In addition to including text and formatting text in a header or footer, you can add automatic page numbering by including ^B ([Ctrl]+[B]) in the header or footer. For example, you can specify the footer to read **Page** ^B, and the pages will be numbered consecutively as Page 1, Page 2, and so on.

You can include automatic page numbering in headers and footers when you first create them or when you edit them, using the procedures just described. To include automatic page numbering, type any text that will precede the page number (such as the word **Page**).

Exercise 3.3: Creating Automatic Page Numbering

To create automatic page numbering, do the following:

1. At the create header screen, type **Page** and press the **space bar** once.
2. Press [Ctrl]+[B].
3. Press [F7] (Exit) to save the changes.

Objective 4: To Number Pages

Numbering pages automatically, not as part of a header or footer, is as easy as telling WordPerfect how and where you want the numbers to appear on the page. Numbering begins with whatever number you choose and appears in the style you specify. Be sure to move the cursor to the top of the document, or go to the Document Initial Codes screen if you want page numbering to begin on the first page.

Page numbers print at the margin. Although page numbers don't appear on-screen, the status line indicates the current page number. You don't see the numbers on the pages until you print the document. You can preview the page numbers, however, with the View Document feature. To preview the page numbers, press [Shift]+[F7] (Print) and choose View Document (6). Alternatively, access the **File** pull-down menu, choose **Print**, and choose View Document (6).

To Number Pages

Choosing a Page Number Position

You can choose from a variety of page number positions. You can position the number at the top or bottom of the page—at the left, right, or center. Or you can have the page number appear at alternating positions—the left side of even pages and the right side of odd pages.

Exercise 4.1: Choosing a Page Number Position

To choose a page number position, follow these steps:

1. Press `Shift`+`F8` to activate the Format command, and choose **P**age (**2**).

   Access the Layout pull-down menu and choose Page.

2. Choose Page **N**umbering (**6**). The Format: Page Numbering screen appears (see fig. 5.13).

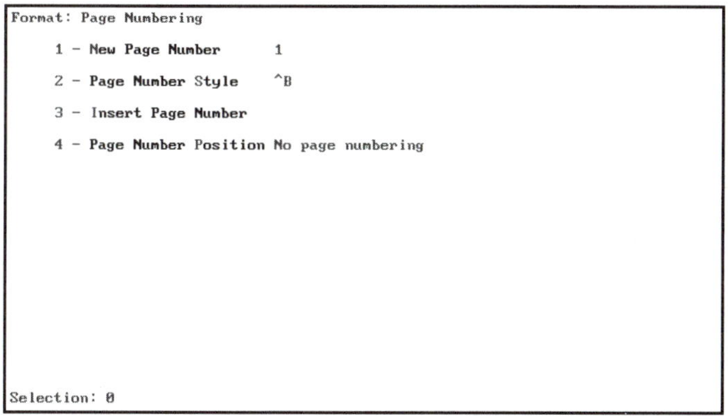

```
Format: Page Numbering
    1 - New Page Number         1
    2 - Page Number Style       ^B
    3 - Insert Page Number
    4 - Page Number Position    No page numbering




Selection: 0
```

Fig. 5.13
The Format: Page Numbering screen.

3. Choose Page Number **P**osition (**4**).
4. Type the number that corresponds to the position where you want page numbers to appear. Refer to figure 5.14 to see your choices.

   WordPerfect positions page numbers at the top or bottom margin and leaves a one-line space between the page number and the body of the text.

5. Press `F7` (Exit) to return to the document.

Formatting Pages

Fig. 5.14
The Format: Page Number Position screen.

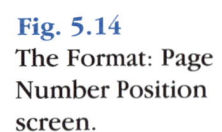

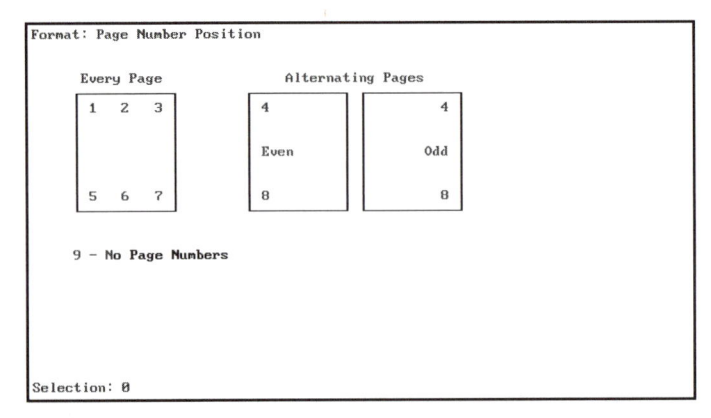

If you turn on page numbering and later decide that you don't want page numbers, you must delete the page-numbering code. To delete the code, first move the cursor to the place where you invoked page numbering. Then press Reveal Codes (Alt + F3 or F11) and delete the [PgNumbering:] code.

Changing the Starting Page Number

You can change page numbers at any point in a document; the change takes effect from that point forward. Keep in mind that you can use Arabic numerals (such as 1, 2, and 3) or upper- or lowercase Roman numerals (such as i and ii, or I and II). If you want Roman numerals for the page numbers, you must use the following procedure to change the starting page number, even if you plan to start with Roman numeral i.

Exercise 4.2: Changing the Starting Page Number

To change the starting page number, follow these steps:

1. Move the cursor to the top of the page where you want to start numbering.
2. Press Shift + F8 to activate the Format command, and choose **P**age (**2**).

    Access the Layout pull-down menu and choose Page.
3. Choose Page **N**umbering (**6**) and then choose **N**ew Page Number (**1**).
4. Type the new starting page number (for example, **1** for Arabic, **i** for lowercase Roman, or **I** for uppercase Roman). Then press Enter.
5. Press F7 (Exit) to return to the document.

124

Exercise 4.3: Suppressing Page Numbering

You can turn off page numbering for an entire document or for a single page. To turn off page numbering for the entire document, follow these steps:

1. Press ⇧Shift + F8 to activate the Format command, and choose **P**age (**2**).

    🖱 Access the Layout pull-down menu and choose Page.

2. Choose Page **N**umbering (**6**).
3. Choose Page Number **P**osition (**4**).
4. Choose **N**o Page Numbers (**9**).
5. Press F7 (Exit) to return to the document.

Exercise 4.4: Suppressing Page Numbering for a Single Page

You can suppress page numbering for a single page so that no number appears for that page, but numbering continues on the following pages. For example, you may not want the title page of a report to have a page number.

To suppress page numbering for a single page, follow these steps:

1. Move the cursor to the top of the page where you want to suppress numbering.
2. Press ⇧Shift + F8 to activate the Format command, and choose **P**age (**2**).

    🖱 Access the Layout pull-down menu and choose Page.

3. Choose S**u**ppress (this page only) (**8**). The menu shown in figure 5.15 appears.

```
Format: Suppress (this page only)
    1 - Suppress All Page Numbering, Headers and Footers
    2 - Suppress Headers and Footers
    3 - Print Page Number at Bottom Center    No
    4 - Suppress Page Numbering               No
    5 - Suppress Header A                     No
    6 - Suppress Header B                     No
    7 - Suppress Footer A                     No
    8 - Suppress Footer B                     No




Selection: 0
```

Fig. 5.15
The Format: Suppress (this page only) menu.

Formatting Pages

4. Choose Suppress **P**age Numbering (**4**).
5. Choose **Y**es to confirm your choice.
6. Press `F7` (Exit) to return to the document.

Objective 5: To Control Page Breaks

WordPerfect provides a number of ways to control where one page ends and the next one begins. You can use automatic page breaks (soft page breaks), hard page breaks, or Widow/Orphan Protection option.

Using Automatic Page Breaks

WordPerfect automatically uses the current paper size and margins to determine where page breaks should go. In addition, WordPerfect calculates the space needed for any headers, footers, or page numbers when determining page breaks.

WordPerfect inserts a dashed line into the document on-screen wherever an automatic page break occurs (see fig. 5.16).

Fig. 5.16
An automatic page break on-screen.

```
         This conference marks the first of its kind in the Midwest.
If you're new to biodynamic gardening, you'll have a rare
opportunity to learn from the experts.  If you're an experienced
biodynamic gardener, you'll be able to mingle and swap secrets with
fellow enthusiasts.
----------------------------------------------------------------
         New Harmony, once the site of two utopian and agrarian
communities in the early nineteenth century is an ideal setting for
our conference.  You'll find a map in the registration packet to
help you find your way here.  Driving time from Chicago is roughly
5 1/2 hours.




C:\WP51\BOOK\HARMONY.LTR                    Doc 1 Pg 2 Ln 1.67" Pos 2.2"
```

This soft page break produces a hidden [SPg] code. When you add or delete text from a page, soft page breaks are recalculated automatically.

Inserting Hard Page Breaks

To force a page break at a certain spot—at the beginning of a new section in a report or after a title page, for example—you enter a hard page break. The page always ends at that point. A hard page break appears on-screen as a line of equal signs.

Exercise 5.1: Inserting a Hard Page Break

To insert a hard page break, follow these steps:

1. Move the cursor to the point where you want the page break to occur.
2. Press Ctrl+⏎Enter to insert a [HPg] code.

Exercise 5.2: Deleting a Hard Page Break

To delete a hard page break, do the following:

1. Use Reveal Codes (Alt+F3 or F11) to find the [HPg] code. Place the cursor on the [HPg] code.
2. Press Del.

Using Widow/Orphan Protection

WordPerfect can automatically prevent single lines from being "stranded" at the top or bottom of a page. In WordPerfect, a paragraph's first line left at the bottom of a page is called a *widow*; a paragraph's last line left at the top of a page is called an *orphan*.

If you want to protect an entire document, either move the cursor to the beginning of the document or go to the Document Initial Codes screen before you complete the following steps. To protect only a portion of the document, move the cursor to the location where you want protection to begin.

Exercise 5.3: Turning On Widow/Orphan Protection

To turn on Widow/Orphan Protection, complete these steps:

1. Press ⇧Shift+F8 to activate the Format command, and choose **L**ine (**1**).

Formatting Pages

    🖱 Access the Layout pull-down menu and choose Line.

2. Choose **W**idow/Orphan Protection (**9**).
3. Choose **Y**es to turn on the feature.
4. Press `F7` (Exit) to return to the document.

To turn off Widow/Orphan Protection, repeat the preceding steps but choose **No** instead of **Yes** in step 3.

Chapter Summary

In this chapter, you learned about various formatting options for use with an entire document or with just a page or a group of pages. You learned how to change the top and bottom margins, center pages top to bottom, design headers and footers, number pages automatically, and control page breaks. The next chapter introduces some of WordPerfect's utilities for checking your work.

Testing Your Knowledge

True/False Questions

1. In WordPerfect, a form definition includes the paper size and type, the location of the paper in the printer, and the orientation of the printing.
2. WordPerfect is preset to leave two-inch margins at the top and bottom of the page.
3. A header is information that prints automatically at the bottom margin of every page.
4. You can add automatic page numbering by including ^B (`Ctrl`+`B`) in the header or footer.
5. A hard page break appears on-screen as a line of equal signs.

Testing Your Knowledge

Multiple Choice Questions

1. A form definition includes the orientation of printing as either
    A. Vertical and Horizontal.
    B. Portrait and Landscape.
    C. Picture and Horizontal.
    D. Portrait and View.
    E. Landscape and 3-D.

2. Pressing [Shift]+[F8], choosing 2, choosing 5, typing 1.5, pressing [Enter], typing 1.5, pressing [Enter], and then pressing [F7]
    A. changes the top and bottom margins to 2 inches.
    B. changes the top and bottom margins to 1.5 inches.
    C. changes the left and right margins to 1.5 inches.
    D. has no effect on the document.
    E. changes the orientation of the document.

3. If you create a header and want it to appear on certain pages, you need to
    A. create a second header.
    B. suppress the header for each page without a header.
    C. set each header to suppress mode.
    D. type page numbers.
    E. designate pages.

4. WordPerfect controls page breaks with
    A. soft page breaks.
    B. hard page breaks.
    C. special codes.
    D. special characters.
    E. A and B.

5. In WordPerfect, a paragraph's first line left at the bottom of the page is called a (an)
    A. orphan.
    B. widow.
    C. parent.
    D. child.
    E. sibling.

Formatting Pages

Fill-in-the-Blank Questions

1. The _____ margin is the distance between the top edge of the paper and the first line of text.
2. Text is centered between the _____ and _____ margins of the page, not between the _____ and bottom edges of the paper.
3. A _____ is information that prints automatically at the bottom of every page.
4. You can add automatic page numbering by typing _____ in the header or footer line.
5. To force a page break at a certain spot on a page, you enter a _____ page break.

Review: Short Projects

1. Set Top and Bottom Margins, Center a Page

   Type the following title page for a report, with the top margin = 2, the bottom margin = 2, and centered on the page. Print the document.

       THE GREAT WAR

       By Tom Angeles

2. Design Headers and Footers

   Retrieve MEMO and add footer A (centered on the page): **January 22, 1992**.

   Add header A: **Page ^ B**.

   Print the document.

3. Create Page Breaks

   Retrieve a document, insert a hard page break, and print both pages.

Review: Long Projects

1. Change Margins, Center a Page

   Create a title page for the document KEYTERMS. Include a two-line title and a two-line byline, as well as the date.

Testing Your Knowledge

2. Design Headers and Footers, and Insert Page Breaks

   Retrieve KEYTERMS. Modify the document by adding header A: **KEY TERMS**. Then add footer A: **Page #**. Create a new page for each chapter term by inserting hard page breaks.

   Add the following text:

   Header

   Information that prints automatically at the top margin of every page.

   Footer

   Information that prints automatically at the bottom margin of every page.

   Soft Page Break

   A page break that occurs automatically. A soft page break appears on-screen as a dashed line.

   Hard Page Break

   A page break you insert to force a break at a certain spot. A hard page break appears on-screen as a line of equal signs.

   Widow

   In WordPerfect, a paragraph's first line at the bottom of a page.

   Orphan

   In WordPerfect, a paragraph's last line at the top of a page.

   After adding the preceding text, print the document and save it as KEYTERMS.

Proofreading

6

WordPerfect makes two powerful tools available every time you begin your editing tasks: Search and Replace. If you have ever experienced the frustration of searching, sentence-by-sentence, for a mistake that you know you made, you will welcome these time-savers. In addition to using the Search and Replace features, you can use the Speller and Thesaurus to check and fine-tune your work.

Caution: Don't rely on WordPerfect to correct all your errors. WordPerfect finds only words that are misspelled, not words that are used incorrectly. Always read your manuscripts carefully.

Objectives

1. To Search for a Word or Phrase
2. To Replace a Word or Phrase
3. To Use the Speller
4. To Use the Thesaurus

Proofreading

Key Terms in This Chapter	
String	A set of characters, including codes and spaces, that WordPerfect uses in search and replace operations.
Synonym	A word with the same or nearly the same meaning as another word. You can use WordPerfect's Thesaurus to find synonyms.
Antonym	A word with the opposite or nearly opposite meaning of another word. WordPerfect's Thesaurus lists both synonyms and antonyms.
Headword	The word you look up with the Thesaurus. The headword has a collection of synonyms attached to it.

Objective 1: To Search for a Word or Phrase

The Search feature enables you to search for a single character, word, phrase, sentence, or code, either forward or backward from the location of the cursor. A group of characters, words, or codes that you want to locate is called a *string*.

Suppose that you want to find where a particular topic, word, or phrase appears in a long document. Searching the document manually is time-consuming. But with WordPerfect's Search feature, you can find character strings, even codes, easily.

Type the text in figure 6.1 to begin the exercises in the chapter.

Exercise 1.1: Launching a Search

You can search for text from any point in a document, and you can search in either direction—forward or backward. To search for text, follow these steps:

1. Press [F2] (Forward Search) to search from the cursor position to the end of the document.

    Alternatively, press [Shift]+[F2] (Backward Search) to search from the cursor position to the beginning of the document.

To Search for a Word or Phrase

> Access the Search pull-down menu and choose Forward or Backward.

If you choose Forward Search, the following prompt appears in the lower left corner of the screen:

→ Srch:

If you choose Backward Search, the following prompt appears:

← Srch:

2. At the prompt shown in figure 6.2, type the text string or code you want to find. You can type as many as 60 characters in the string.

```
Brainstorming
When you have trouble determining a sharp focus for a document—
when you are uncertain what you want to say—consider trying a
semistructured writing exercise known as "brainstorming."

When you brainstorm a writing assignment on-screen, you record your
ideas in list form as they occur to you.  When you brainstorm, you
don't worry about typos, spelling errors, or style.  You turn off
the inclination to hone each sentence before you move on to the
next one.  You can handle those matters later.  Your goal is,
rather to generate as many ideas as possible about the topic, the
purpose, or the audience.

Keeping an Idea File

An idea file is an extension of a brainstorming file.  You can save
an idea file and retrieve it when you want to add more ideas later.

Using a Prewriting Template

Prewriting is everything you do up to the actual step of writing
that first draft.  It is very much a part of the planning stage.

-> Srch:
```

Fig. 6.1
The text of the document.

```
Brainstorming
When you have trouble determining a sharp focus for a document—
when you are uncertain what you want to say—consider trying a
semistructured writing exercise known as "brainstorming."

When you brainstorm a writing assignment on-screen, you record your
ideas in list form as they occur to you.  When you brainstorm, you
don't worry about typos, spelling errors, or style.  You turn off
the inclination to hone each sentence before you move on to the
next one.  You can handle those matters later.  Your goal is,
rather to generate as many ideas as possible about the topic, the
purpose, or the audience.

Keeping an Idea File

An idea file is an extension of a brainstorming file.  You can save
an idea file and retrieve it when you want to add more ideas later.

Using a Prewriting Template

Prewriting is everything you do up to the actual step of writing
that first draft.  It is very much a part of the planning stage.

-> Srch: prewriting
```

Fig. 6.2
Typing the string you want to find.

3. To begin the search, press F2 (Forward Search) again or press F2.

At this point, pressing F2 works for both Forward Search and Backward Search.

> Press the right mouse button, or double-click the left button to begin the search.

Proofreading

When WordPerfect finds the first occurrence of the search string, the search stops. You then can edit and move around in the document.

If you want to continue the search, press (F2) (Forward Search) again. You don't need to retype the text string or code because WordPerfect remembers your last search request. Press (F2) (Forward Search) or (Esc) again to find the next occurrence of the text string or code. If you use a mouse, repeat the search by accessing the **Search** pull-down menu and choosing **Next** or **Previous**.

If WordPerfect cannot find the search string, a * Not found * message appears.

To return the cursor to its location before the search, press (Ctrl)+(Home) (GoTo) twice.

Guidelines for Defining a Search String

To use the Search feature effectively, you need to know how WordPerfect interprets a string. Here are some of the rules that WordPerfect follows:

- If you type a string in lowercase letters, WordPerfect looks for either upper- or lowercase characters. For example, if you ask the program to find *search*, WordPerfect stops at *search*, *Search*, and *SEARCH*. But if you ask the program to find *Search*, WordPerfect stops at *Search* and *SEARCH*.

- Be careful how you enter a search string. If you enter the string *the*, for example, WordPerfect matches the string to every occurrence of the word *the* as well as to words that contain the string, such as *anesthesia*. To locate only the word *the*, enter a space before and after the word: *<space>***the***<space>*.

- If you think that the string you're looking for might be in a header, a footer, a footnote, an endnote, a graphics box caption, or a text box, you must perform an *extended search*. This search is the same as a regular search except that you must press (Home) and then (F2) (Forward Search) for an extended forward search, or (Home) and then (Shift)+(F2) (Backward Search) for an extended backward search. You also can perform an extended search by choosing the **Extended** option on the **Search** pull-down menu.

- If you need to find a hidden code, such as a margin setting, use the normal search procedure, but when the search prompt appears, press the function key or key combination that creates the hidden code.

When WordPerfect finds the hidden code, use Reveal Codes to view the code and to perform any editing.

- When searching for paired codes, you can insert an ending code at the search (or replace) prompt by pressing the corresponding function key or key combination twice. For example, you can press [F6] (Bold) once to insert a [BOLD] code, or twice to insert a [bold] code. To remove the [BOLD] code, press the left-arrow key and then press the [Backspace] key to leave only the [bold] code in the search string.

- If you are searching for text that includes an element that changes from one occurrence to the next—for example, (1), (2), and (3)—or if you are uncertain about the correct spelling of a word, use the matching character ^X (press [Ctrl]+[V] and then [Ctrl]+[X]). This wild-card character matches any single character within a character string. If you enter (^X) at the → Srch: prompt, the cursor stops at *(1)*, *(2)*, *(3)*, and so on. When you are uncertain about the spelling, use ^X in the string. For example, if you enter **c^Xt** at the → Srch: prompt, the cursor stops at words such as *cat*, *CAT*, *Cat*, *cot*, *cattle*, and *cutting*. Be as specific about the character string as you can.

- To find a word at the end of a paragraph, type the word at the search prompt, along with any following punctuation, and then press [Enter] to insert a hard return code ([HRt]). For example, type **Einstein**, press the period key (.), and press [Enter]. The search finds only occurrences of *Einstein* that are followed by a period and a hard return.

- At the search prompt, you can change the direction of the search with the up- or down-arrow key. Enter the search string, press the up- or down-arrow key, and then press [F2] (Forward Search) or [Esc] to begin the search.

- A common mistake is to press [Enter] instead of [F2] (Forward Search) or [Esc] to start the search. Pressing [Enter] inserts a [HRt] code in the search string, which may not be what you want.

Objective 2: To Replace a Word or Phrase

WordPerfect's Replace feature automatically finds every occurrence of a string or code and replaces it with another string or code. You can also use the Replace feature to remove a string or code completely. For example, if you complete a long sales report and then need to remove all the boldfacing, you can use a replace operation to find all occurrences of the code and replace them with nothing.

Proofreading

Exercise 2.1: Replacing a String

Sometimes you may want to replace the text that you find with different text. To replace a string, follow these steps:

1. Press Alt + F2 to activate the Replace command.

    Access the Search pull-down menu and choose Replace.

    WordPerfect displays a confirmation prompt at the bottom of the screen (see fig. 6.3).

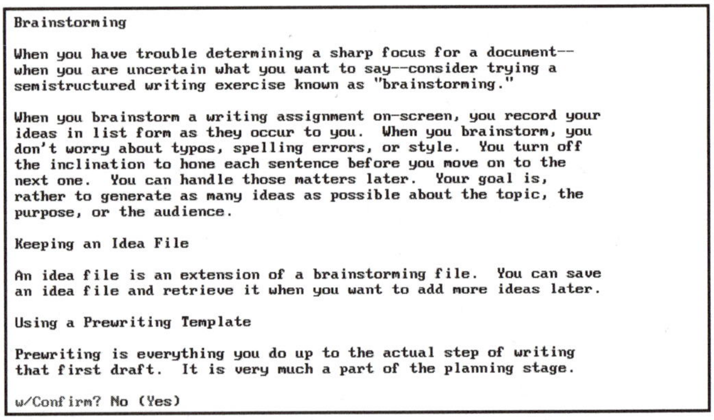

Fig. 6.3
Confirming that you want to replace a string.

```
Brainstorming

When you have trouble determining a sharp focus for a document--
when you are uncertain what you want to say--consider trying a
semistructured writing exercise known as "brainstorming."

When you brainstorm a writing assignment on-screen, you record your
ideas in list form as they occur to you.  When you brainstorm, you
don't worry about typos, spelling errors, or style.  You turn off
the inclination to hone each sentence before you move on to the
next one.  You can handle those matters later.  Your goal is,
rather to generate as many ideas as possible about the topic, the
purpose, or the audience.

Keeping an Idea File

An idea file is an extension of a brainstorming file.  You can save
an idea file and retrieve it when you want to add more ideas later.

Using a Prewriting Template

Prewriting is everything you do up to the actual step of writing
that first draft.  It is very much a part of the planning stage.

w/Confirm? No (Yes)
```

2. Choose **Y**es if you want to approve each replacement separately. Choose **N**o or press ⏎Enter if you want to replace all occurrences without confirming them.

3. At the → Srch: prompt, shown in figure 6.4, type your search string, which can contain up to 60 characters.

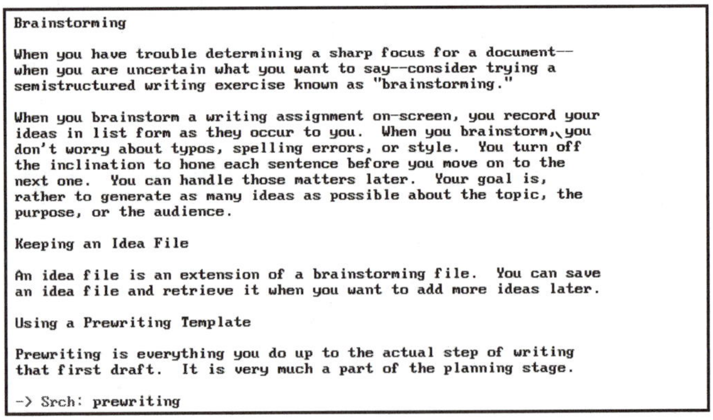

Fig. 6.4
Entering the search string.

```
Brainstorming

When you have trouble determining a sharp focus for a document--
when you are uncertain what you want to say--consider trying a
semistructured writing exercise known as "brainstorming."

When you brainstorm a writing assignment on-screen, you record your
ideas in list form as they occur to you.  When you brainstorm, you
don't worry about typos, spelling errors, or style.  You turn off
the inclination to hone each sentence before you move on to the
next one.  You can handle those matters later.  Your goal is,
rather to generate as many ideas as possible about the topic, the
purpose, or the audience.

Keeping an Idea File

An idea file is an extension of a brainstorming file.  You can save
an idea file and retrieve it when you want to add more ideas later.

Using a Prewriting Template

Prewriting is everything you do up to the actual step of writing
that first draft.  It is very much a part of the planning stage.

-> Srch: prewriting
```

To Replace a Word or Phrase

4. Press `F2` (Forward Search) or `Esc`.

    🖱 Press the right mouse button or double-click the left button.

5. At the `Replace with:` prompt, type the replacement string (see fig. 6.5). If you want the search string deleted and not replaced with anything, don't enter anything in response to this prompt.

```
Brainstorming
When you have trouble determining a sharp focus for a document--
when you are uncertain what you want to say--consider trying a
semistructured writing exercise known as "brainstorming."

When you brainstorm a writing assignment on-screen, you record your
ideas in list form as they occur to you.  When you brainstorm, you
don't worry about typos, spelling errors, or style.  You turn off
the inclination to hone each sentence before you move on to the
next one.  You can handle those matters later.  Your goal is,
rather to generate as many ideas as possible about the topic, the
purpose, or the audience.

Keeping an Idea File

An idea file is an extension of a brainstorming file.  You can save
an idea file and retrieve it when you want to add more ideas later.

Using a Prewriting Template

Prewriting is everything you do up to the actual step of writing
that first draft.  It is very much a part of the planning stage.

Replace with: prewriting
```

Fig. 6.5
The Replace with: prompt.

6. Press `Esc` (Forward Search) or `Esc` to begin the search.

    🖱 Press the right mouse button, or double-click the left button to continue the search operation.

    If you chose **N**o at the `w/Confirm? No (Yes)` prompt in step 2, WordPerfect replaces all occurrences automatically. If you chose **Y**es at that prompt, the cursor stops at each occurrence of the search string, and WordPerfect displays the prompt `Confirm? No (Yes)`.

7. If you are prompted, choose **Y**es to replace the string or **N**o if you don't want to replace it. If you want to cancel the replace operation, press `F1` (Cancel) or `F7` (Exit); otherwise, WordPerfect continues to search the document.

    🖱 Click the right mouse button to reject the change, or click Yes or No with the left button.

After WordPerfect has found all the occurrences of the string, the operation stops.

To return the cursor to its location before the replace operation, press `Ctrl`+`Home` (GoTo) twice.

Proofreading

Exercise 2.2: Replacing Hidden Codes

You can use the Replace feature to replace hidden codes for any commands accessed through the function keys. You cannot replace codes entered through the pull-down menus.

To replace hidden codes, follow these steps:

1. Press [Alt]+[F2] to activate the Replace command.

    ⌨ Access the Search pull-down menu and choose Replace.

2. At the prompt, choose **Y**es if you want to confirm each replacement, or choose **N**o if you want to replace all occurrences automatically.

3. At the → Srch: prompt shown in figure 6.6, press the function key or key combination that activates the desired command—for example, to search for the bold codes, press [F6] (Bold).

Fig. 6.6
The Search prompt.

```
Brainstorming

When you have trouble determining a sharp focus for a document—
when you are uncertain what you want to say—consider trying a
semistructured writing exercise known as "brainstorming."

When you brainstorm a writing assignment on-screen, you record your
ideas in list form as they occur to you. When you brainstorm, you
don't worry about typos, spelling errors, or style. You turn off
the inclination to hone each sentence before you move on to the
next one. You can handle those matters later. Your goal is,
rather to generate as many ideas as possible about the topic, the
purpose, or the audience.

Keeping an Idea File

An idea file is an extension of a brainstorming file. You can save
an idea file and retrieve it when you want to add more ideas later.

Using a Prewriting Template

Prewriting is everything you do up to the actual step of writing
that first draft. It is very much a part of the planning stage.

-> Srch: [BOLD]
```

If the command accessed with a function key or key combination leads to a submenu, WordPerfect displays a list of menu items for entry into the search string. Press the number or letter of the menu item that represents the hidden code you want to replace. WordPerfect enters the appropriate code in the search string.

4. At the Replace with: prompt, type the replacement string and press [↵Enter]. To delete the hidden code and replace it with nothing, don't enter anything in response to this prompt.

5. To begin the replace operation, press [F2] (Forward Search) or [Esc].

    ⌨ Press the right mouse button, or double-click the left button to begin the replace operation.

Guidelines for Using Replace

To use the Replace feature effectively, you need to keep in mind the following basic guidelines:

- WordPerfect doesn't allow you to search for codes with specific settings, such as [Margin Set:1,65], but you can find all occurrences of the command code [Margin Set].
- To limit a replace operation to a specific section of a document, first define the text with the Block command, and then proceed with the replace operation.
- Use the Replace feature to enter a string of text that occurs frequently in a document. For example, you can enter a backslash (\) wherever you want *methyl ethyl chloride* to appear. When you finish typing, replace the backslash with the chemical term.
- WordPerfect's Replace feature doesn't replace text in headers, footers, footnotes, endnotes, graphics box captions, or text boxes. To replace a character or string of characters in these locations, you must use an extended replace operation. The procedure is the same as for a replace operation, except that you initiate an extended replace operation by first pressing [Home] and then [Alt]+[F2] (Replace). You also can perform an extended replace operation by choosing the Extended option on the Search pull-down menu.

Objective 3: To Use the Speller

WordPerfect's Speller contains a dictionary of 115,000 words. You can use the Speller to search for spelling mistakes and common typing errors, such as transposed, missing, extra, or wrong letters—even typing errors such as double words (*the the*) or irregular capitalization (*BOston* or *bOSTON*). You also can use the Speller when you know what a word sounds like but are unsure of its spelling. WordPerfect's Speller can check a single word, a page, a block of text, or an entire document.

The Speller compares each word in the document with the words in WordPerfect's dictionary. This dictionary contains a file that lists common words (words most frequently used) and main words (words generally found in dictionaries). WordPerfect checks every word against its list of common words; and if the program doesn't find the word there, WordPerfect looks in its dictionary of main words. WordPerfect enables you to create a

Proofreading

supplemental dictionary to save words that are not in the WordPerfect dictionary. If you have created a supplemental dictionary, the program looks there as well. Words found in any of the dictionaries are considered correct.

Exercise 3.1: Checking a Word, Page, or Document

You can check a word, a page, or an entire document. To check a word, page, or document, follow these steps:

1. Position the cursor anywhere in the word or on the page. When you check an entire document, the position of the cursor doesn't matter.

2. Press Ctrl + F2 to activate the Spell command.

    Access the Tools pull-down menu and choose Spell (see fig. 6.7).

    The Spell menu appears at the bottom of the screen (see fig. 6.8).

3. Choose the menu option you want.

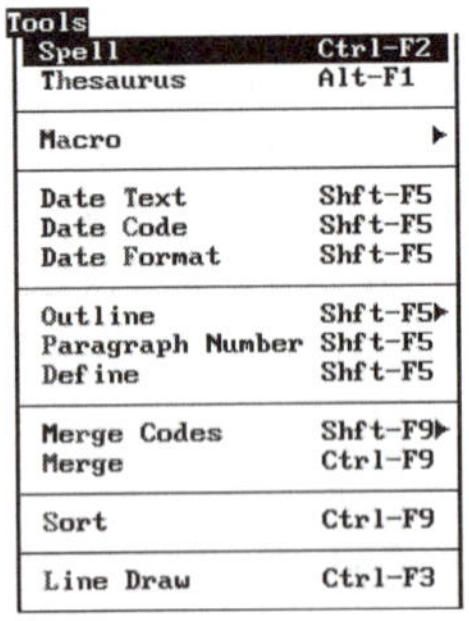

Fig. 6.7
Choosing Spell from the Tools pull-down menu.

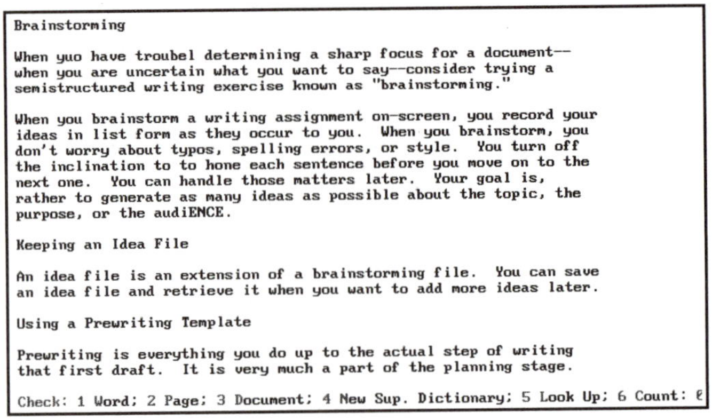

Fig. 6.8
The Spell menu.

142

The following options are available on the Spell menu:

- Choose **Word** (**1**) to check the word on which the cursor is located. If WordPerfect finds the word in its dictionaries, the cursor moves to the next word, and the Spell menu remains displayed. You can continue checking word-by-word or choose another option from the Spell menu. If the word isn't found, WordPerfect offers alternative spellings.
- Choose **Page** (**2**) to check every word on the page. After the page is checked, the Spell menu remains displayed. Continue checking words or choose another option.
- Choose **Document** (**3**) to check every word in the document.
- Choose **New Sup. Dictionary** (**4**), type the name of the supplemental dictionary you want to use, and press ⏎Enter. Generally, you create supplemental dictionaries to contain words pertaining to specialized or technical areas, such as medicine, law, or science.
- Choose **Look Up** (**5**), and at the prompt Word or word pattern:, type your rough guess of the word's spelling and then press ⏎Enter. You can type a word pattern that includes an asterisk (*) to represent several unknown letters, or a question mark (?) to represent a single unknown letter. WordPerfect offers a list of words that fit the pattern.
- Choose **Count** (**6**) to count the number of words in the document. Note that after a spelling check, WordPerfect displays the number of words automatically.

When the Speller finds a word not in its dictionary, the Speller stops, highlights the word, usually provides a list of alternative spellings, and displays the Not Found menu.

Exercise 3.2: Choosing from the Alternatives List

To choose a word from the alternatives list, first look for the correct spelling from the list (see fig. 6.9).

If you do not see the correct spelling and WordPerfect prompts you to Press Enter for more words, press ⏎Enter. When the correct spelling appears, type the letter next to the alternative you want to choose.

After you correct the word, the Speller continues checking the rest of the document (see fig. 6.10).

Proofreading

Fig. 6.9
An example of the Speller's alternatives list.

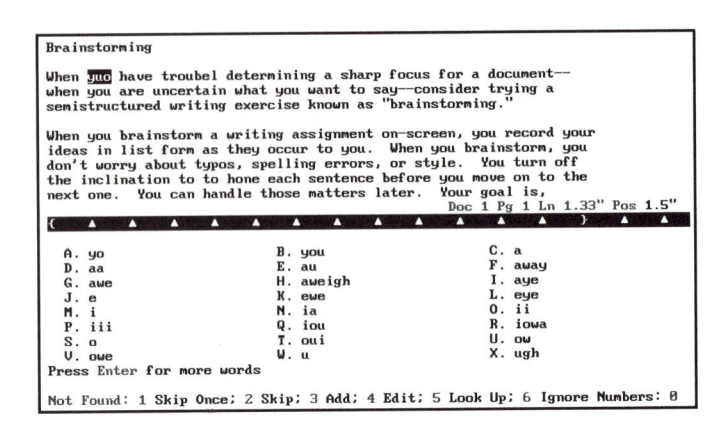

Fig. 6.10
WordPerfect finds another misspelled word.

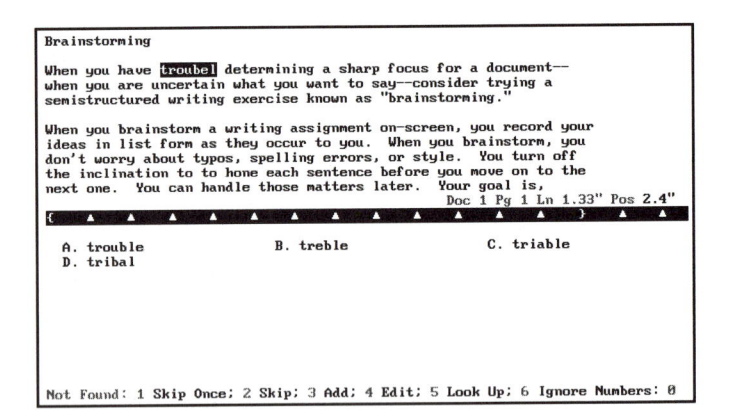

Exercise 3.3: Selecting Other Speller Options

Many correctly spelled words do not appear in WordPerfect's dictionary. Even though it contains 115,000 words, some words must be omitted. If the correct spelling is not displayed, you can choose from the options on the Not Found menu:

- Choose Skip Once (**1**) to have the Speller ignore the word once but stop at every occurrence of the word thereafter. This option enables you to verify your spelling of the word; verification is a good idea if the word is a difficult technical term.

- Choose Skip (**2**) to skip all occurrences of what you know to be a correctly spelled word.

- Choose Add (**3**) to add a frequently used word to your supplemental dictionary. WordPerfect stores the word in memory and ignores all

To Use the Speller

future occurrences. At the end of the check, all words added are saved to the current supplemental dictionary.

- Choose Edit (**4**) when the correct alternative is not offered and when you know that the spelling is incorrect. You must make the correction yourself. When you choose Edit, the cursor moves to the word in question. Make the correction with the right- and left-arrow keys. Press [F7] (Exit) to continue the spelling check.

- Choose Look Up (**5**) to look up a word. WordPerfect prompts you to enter a word or word pattern. Type your rough guess and press [⏎Enter]. WordPerfect then displays all the possible matches. You can choose one of the alternative words. If you don't find the correct spelling, press [F1] (Cancel) twice; then choose Edit (**4**) and enter the correction manually.

- Choose Ignore Numbers (**6**) if you want WordPerfect to ignore all words that contain numbers (such as *RX7* or *LPT1:*).

Exercise 3.4: Finding Double Words

In addition to identifying misspelled words, the Speller finds double words, such as *the the*. When the Speller encounters a double word, as shown in figure 6.11, the program doesn't offer alternatives. Instead, WordPerfect displays a different Not Found menu.

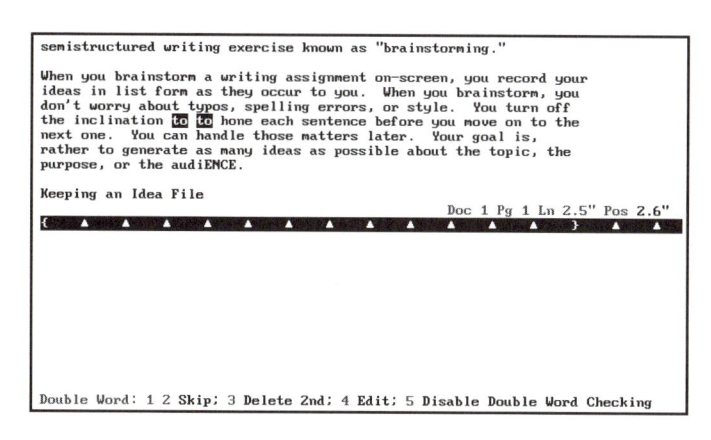

Fig. 6.11
The Not Found menu for double words.

You can choose from these options:

- Choose Skip (**1** or **2**) if the double word is legitimate.

- Choose Delete 2nd (**3**) if you accidentally typed two words instead of one. WordPerfect deletes the second word.

145

Proofreading

- Choose Edit (**4**) and make the appropriate correction if one of the words is a typographical error.
- Choose Disable Double Word Checking (**5**) if the document contains many legitimate double words and you are confident in your proofreading skill.

Exercise 3.5: Correcting Irregular Case

The Speller also checks for some common errors in capitalization. Figure 6.12, for example, shows that the Speller stops at words with irregular case and enables you to replace each word with the Speller's guess about the correct case. For example, *cAse* is changed to *Case*, *CAse* to *Case*, *cASE* to *CASE*, and *caSE* or *caSe* to *case*. In this example, the program stops at the word *BOston* and displays the Irregular Case menu.

Fig. 6.12
The Irregular Case menu.

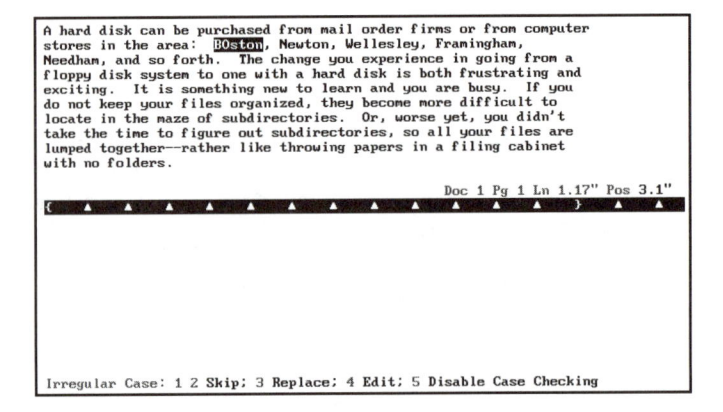

```
A hard disk can be purchased from mail order firms or from computer
stores in the area: BOston, Newton, Wellesley, Framingham,
Needham, and so forth.  The change you experience in going from a
floppy disk system to one with a hard disk is both frustrating and
exciting.  It is something new to learn and you are busy.  If you
do not keep your files organized, they become more difficult to
locate in the maze of subdirectories.  Or, worse yet, you didn't
take the time to figure out subdirectories, so all your files are
lumped together--rather like throwing papers in a filing cabinet
with no folders.
                                              Doc 1 Pg 1 Ln 1.17" Pos 3.1"
Irregular Case: 1 2 Skip; 3 Replace; 4 Edit; 5 Disable Case Checking
```

If the unusual capitalization is actually correct for the word, choose Skip (**1** or **2**). If you have many words with odd case selections, you may instead want to choose Disable Case Checking (**5**). You can choose Replace (**3**) to have the case for the word corrected. Note, however, that the Speller does not show you how it will correct the word. If you are not sure how the word will be corrected, choose Edit (**4**) instead and then correct the word yourself.

Exercise 3.6: Checking a Block

To check the spelling of a block, follow these steps:

1. Highlight the block by pressing [Alt]+[F4] or [F12] to activate the Block command, or by dragging the mouse.

2. Press Ctrl+F2 to activate the Spell command.

🖰 Access the Tools pull-down menu and choose Spell.

When you check a block, you skip the Spell menu because you already have told WordPerfect how much of the document you plan to check. Otherwise, the Speller operates as usual.

Objective 4: To Use the Thesaurus

The Thesaurus is similar to the Speller except that the Thesaurus lists alternative word choices instead of alternative spellings. The Thesaurus displays synonyms (words with the same or nearly the same meanings) and antonyms (words with opposite or nearly opposite meanings) for the selected word. The Thesaurus only lists these words; you must decide which one best fits your meaning.

Displaying Synonyms and Antonyms

If you are using a hard disk system, the Thesaurus files are immediately available. WordPerfect's standard installation procedure puts those files in the C:\WP51 directory.

Exercise 4.1: Using the Thesaurus

To use the Thesaurus, follow these steps:

1. Place the cursor anywhere in the word you want to look up.
2. Press Alt+F1 to activate the Thesaurus command.

🖰 Access the Tools pull-down menu and choose Thesaurus.

In figure 6.13, the word is highlighted and the screen is split. The document text appears at the top; the Thesaurus menu and word list (in columns) are displayed at the bottom.

The word you look up is called the *headword* because it has a body of similar words attached to it. The headword appears at the top of the column. WordPerfect also notes synonyms and antonyms for the headword. Words are divided into numbered groups and parts of speech. The column of letters to the left of the words is called the Reference menu. Words marked with a bullet (the dot next to the word) are headwords too; you can look up any of these words.

Proofreading

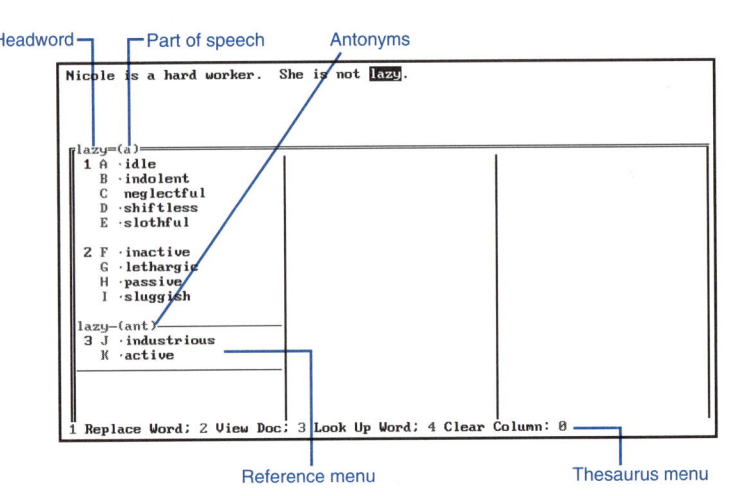

Fig. 6.13
The Thesaurus menu and word list.

```
                    Headword    Part of speech    Antonyms
            Nicole is a hard worker. She is not lazy.

            ┌lazy=(a)═══════════════════════════════════════
            │ 1 A ·idle
            │   B ·indolent
            │   C  neglectful
            │   D ·shiftless
            │   E ·slothful
            │
            │ 2 F ·inactive
            │   G ·lethargic
            │   H ·passive
            │   I ·sluggish
            │ lazy-(ant)
            │ 3 J ·industrious
            │   K ·active
            │
            │
            │ 1 Replace Word; 2 View Doc; 3 Look Up Word; 4 Clear Column: 0
                              Reference menu              Thesaurus menu
```

If the columns are empty and `Word:` appears at the bottom of the screen, either the cursor was not placed within the word, or the Thesaurus cannot find the word you want to look up. In either case, type the word you want to look up at the `Word:` prompt, and then press `↵Enter`.

Exercise 4.2: Selecting More Words

If you don't see a word that is exactly right, or if you want to try other words, you can expand the word list. You can display more alternatives for any headword (the words with a bullet next to them). Follow these steps:

1. Choose the headword that is closest to the meaning of the word in question, and press the letter next to that word. A new word list appears in the column to the right of the previous headword.

2. Use the right- or left-arrow key to move the letter choices to other columns.

Exercise 4.3: Using the Thesaurus Menu

With the Thesaurus menu displayed, you can choose from the following options:

- Choose Replace Word (**1**) to replace the highlighted word. At the prompt `Press letter for word`, type the letter (from the Reference menu) that corresponds to the replacement word. The Thesaurus menu disappears, and the program inserts the word you selected into the text.

- Choose View Doc (**2**) if you are unsure of a word's exact meaning in the context of your writing. The cursor moves back to the document, and you can use the cursor keys to move around and view the surrounding text. Press `F7` (Exit) to return to the Thesaurus menu.
- Choose Look Up Word (**3**) to look up other words that come to mind. At the `Word:` prompt, type the word you want to look up. If the word is a headword, the Thesaurus displays the word with all its subgroups of synonyms and antonyms. If the word is not a headword, WordPerfect either looks up another similar word or displays the message `Word not found`.
- Choose Clear Column (**4**) if you want WordPerfect to clear a column and make room for additional word columns.

Chapter Summary

This chapter introduces you to WordPerfect's features for checking a document. You have learned how to use the Search feature to search for a string—a single character, word, phrase, sentence, code, or combination of these. You also learned how to use the Replace feature to replace a string with another string. You then explored the many options available through WordPerfect's Speller and Thesaurus. The next chapter discusses WordPerfect's printing features.

Testing Your Knowledge

True/False Questions

1. A group of characters, words, or codes that you want to locate is called a string.
2. Pressing `Shift`+`F2` begins searching a document from the cursor position to the end of the document.
3. WordPerfect's Replace feature automatically finds every occurrence of a string or code and replaces it with another string or code.
4. WordPerfect's Speller automatically chooses the correct spelling of a word in the document.
5. The Thesaurus lists alternative word choices, such as synonyms and antonyms.

Proofreading

Multiple Choice Questions

1. The Search feature enables you to search for
   - A. a single character.
   - B. a word or phrase.
   - C. a sentence.
   - D. a code.
   - E. all of the above.

2. Pressing [F2], typing the string **She**, and pressing [F2]
   - A. causes WordPerfect to stop at *She*.
   - B. causes WordPerfect to stop at *SHE*.
   - C. causes WordPerfect to stop at *she*, *She*, and *SHE*.
   - D. causes WordPerfect to stop at *SHE* or *She*.
   - E. does none of the above.

3. To replace the word *You* with *We*, you
   - A. press [Alt]+[F2], choose **Y**es to approve replacement, and enter the search string.
   - B. press [F2], enter the replacement string, and press [F2].
   - C. press [Alt]+[F2], type the search string, press [F2], and choose the word to change from the list displayed.
   - D. can do A and B only.
   - E. can do A and C only.

4. You can use the WordPerfect Speller to check
   - A. a word.
   - B. a word, page, document, and block.
   - C. an entire document.
   - D. a sentence.
   - E. a block.

5. The Thesaurus menu displays
   - A. the part of speech of the headword.
   - B. definitions in paragraph form.
   - C. five choices for each word.
   - D. multiple screens of words at once.
   - E. an error message if a selection is not made.

Testing Your Knowledge

Fill-in-the-Blank Questions

1. You can search for text from any point in a document, and you can search either _____ or _____ in direction.
2. To activate the Replace command, press _____ or access the _____ pull-down menu and choose _____.
3. You can check a _____ or _____ by using the WordPerfect Speller.
4. The WordPerfect Thesaurus lists alternative word choices, displaying both _____ and _____.
5. The word you look up is called the _____ because it has a body of similar words attached to it.

Review: Short Projects

1. Search

   Retrieve a document from your disk, and search for words, using various searches.

2. Search and Replace

   Retrieve the document SETUP, find the string *you*, and replace with *they*. Be sure to choose Confirm before replacing so that you can check the grammar.

3. Use the Speller

   Retrieve any document, use the Speller, and record the word count.

Review: Long Projects

1. Search and Replace

   Retrieve the document LETTER. Search for the string *you'll* and replace it with *you will*. Save the document as NEWLET. Search the document for a word or group of words, and note the number of occurrences. Check the spelling of the document.

2. Search, Replace, and Use the Speller and Thesaurus

   Type the following text. Use the Search feature to search for *writing*, and note the number of occurrences. Next, use the Search and Replace feature to search for the word *important*, and replace it with *valuable*.

Proofreading

Use the Speller, and record the number of words. Finally, use the Thesaurus to find synonyms or antonyms for the following words: *length*, *tasks*, *organize*.

Coherent Organization

Letters can vary in length from one paragraph to several pages, although many business letters are no longer than a page. But whatever the length, be certain about what you want to include before you begin; then you won't forget something **important**.

As with other writing tasks, you'll need to analyze the purpose of your letter before you write it. If you are answering another person's letter, it will help to have that letter before you and note any comments to which a reply is needed. Finally, jot down a brief outline to organize the material logically.

It's also important to think about who the reader of your letter will be, especially when you are writing about a technical topic. The **knowledge** and **experience** of your readers will determine how detailed the explanations of technical material will be.

After typing the preceding text and performing all the operations, save the document as ORGANIZE.

Printing

For most documents, you probably will need a printout, or *hard copy*. This chapter explains how to designate the many printing specifications, such as number of copies and print quality, that you need to print your document.

You can print directly from the screen all or part of the document that currently shows, or you can print all or part of a document you have previously stored to disk. WordPerfect can keep track of multiple print jobs and print them in the order you specify. Before you print, you can use WordPerfect's View Document feature to preview how the printed document will look, avoiding waste of time and paper.

Objectives

1. To Print from the Screen
2. To Print from Disk
3. To Control the Printer
4. To Preview a Document

Printing

Key Terms in This Chapter	
Print queue	An internal list of jobs to be printed.

Objective 1: To Print from the Screen

Printing a document from the screen is quicker than printing a document from disk—especially if the document is short. From the screen, you can print an entire document, a single page, or selected pages.

Exercise 1.1: Printing an Entire Document

To print an entire document from the screen, follow these steps:

1. Display the document.
2. Press ⇧Shift + F7 to activate the Print command.
   - Access the File pull-down menu and choose Print.
3. Choose Full Document (1).

Exercise 1.2: Printing a Single Page

To print a single page from a document on-screen, follow these steps:

1. Display the document, and position the cursor anywhere within the page you want to print.
2. Press ⇧Shift + F7 to activate the Print command.
   - Access the File pull-down menu and choose Print.
3. Choose Page (2).

If the page you chose isn't near the beginning of the document, you may notice a short pause before the page prints. WordPerfect scans the document for the last format settings (such as margins and tabs) before printing the page.

Exercise 1.3: Printing Selected Pages

To print selected pages from a document on-screen, follow these steps:

To Print from the Screen

1. Display the document.
2. Press `Shift`+`F7` to activate the Print command.
   🖱 Access the File pull-down menu and choose Print.
3. Choose **M**ultiple Pages (**5**).
4. Type the page numbers of the pages you want to print. Then press `Enter`.

   Type the page numbers according to the following specifications:

Specification	Page(s) Selected for Printing
5	Page 5 only
2,25	Pages 2 and 25 only
3-	Pages 3 through the end of the document
1-10	Pages 1 through 10
-3	Pages from the beginning of the document through page 3

Adding a Print Job to the Queue

You can continue working on the document (or another document) while you print. If you finish working on a second document before the first document has finished printing, you can print the second file just as you did the first. WordPerfect adds the print job to the *print queue*, which is a "holding area" for documents waiting to print.

Making a Screen Print

When you need a quick printout of whatever appears on-screen (for example, a hard copy of a WordPerfect Help screen), you can press `PrtSc` (on an enhanced keyboard) or `Shift`+`PrtSc` (on a PC keyboard). This kind of printout doesn't show formatting codes, but it includes the information that appears on the status line.

Exercise 1.4: Specifying the Number of Copies

If you need more than one copy of a document, you can change the number of copies through the Print menu. When you use the **N**umber of Copies

Printing

option, the pages in each copy of the print job are *collated*. Collating the pages means that the printed copies will be printed in ordered packets. Until you change the number back to one, WordPerfect continues to print the number of copies you specify on the Print menu for all print jobs.

To specify the number of copies to print, follow these steps:

1. Press ⇧Shift + F7 to activate the Print command.
   Access the File pull-down menu and choose Print.
2. Choose **N**umber of Copies (**N**).
3. Type the number of copies you want to print. Then press ⏎Enter.

Exercise 1.5: Printing Multiple Copies of a Print Job

Some printers are capable of printing multiple copies after receiving the printer information only once. If your printer has that capability, you can use the M**u**ltiple Copies Generated By option to increase print speed. The copies, however, are not collated. Follow these steps to generate multiple copies of a print job:

1. Press ⇧Shift + F7 to activate the Print command.
   Access the File pull-down menu and choose Print.
2. Choose M**u**ltiple Copies Generated By (**U**).
3. Choose **P**rinter (**2**).

Objective 2: To Print from Disk

With WordPerfect, you can print a document from disk without displaying the document on-screen. You can print from either the Print menu or the List Files screen. With both methods, you can specify which pages to print.

Note: If you want to reduce your printing time, you can turn off the Fast Save feature from the Setup: Environment menu. The Fast Save feature, which usually is turned on, enables WordPerfect to save a file quickly by storing an unformatted version of the file. At print time, however, WordPerfect must take time to construct and format a temporary file before sending the job to the printer.

Exercise 2.1: Printing from the Print Menu

When you print from the Print menu, you must know the complete file name before starting the operation. You cannot use the List Files screen to look up the file after you have pressed Print (Shift+F7).

To use the Print menu to print a document from disk, follow these steps:

1. Press Shift+F7 to activate the Print command.

    ⌨ Access the File pull-down menu and choose Print.

2. From the Print menu, choose **D**ocument on Disk (**3**).

3. Type the file name and press Enter.

    Note: If the document is stored in a directory other than the current directory, you must type the drive, path name, and directory name.

    The prompt Page(s): (All) appears on the status line.

4. If you want to print the entire document, press Enter. If you want to print particular pages only, type the pages you want to print, and then press Enter.

    Type the page numbers according to the specifications given in the section "Exercise 1.3: Printing Selected Pages."

WordPerfect reads the file from disk, creates a print job, and adds the document to the print queue.

Exercise 2.2: Printing from the List Files Screen

In addition to printing from the Print menu, you can print from the List Files screen. Printing from that screen has two advantages: You don't need to remember the name of the file you want to print, and you can mark any number of files to print. The files are printed in the order in which they appear on the List Files screen.

To use the List Files screen to print a document from disk, follow these steps:

1. Press F5 to activate the List command.

    ⌨ Access the File pull-down menu and choose List Files.

2. If the file resides in the current drive and directory, press Enter. If the file is in a different directory, type the drive, path name, and directory name; then press Enter.

    WordPerfect displays the List Files screen (see fig. 7.1).

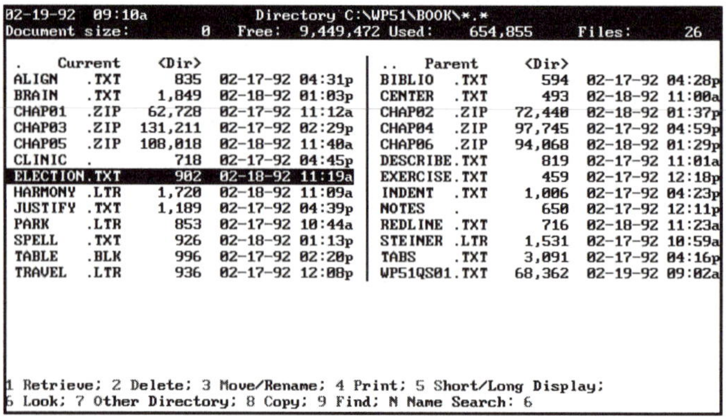

Printing

Fig. 7.1
The List Files screen.

3. Use the cursor keys to highlight the name of the file you want to print.

   Alternatively, choose Name Search (N), and begin typing the file name. When the file you want is highlighted, press ⏎Enter.

4. Choose Print (4) from the menu at the bottom of the screen.

5. At the prompt Page(s): (All), press ⏎Enter to print the entire document; alternatively, just type the pages you want to print, and then press ⏎Enter.

Exercise 2.3: Marking Files To Print

From the List Files screen, you can mark several files to print. To mark each file, do the following:

1. Use the cursor keys to highlight the name of the file.
2. Press ⇧Shift+8—the asterisk (*) key.

   Alternatively, you can press Home and then press ⇧Shift+8 to mark *all* the files on the List Files screen.

3. After you mark the files, choose Print (4).
4. To confirm printing, choose Yes.

WordPerfect adds the marked files to the print queue and prints them in the order in which they appear on the List Files screen. To unmark all files, press Home and then ⇧Shift+8 again.

Exercise 2.4: Printing a Disk Directory

For a neatly formatted printout of a disk directory, follow these steps:

To Control the Printer

1. Press [F5] to activate the List command.

   ⌨ Access the File pull-down menu and choose List Files.

2. Press [↵Enter].
3. Press [⇧Shift]+[F7] to activate the Print command.

   ⌨ Access the File pull-down menu and choose Print.

Objective 3: To Control the Printer

WordPerfect's Control Printer feature is a powerful tool for managing your printing activities. Using this feature, you can cancel print jobs, display a list of jobs waiting to be printed, and suspend and then resume printing. You perform all these operations from the Print: Control Printer screen.

Exercise 3.1: Accessing the Print: Control Printer Screen

To access the Print: Control Printer screen, follow these steps:

1. Press [⇧Shift]+[F7] to activate the Print command.

   ⌨ Access the File pull-down menu and choose Print.

2. Choose **C**ontrol Printer (**4**).

The Print: Control Printer screen is divided into three sections (see fig. 7.2).

```
Print: Control Printer
Current Job

Job Number: 1                    Page Number:  2
Status:    Printing              Current Copy: 1 of 1
Message:   None
Paper:     Standard 8.5" x 11"
Location:  Continuous feed
Action:    None

Job List

Job  Document            Destination    Print Options
 1   C:\...\WP51QS01.TXT  LPT 1
 2   C:\...\NELECTION.TXT LPT 1
 3   C:\...\HARMONY.LTR   LPT 1

Additional Jobs Not Shown: 3


1 Cancel Job(s); 2 Rush Job; 3 Display Jobs; 4 Go (start printer); 5 Stop: 0
```

Fig. 7.2
The Print: Control Printer screen.

The Current Job portion of the screen, which is the top section, gives you information about the job that is currently printing.

159

Printing

The Job List portion, which is in the middle, displays information about the next three print jobs.

The Control Printer menu at the bottom of the screen gives you the options you need for managing your printing activities.

Exercise 3.2: Canceling a Print Job

With the Print: Control Printer screen displayed, choose **Cancel Job(s)** (**1**) to cancel individual print jobs or all print jobs while they are printing. WordPerfect displays a message that tells you the number of the job currently being printed. Press [Enter] to cancel the current job, or type the number of the job you want to cancel. You can cancel all jobs by pressing [Shift]+[8] (*) and choosing **Yes** to confirm the cancellation.

Suspending Printing

If your printer has jammed or needs a new ribbon, you may need to suspend and then resume printing. In this case, choose **Stop** (**5**) from the menu at the bottom of the Print: Control Printer screen. Then you can correct the problem.

Before you resume printing, you must position the print head at the top of the next page. Then press G to restart the printer. Printing resumes on page one if the document consists of only one page or if you stopped printing on page one.

Otherwise, WordPerfect prompts you to enter the number of the page where you want printing to resume. At the prompt `Restart on page:`, type the page number and press [Enter] (see fig. 7.3).

Objective 4: To Preview a Document

Another option on the Print menu is **View Document** (**6**). Use this option to preview a document before you print it.

With the View Document option, you save costly printer paper and time by first previewing the document, making changes if needed, and then printing the document when you are certain that it's perfect. Document pages appear on-screen as they will appear when printed on paper, including graphics (if your system can display graphics), footnotes, page numbers, line numbers, headers, footers, and justification.

To Preview a Document

```
Print: Control Printer

Current Job

Job Number:  1                         Page Number:  2
Status:      Stopped                   Current Copy: 1 of 1
Message:     None
Paper:       Standard 8.5" x 11"
Location:    Continuous feed
Action:      Reset printer (press RESET or turn printer OFF and ON)
             Press "G" to restart, "C" to cancel
             Press Help for additional information
Job List

Job  Document              Destination      Print Options
 1   C:\...\WP51QS01.TXT   LPT 1
 2   C:\...\ELECTION.TXT   LPT 1
 3   C:\...\HARMONY.LTR    LPT 1

Additional Jobs Not Shown: 3


Restart on page: 3
```

Fig. 7.3
Entering the number of the page where you want printing to resume.

Exercise 4.1: Previewing a Document

To preview a document, follow these steps:

1. Display the document you want to view.
2. Position the cursor anywhere on the page you want to view.
3. Press ⇧Shift+F7 to activate the Print command.

   ⌨ Access the File pull-down menu and choose Print.

4. Choose **V**iew Document (**6**).
5. Choose one of the four options available, which are the following:

   Choose 100% (**1**) to view the document at its actual size (see fig. 7.4).

   Choose 200% (**2**) to view the document at twice its actual size (see fig. 7.5).

   Choose Full Page (**3**) to view the entire page (see fig. 7.6).

   Choose Facing Pages (**4**) to view the current page and its facing page (odd-numbered pages are displayed on the right side of the screen; even-numbered pages are displayed on the left). Figure 7.7 shows a document that is at least two pages in length.

6. Press PgUp, PgDn, or Ctrl+Home (GoTo) to view other pages of the document.

   Note that you cannot edit this preview version of the document.

7. When you have finished previewing the document, press F7 (Exit) to return to the editing screen.

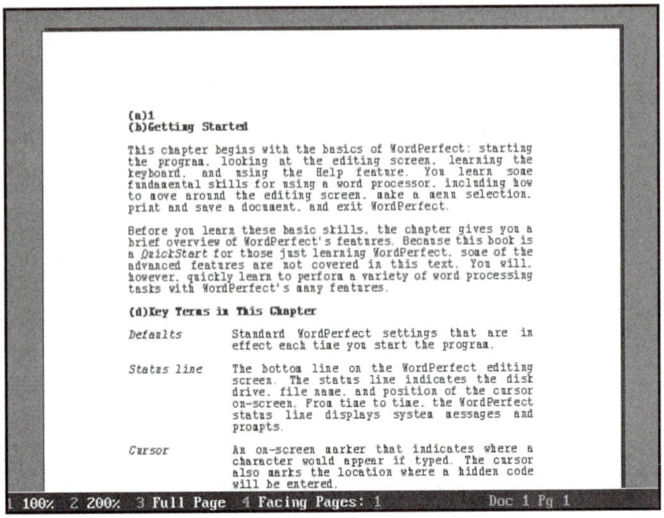

Printing

Fig. 7.4
The actual size of the document.

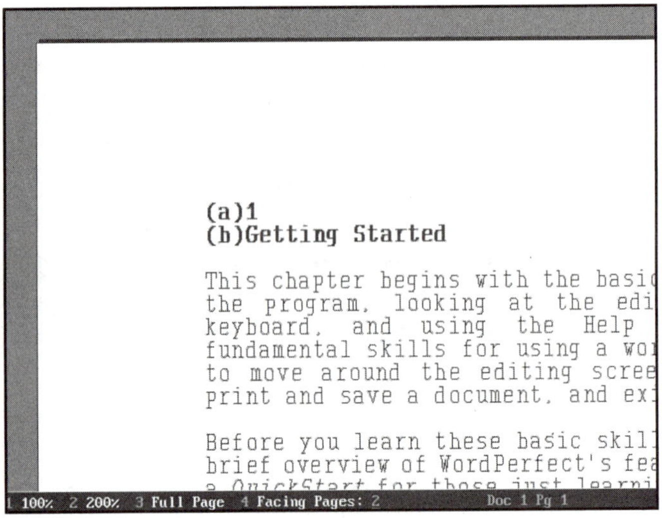

Fig. 7.5
The document at twice its actual size.

To Preview a Document

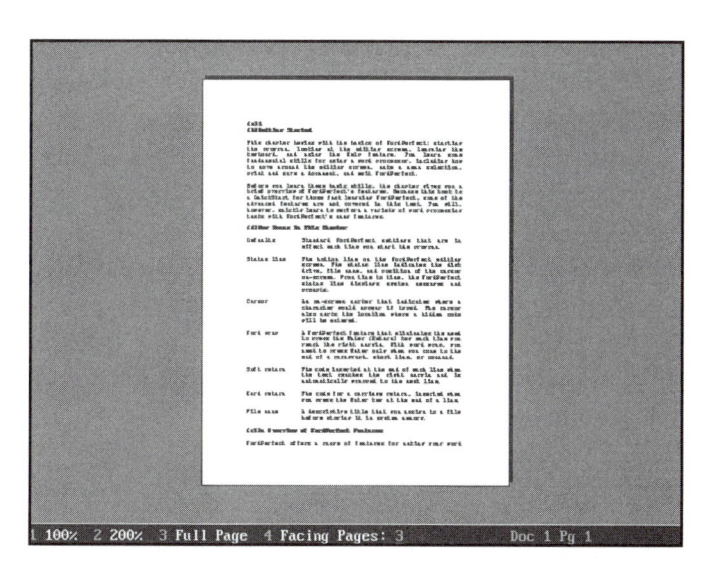

Fig. 7.6
Viewing the entire page.

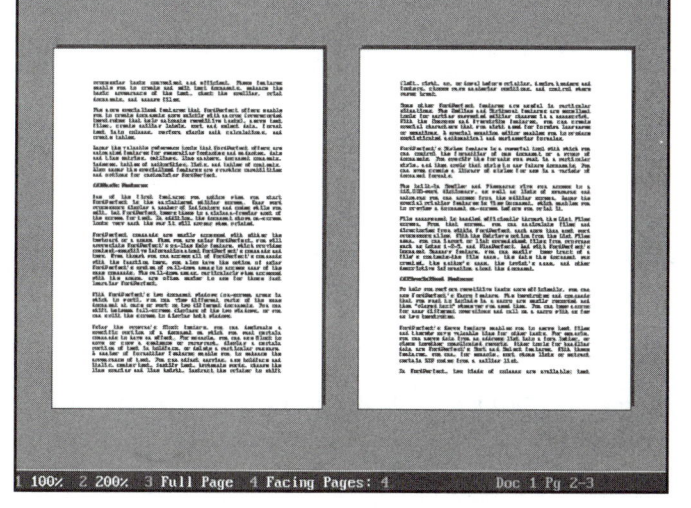

Fig. 7.7
Viewing facing pages.

Chapter Summary

In this chapter, you have learned how to print the test document. You have examined some of WordPerfect's many printing features, learning how to print, first from the screen and then from disk. You explored various ways to control your print jobs and to specify the options you want, and you learned how to preview a document before printing.

In the next chapter, you learn how to merge documents.

Testing Your Knowledge

True/False Questions

1. Printing a document from a disk is quicker than printing a document from the screen.
2. With the document on-screen, pressing ⇧Shift+F7 and then typing **2** prints a single page of the document.
3. Printing a document from the List Files screen enables you to print a document from disk.
4. Using the **C**ancel Job(s) option on the Print: Control Printer menu deletes the document.
5. You can save printer paper and time by first previewing the document.

Multiple Choice Questions

1. WordPerfect enables you to print a document from
    - A. the screen or the disk.
    - B. the DOS prompt.
    - C. the screen.
    - D. disk.
    - E. the printer companion program.
2. To print a single page from a document on-screen, you
    - A. press ⇧Shift+F7, and then choose **F**ull Document (**1**).
    - B. press ⇧Shift+F7, and then choose **P**age (**2**).

Testing Your Knowledge

C. press `Shift`+`F7`, and then choose **C**ontrol Printer (4).
D. press `Shift`+`F7`, and then choose **M**ultiple Page (5).
E. choose **V**iew Document (6).

3. The list files screen enables you to
   A. delete and print a file.
   B. retrieve a file.
   C. copy a file.
   D. look at a file.
   E. do all the above.

4. If you press `Shift`+`F7` and then press 4, you will
   A. copy a file to a disk.
   B. print a file.
   C. view a file.
   D. activate the Print: Control Printer menu.
   E. cancel the Print command.

5. Viewing a document enables
   A. you to view and print the document.
   B. you to view the document on-screen as it will appear on paper.
   C. you to send the document to two locations.
   D. you to make changes to the document.
   E. you to do none of the above.

Fill-in-the-Blank Questions

1. To print an entire document from the screen, press _____ to activate the Print command and then choose _____.
2. When you need a quick printout of whatever appears on-screen, you can press _____.
3. To activate the List Files screen to print a document when using a mouse, access the _____ pull-down menu and choose _____ files.
4. Using the _____ Document option, you can save costly printer paper and time by previewing the document before printing.

Printing

5. To view a document at twice its actual size, choose _____ from the View Document screen.

Review: Short Projects

1. Retrieve a file from your disk and print it by using the Print menu.
2. Using the List Files screen, choose a file and print it from this screen.
3. Retrieve a file, view it in various sizes, and print the file.

Review: Long Projects

1. Printing and the Print Screen

   Retrieve LETTER and print it by using the Print menu and the `PrtSc` key.

2. Retrieve, View, and Print a Document

   Retrieve KEYTERMS. View and then print the document. Notice that this document will have multiple pages. Print two copies of the document by using **N**umber of Copies.

Merging Documents

8

The Merge feature, frequently referred to as mail merge, is one of WordPerfect's most versatile tools for increasing office productivity. You use Merge whenever you need to insert variable data into a fixed format. For example, you can use Merge to create personalized form letters from an address list, produce phone lists, address envelopes, print mailing labels, piece together complicated reports, or fill in forms.

Objectives

1. To Create a Secondary Merge File
2. To Create a Primary Merge File
3. To Merge the Primary and Secondary Files
4. To Merge from the Keyboard
5. To Address Envelopes
6. To Print Mailing Labels

Merging Documents

Key Terms in This Chapter	
Merge	To assemble a document by inserting variable data into a fixed format.
Primary merge file	A skeleton document containing the fixed format into which pieces of data are merged.
Secondary merge file	A file containing the data (or variable information) that is merged into the primary merge file. The variable information is organized into records and fields.
Field	A unit of information that is part of a record. Each field contains the same type of information, such as a person's name; a street address; or a city, state, and ZIP code.
Record	A collection of fields with related information, such as a line of data, a paragraph, or a name and address in a secondary merge file.

8

Understanding the Basics

A merge operation requires a primary merge file, in combination with a secondary merge file. The primary merge file is a skeleton document containing the fixed format into which pieces of data are merged (see fig. 8.1). The secondary merge file contains data (or variable information) that is merged into the primary document (see fig. 8.2).

```
{DATE}

{FIELD}FullName~
{FIELD}Company?~
{FIELD}Street~
{FIELD}City~

Dear {FIELD}FirstName~:

Simpson Travel and Tours want to help with all of your travel
plans.  Whether you are going across the state, across the country,
or around the world, give me a call.  I'll guarantee you the best
fares and the most convenient connections.

Enclosed is a brochure that describes some of this season's best
travel bargains.  Call me for additional details on prices and
schedules.

Sincerely,

Sally Oceans
Travel Agent
C:\WP51\BOOK\TRAVEL.PMF                           Doc 1 Pg 1 Ln 1" Pos 1"
```

Fig. 8.1
The primary merge file.

Merging Text Files

```
{FIELD NAMES}FullName~Company~Street~City~FirstName~~{END RECORD}
================================================================
Ms. Katherine Haley{END FIELD}
Town Investments Company{END FIELD}
5 Waverly Place{END FIELD}
New York, NY  10022{END FIELD}
Kathy{END FIELD}
{END RECORD}
================================================================
Mr. Dave Acevedo{END FIELD}
Theatrical Productions{END FIELD}
1120 E. Broadway{END FIELD}
Sacramento, CA  95899{END FIELD}
Dave{END FIELD}
{END RECORD}
================================================================
Mr. John Quigley{END FIELD}
{END FIELD}
1423 So. Spencer St.{END FIELD}
Euclid, OH  46666{END FIELD}
John{END FIELD}
{END RECORD}
================================================================
C:\WP51\BOOK\ADDRESS.SMF              Doc 1 Pg 1 Ln 1" Pos 1"
```

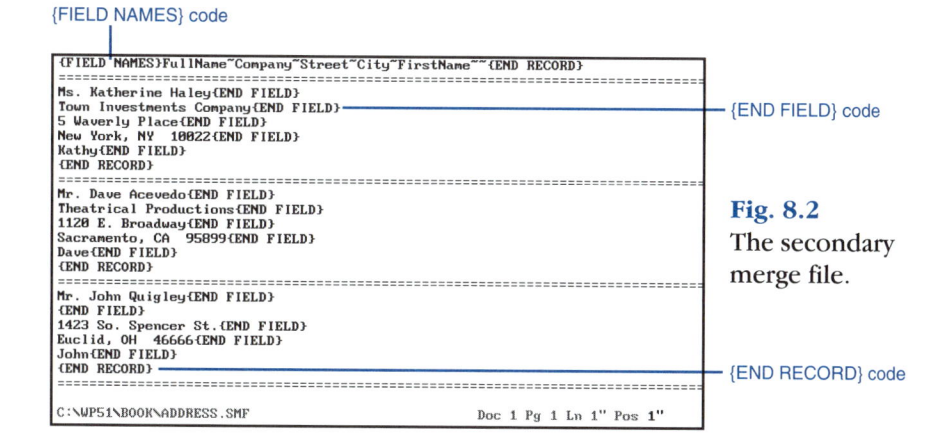

{FIELD NAMES} code — {END FIELD} code — {END RECORD} code

Fig. 8.2
The secondary merge file.

The primary merge file contains fixed text and merge codes. You place *merge codes* where you want to insert variable items into the fixed text. When a merge is completed, the codes are replaced with entries from a secondary merge file or from the keyboard.

The most typical and time-saving merge uses a secondary merge file that contains related variable data, such as an address list. All the information relating to one person makes up a *record*. Within each record, the separate items, such as a person's name or street address, are known as *fields*. WordPerfect inserts these items into the primary merge file by matching the codes in the primary and secondary merge files.

Fields, records, and certain merge operations are controlled by merge codes. You must put these codes in the right places and in the right order to ensure the success of a merge.

Merging Text Files

A *text file merge* combines two existing files—a primary merge file and a secondary merge file. Before you can execute such a merge, you must create these files. Create the secondary merge file first so that you know the field layout before you create the primary merge file.

After you create the secondary merge file, such as an address list, you can use the data in that file for a number of applications. For example, you can merge the data with a form letter for a mass mailing, and you can use the address data to print envelopes or mailing labels.

Merging Documents

Objective 1: To Create a Secondary Merge File

A *secondary merge file*, or *secondary file*, consists of records, each of which contains a number of fields. The structure must be uniform; otherwise, the merge will not work properly. Every record must have the same number of fields, and the fields must be in the same order in all records. If, for example, the first name is in the first field, but one record has the last name in the first field, WordPerfect prints that last name where the first name should be.

Suppose that you are creating a secondary file that contains address information. Each record in the file will contain the same units of information (or fields). The following is a list of the fields in each record:

FullName

Company

Street

City

FirstName

When you create a secondary file, you can name each field and include at the top of the file a list of all the field names. You also include certain codes to indicate where each record ends and where each field ends (refer to fig. 8.2).

A {FIELD NAMES} record displays the names of each field in the secondary file. Use {END FIELD} to indicate the end of a field and to enter a hard return code. Use {END RECORD} to indicate the end of a record and to enter a hard page code.

Exercise 1.1: Creating the {FIELD NAMES} Record for a Secondary File

To create the {FIELD NAMES} record for the sample secondary file, follow these steps:

1. Clear the screen, and place the cursor at the top left margin.
2. Press ⇧Shift+F9 to activate the Merge Codes command.

    The Merge Codes menu appears at the bottom of the screen.

To Create a Secondary Merge File

🖰 Access the Tools pull-down menu, and choose Merge Codes to display the Merge Codes pop-out menu.

3. Choose **M**ore (**6**).

   The Merge Codes selection box appears (see fig. 8.3).

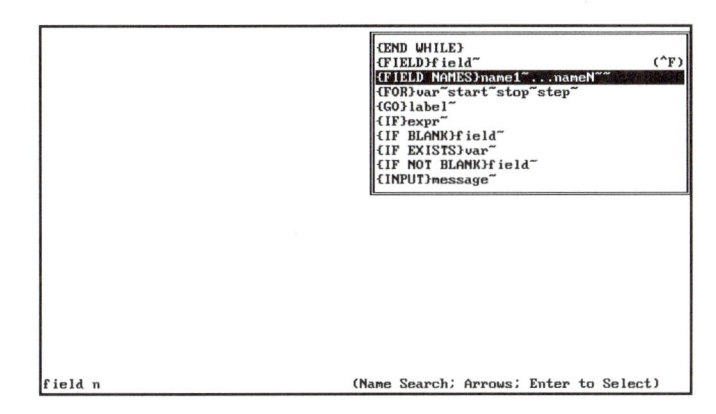

```
{END WHILE}
{FIELD}field~
{FIELD NAMES}name1~...nameN~~        (^F)
{FOR}var~start~stop~step~
{GO}label~
{IF}expr~
{IF BLANK}field~
{IF EXISTS}var~
{IF NOT BLANK}field~
{INPUT}message~
```
field n   (Name Search; Arrows; Enter to Select)

Fig. 8.3
The Merge Codes selection box.

4. Highlight the {FIELD NAMES} code in the Merge Codes selection box. Either use the arrow keys to move the highlight bar to {FIELD NAMES}, or start typing the words **field names**.

   🖰 Move the mouse pointer to the Merge Codes selection box. Drag the mouse to move the highlight bar to the {FIELD NAMES} code.

5. With the highlight bar on the {FIELD NAMES} code, press ⏎Enter.

   🖰 Double-click the {FIELD NAMES} code.

6. At the Enter Field 1 prompt, type the name of the first field. For this example, type **FullName** and press ⏎Enter.

7. At the Enter Field 2 prompt, type the name of the second field. In this case, type **Company** and press ⏎Enter.

8. If you have more fields, continue to enter their names at the prompts. For this example, type **Street** for Field 3, type **City** for Field 4, and type **FirstName** for Field 5.

9. After you type the last field name, press ⏎Enter at the next prompt for a field name. Pressing ⏎Enter tells WordPerfect that you have finished entering field names.

WordPerfect inserts a {FIELD NAMES} record at the top of the document (refer to fig. 8.2).

Merging Documents

Exercise 1.2: Creating the Rest of the Records for a Secondary File

To create the rest of the records for the secondary file, follow these steps:

1. Make sure that the cursor is at the top of page 2, immediately following the page break.
2. Type the name for the first record. For this example, type **Ms. Katherine Haley**. Do *not* press ⏎Enter.
3. Press F9 to activate the End Field command. WordPerfect inserts an {END FIELD} code and a hard return code after the name you typed.
4. Notice that the field name indicator in the lower left corner has changed to Company. Type the name of the company. In this case, type **Town Investments Company**.
5. Press F9 again.
6. Type the rest of the information for the first record. Make sure that you press F9 at the end of each field, including the last one. Use the following data:

    5 Waverly Place

    New York, NY 10022

    Kathy

7. When you have entered all the fields for Katherine Haley's record, press ⇧Shift + F9 (Merge Codes).

    🖰 Access the Tools pull-down menu, and choose Merge Codes to display the Merge Codes pop-out menu.

8. Choose **E**nd Record (**2**).

    An {END RECORD} code appears, followed by a hard page code (see fig. 8.4).

9. Repeat steps 2 through 8 for each of the remaining records. Make sure that you start each record on a separate page. Use the following data:

    Mr. Dave Acevedo

    Theatrical Productions

    1120 E. Broadway

    Sacramento, CA 95899

    Dave

Mr. John Quigley

{END FIELD}

1423 So. Spencer St.

Euclid, OH 46666

John

Note: If your records contain any blank fields, such as a field without an entry for the company name, you must acknowledge the presence of those fields. Press `F9` (End Field) to insert an {END FIELD} code into the blank field.

```
{FIELD NAMES}FullName~Company~Street~City~FirstName~~{END RECORD}
================================================================
Ms. Katherine Haley{END FIELD}
Town Investments Company{END FIELD}
5 Waverly Place{END FIELD}
New York, NY  10022{END FIELD}
Kathy{END FIELD}
{END RECORD}
================================================================




















Field: FullName                               Doc 1 Pg 3 Ln 1" Pos 1"
```

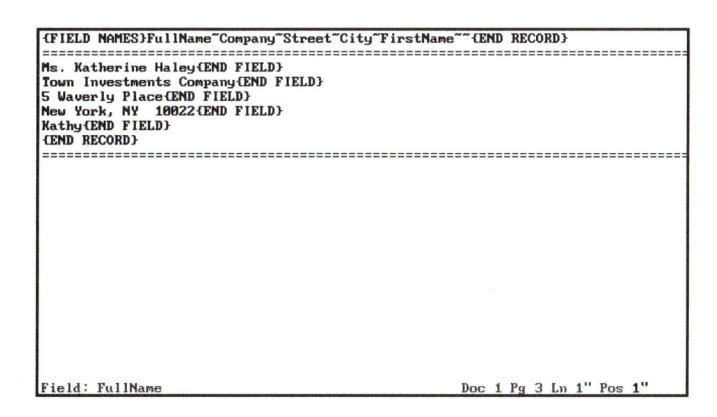

Fig. 8.4
The inserted {END RECORD} and hard page codes.

10. When you finish entering records, press `F7` (Exit) and give the file a descriptive name, such as ADDRESS.SMF. The SMF extension can remind you that the file is a secondary merge file.

Objective 2: To Create a Primary Merge File

A *primary merge file*, or *primary file*, contains fixed text and merge codes. Each merge code tells WordPerfect to insert a certain item from the secondary file into the primary file. The item is inserted at the location of the code.

Use a {DATE} code to insert the current date. Use a {FIELD}*fieldname*~ code to tell WordPerfect to insert an item from the secondary file into the primary file at the location of the code. Use a {FIELD}*fieldname?*~ code to prevent a blank line from appearing where an empty field exists in the secondary file.

173

Merging Documents

By splitting the screen, you can see the relationship between the two merge files. The field names in the primary file are evident in the top half, and the variable data fields in the secondary file are visible in the bottom half (see fig. 8.5).

Fig. 8.5
Splitting the screen to see the primary and secondary files.

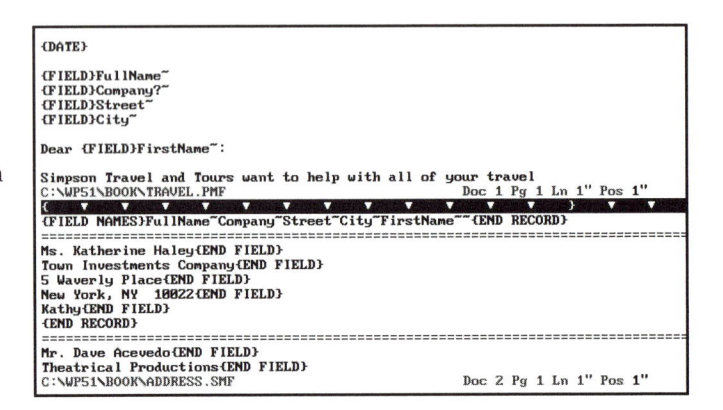

```
{DATE}
{FIELD}FullName~
{FIELD}Company?~
{FIELD}Street~
{FIELD}City~

Dear {FIELD}FirstName~:

Simpson Travel and Tours want to help with all of your travel
C:\WP51\BOOK\TRAVEL.PMF                          Doc 1 Pg 1 Ln 1" Pos 1"
================================================================
{FIELD NAMES}FullName~Company~Street~City~FirstName~~{END RECORD}
================================================================
Ms. Katherine Haley{END FIELD}
Town Investments Company{END FIELD}
5 Waverly Place{END FIELD}
New York, NY  10022{END FIELD}
Kathy{END FIELD}
{END RECORD}
================================================================
Mr. Dave Acevedo{END FIELD}
Theatrical Productions{END FIELD}
C:\WP51\BOOK\ADDRESS.SMF                         Doc 2 Pg 1 Ln 1" Pos 1"
```

The most commonly used code is the field name code {FIELD}*fieldname~*. The *fieldname* indicates the field name of each record in the secondary file. For example, when you specify {**FIELD**}**Street~**, you instruct WordPerfect to enter at that particular location the information found in the Street field.

If a record contains a blank field followed by a hard return, the empty field is printed as a blank line. To prevent a blank line from appearing, add a question mark after the field name. For example, you might use the code {FIELD}Company?~ in your primary file because some records in your secondary file are missing a company name.

Make sure that you correctly enter the field names in the primary file. Each field name must match the appropriate field in the secondary file; otherwise, an incorrect item will be merged.

Exercise 2.1: Creating the Primary File

To create the primary file, follow these steps:

1. Position the cursor at the place in the document where you want the current date entered.

2. Press ⇧Shift + F9 to activate the Merge Codes command, and choose **M**ore (6).

To Merge the Primary and Secondary Files

    🖰 Access the Tools pull-down menu, choose Merge Codes, and choose More.

    The Merge Codes selection box appears.

3. Highlight the {DATE} code in the Merge Codes selection box. Either use the arrow keys to move the highlight bar to {DATE}, or start typing the word **date**.

    🖰 Move the mouse pointer to the Merge Codes selection. Drag the mouse to move the highlight bar to the {DATE} code.

4. With the highlight bar on {DATE}, press ⏎Enter.

    🖰 Double-click {DATE}.

    A {DATE} code appears in the document.

5. Press ⏎Enter twice to skip a line and to position the cursor where you want to begin entering the name and address.

6. Press ⇧Shift + F9 (Merge Codes), and choose **F**ield (**1**).

    🖰 Access the Tools pull-down menu, choose Merge Codes, and choose Field.

7. At the Enter Field prompt, type the name of the field exactly as you have defined it. For this example, to enter the name of the first field, type **FullName**.

8. Press ⏎Enter.

    WordPerfect inserts a {FIELD} code, followed by the name of the field and a tilde (~).

9. Continue typing the sample letter, entering the {FIELD}*fieldname*~ codes as they appear. Repeat steps 6 through 8 to enter the codes. Be sure to add a question mark (?) when you enter the Company field. At the Enter Field prompt for that field, type **Company?**.

10. When you finish creating the primary file, press F7 (Exit), and save the file with a name that indicates the file's purpose. For example, use the name TRAVEL.PMF; the PMF extension serves as a reminder that this file is a primary merge file.

Objective 3: To Merge the Primary and Secondary Files

After you create the primary and secondary files, you are ready to start the merge. If you have a small secondary file, you can merge the files to the screen. If you have a large secondary file, you can merge directly to the printer.

Merging Documents

Merging to the Screen

When you merge files to the screen, you can check for errors in the merge before you print. You can view each merged file to be sure that the correct information is being merged. If you find errors, you can edit either file and merge again to conserve paper.

Exercise 3.1: Merging the Text Files to the Screen

To merge the text files to the screen, follow these steps:

1. Clear the screen.
2. Press `Ctrl`+`F9` to activate the Merge/Sort command, and choose **M**erge (**1**).

   🖱 Access the Tools pull-down menu, and choose Merge.

3. At the `Primary file` prompt, type the name of the primary file and press `⏎Enter`. For this example, type **TRAVEL.PMF** and press `⏎Enter`.
4. At the `Secondary file` prompt, type the name of the secondary file. In this case, type **ADDRESS.SMF** and press `⏎Enter`.

WordPerfect merges the primary file with the secondary file. While this is happening, the program displays the message * Merging * in the lower left corner of the screen.

When the merging process reaches the {DATE} code, WordPerfect automatically replaces the code with the current date. If your computer has a battery-powered clock/calendar or if you enter the correct date at the beginning of each session, the display shows the correct date; otherwise, an incorrect date may appear. At each {FIELD} code, WordPerfect substitutes the appropriate information from the secondary file.

When the merge is completed, the screen displays the last letter in the merge operation.

If you move the cursor to the beginning of the document, you will find the first completed letter. Notice that all the necessary items are filled in, and each letter is separated from the others by a hard page code. The letters are ready to print, and each letter will be printed on a separate page.

Merging to the Printer

When you are creating a large number of form letters, all the merged letters may not fit into memory. WordPerfect therefore cannot complete the merge

To Merge the Primary and Secondary Files

and display the letters on-screen. To solve this problem—or just to save time by eliminating the step of displaying the letters on-screen—you can send the results of a merge operation directly to the printer.

Create a merge to the printer by inserting into the primary file a {PRINT} code, which instructs WordPerfect to send to the printer any text merged up to that point.

You also must include a {PAGE OFF} code so that the printer properly prints consecutive sheets one at a time (see fig. 8.6).

```
{DATE}

{FIELD}FullName~
{FIELD}Company?~
{FIELD}Street~
{FIELD}City~

Dear {FIELD}FirstName~:

Simpson Travel and Tours want to help with all of your travel
plans. Whether you are going across the state, across the country,
or around the world, give me a call. I'll guarantee you the best
fares and the most convenient connections.

Enclosed is a brochure that describes some of this season's best
travel bargains. Call me for additional details on prices and
schedules.

Sincerely,


Sally Oceans
Travel Agent
{PAGE OFF}{PRINT}
C:\WP51\BOOK\TRAVEL.PMF                    Doc 1 Pg 1 Ln 4.83" Pos 1"
```

Fig. 8.6

The {PAGE OFF} and {PRINT} codes in the primary document.

Exercise 3.2: Adding the Codes for Merging Directly to the Printer

To add the codes for merging directly to the printer, follow these steps:

1. Press Home, Home, ↓ to move the cursor to the bottom of the primary file.

2. Press ⇧Shift + F9 to activate the Merge Codes command, and choose **P**age Off (**4**).

   ▭ Access the Tools pull-down menu, choose Merge Codes, and choose Page Off.

   A {PAGE OFF} code appears at the bottom of the document.

3. Press ⇧Shift + F9 again, and choose **M**ore (**6**).

   ▭ Access the Tools pull-down menu, choose Merge Codes, and choose More.

4. Highlight the {PRINT} code in the Merge Codes selection box. Either use the arrow keys to move the highlight bar to {PRINT}, or start typing the word **print**.

Merging Documents

    🖱 Move the mouse pointer to the Merge Codes selection box. Drag the mouse to move the highlight bar to the {PRINT} code.

5. With the highlight bar on {PRINT}, press ⏎Enter.

    🖱 Double-click the {PRINT} code.

A {PRINT} code appears at the end of the document.

After you add the merge codes for printing, save the letter (again using the file name TRAVEL.PMF), turn on the printer, and merge the text files with the same procedure you used to merge the files to the screen. WordPerfect then prints your letters.

If your computer freezes while the screen displays the `* Merging *` message, don't panic—you probably forgot to turn on the printer, or it is not on line. If you turn on the printer, the document starts to print, and the screen returns to normal.

Merging to the printer is an excellent way to automate certain tasks. If you have a fast printer, you can print many personalized letters with minimum effort.

8   Objective 4: To Merge from the Keyboard

The simplest form of merge is the keyboard merge. This kind of merge uses a special merge code that makes the merge-printing pause so that you can enter information from the keyboard. Keyboard merges are useful for filling in preprinted forms, addressing memos, and entering frequently updated information in a form letter.

Exercise 4.1: Preparing the Primary File for a Keyboard Merge

For a keyboard merge, you need only a primary file with text and a few merge codes. Suppose that you regularly send a memo announcing the time, date, and subject of a monthly meeting. Your primary file can contain the regular text of a letter and the merge codes that hold the places for the variable information.

The following two kinds of merge codes are useful in the primary file for the memo (see fig. 8.7):

- The {DATE} code to indicate where the current date is displayed
- The {INPUT} code to indicate where an entry from the keyboard is placed

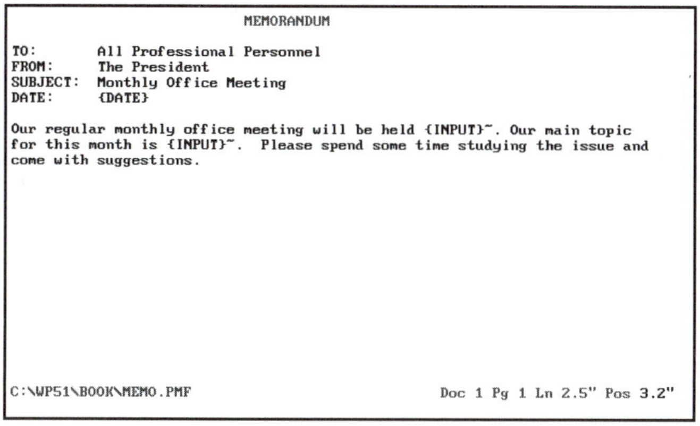

```
                              MEMORANDUM

TO:        All Professional Personnel
FROM:      The President
SUBJECT:   Monthly Office Meeting
DATE:      {DATE}

Our regular monthly office meeting will be held {INPUT}~. Our main topic
for this month is {INPUT}~.  Please spend some time studying the issue and
come with suggestions.

C:\WP51\BOOK\MEMO.PMF                          Doc 1 Pg 1 Ln 2.5" Pos 3.2"
```

Fig. 8.7
Using the {DATE} and {INPUT} codes in the merge file.

The {DATE} code indicates where the current date is displayed. {INPUT} code indicates where an entry from the keyboard is placed.

To prepare the primary file for the keyboard merge, follow these steps:

1. Type the memo up to the date entry (see fig. 8.8).

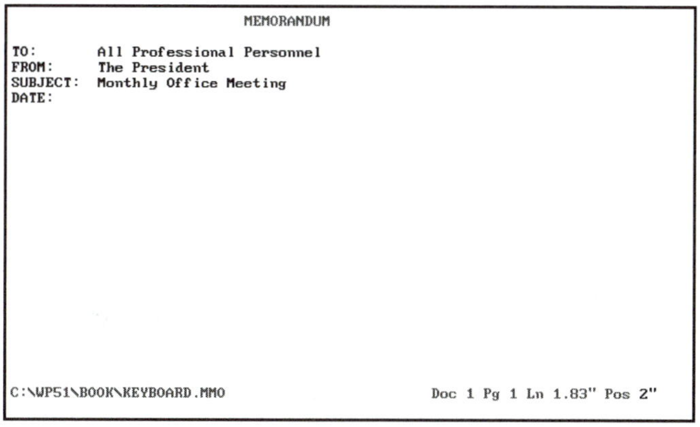

```
                              MEMORANDUM

TO:        All Professional Personnel
FROM:      The President
SUBJECT:   Monthly Office Meeting
DATE:

C:\WP51\BOOK\KEYBOARD.MMO                      Doc 1 Pg 1 Ln 1.83" Pos 2"
```

Fig. 8.8
The heading of the memo.

2. To enter the date merge code, press Shift + F9 to activate the Merge codes command.

   Access the Tools pull-down menu, and choose Merge Codes.

Merging Documents

3. Choose **M**ore (**6**).

   The Merge Codes selection box appears.

4. Highlight the {DATE} code in the Merge Codes selection box. Either use the arrow keys to move the highlight bar to {DATE}, or start typing the word **date**.

   🖰 Move the mouse pointer to the Merge Codes selection box. Drag the mouse to move the highlight bar to the {DATE} code.

5. With the highlight bar on the {DATE} code, press ⏎Enter.

   🖰 Double-click the {DATE} code.

6. Continue typing the memo up to where you want to insert the first {INPUT} merge code.

7. To enter a merge code that pauses for keyboard input ({INPUT}), position the cursor at the first spot where you want the merge to pause.

8. To enter the first {INPUT} merge code, press ⇧Shift + F9 to activate the Merge Codes command.

   🖰 Access the Tools pull-down menu, and choose Merge Codes.

9. Choose **M**ore (**6**).

   The Merge Codes selection box appears again

10. Highlight the {INPUT} code in the Merge Codes selection box. Either use the arrow keys to move the highlight bar to {INPUT}, or start typing the word **input**.

    🖰 Move the mouse pointer to the Merge Codes selection box. Drag the mouse to move the highlight bar to the {INPUT} code.

11. With the highlight bar on the {INPUT} code, press ⏎Enter.

    🖰 Double-click the {INPUT} code.

    At this point, you could enter a message to be displayed during the merge. But for this exercise, no message is needed.

12. At the `Enter Message` prompt, press ⏎Enter.

13. Continue typing the memo, and repeat steps 7 through 12 to enter any other {INPUT} codes.

14. Finish typing the memo and save it. Name the memo MEMO.PMF.

Exercise 4.2: Running a Keyboard Merge

When you run the keyboard merge, WordPerfect pauses and waits for keyboard input whenever the program reaches an {INPUT} code.

To merge-print the memo, follow these steps:

1. Clear the screen.
2. Press `Ctrl`+`F9` to activate the Merge/Sort command, and choose **M**erge (**1**).

   📼 Access the Tools pull-down menu, and choose Merge.
3. Type the name of the primary file, and press `↵Enter`. For this example, type **memo.pmf** and press `↵Enter`.
4. Because you are not using a secondary merge file, press `↵Enter` again.

   The cursor replaces the {INPUT} code with the primary document screen and is positioned at the appropriate place in your document.
5. Enter the first segment of the variable text.
6. Press `F9` (End Field) to continue the merge.

   The cursor goes to the position of the next {INPUT} code (which is no longer displayed) so that you can type the text for this code.
7. Enter any other segments of variable text.
8. Press `F9` (End Field).
9. Save and print the memo.

While the merge is in progress, WordPerfect displays the message * Merging * on the status line. When you enter the last item and press `F9` (End Field), the message disappears.

After you have created a secondary file, you can use that file to automate a number of other tasks. Two common tasks that you may want to automate are addressing envelopes and printing mailing labels.

Objective 5: To Address Envelopes

The procedure for addressing envelopes begins with selecting the paper form. You must edit or create a form definition for envelopes (if your printer doesn't already have an appropriate definition). Next, you need to create a primary file that chooses the envelope definition, specifies the location on the envelope where the address should be printed, and specifies which fields should be merged from the secondary file. Finally, you need to merge the secondary file of addresses directly to the printer to print your envelopes.

Merging Documents

Creating an Envelope Form Definition

Depending on what kind of printer you are using, you may already have a form definition for envelopes. If you have one, you still may need to use the first procedure described here, showing how to edit your form definition so that it will work properly for printing envelopes. If you don't have an envelope definition, use the second procedure to create the definition. These procedures define a form for a standard 9 1/2-by-4-inch business envelope that you can feed manually into your printer. The printer prompts you to insert each envelope. Note that these procedures may vary according to your printer. The steps that follow are designed for a Hewlett-Packard LaserJet Series II printer.

Exercise 5.1: Editing a Form Definition for Envelopes

Follow these steps to edit a form definition for envelopes:

1. Press Shift + F8 to activate the Format command; choose **P**age (**2**), and choose Paper **S**ize/Type (**7**).

    Access the Layout pull-down menu, choose Page, and choose Paper Size/Type (7).

2. Use the arrow keys to highlight the envelope definition, and choose **E**dit (**5**).
3. Choose **L**ocation (**5**), and choose **M**anual (**3**).
4. Choose **P**rompt to Load (**4**), and choose **N**o.
5. Press F7 (Exit) three times to return to the editing screen.

Exercise 5.2: Creating a Form Definition for Envelopes

Follow these steps to create a form definition for envelopes:

1. Press Shift + F8 to activate the Format command, choose **P**age (**2**), and choose Paper **S**ize/Type (**7**).

    Access the Layout pull-down menu, choose Page, and choose Paper Size/Type (7).

2. Choose **A**dd (Create) (**2**), choose **E**nvelope (**5**), and choose Paper **S**ize (**1**).
3. Choose **E**nvelope (**5**).
4. Choose **F**ont Type (**3**), and choose **L**andscape (**2**).

To Address Envelopes

5. Choose **L**ocation (**5**), and choose **M**anual (**3**).
6. Choose P**r**ompt to Load (**4**), and choose **N**o.

    The Format: Edit Paper Definition menu appears, with your selections indicated.

7. Press ⏎Enter to return to the list of form definitions.

    The definition you created for envelopes is highlighted.

8. Press F7 (Exit) twice to return to the editing screen.

Creating the Envelope Primary File

After you have defined the envelope form, you need to choose the definition and then format your page for printing the address on the envelope. This section takes you step-by-step through the procedure for choosing the form and positioning the address on a standard 9 1/2-by-4-inch business envelope. The address will be printed 2 inches from the top of the envelope and 4 1/2 inches from the left side of the envelope. After you accomplish the formatting, you need to specify which fields should be used from the secondary file (in this example, ADDRESS.SMF) for merge printing the addresses.

Exercise 5.3: Choosing the Envelope Definition

To choose the envelope definition, follow these steps:

1. Begin a new document. This document will become the primary file.
2. Access the Document Initial Codes screen by pressing ⇧Shift + F8 to activate the Format command, choosing **D**ocument (**3**), and choosing Initial **C**odes (**3**).

    🖱 Access the Layout pull-down menu, choose Document, and choose Initial Codes (2).

    Note: Putting the formatting codes for the primary document into Document Initial Codes is important. Otherwise, all formatting codes will be repeated at the top of every page in the final document.

3. Press ⇧Shift + F8 again, and choose **P**age (**2**).

    🖱 Access the Layout pull-down menu, and choose Page.

4. Choose Paper **S**ize/Type (**7**).
5. Use the arrow keys to highlight the envelope definition, and choose **S**elect (**1**).
6. Press F7 (Exit) to return to the Document Initial Codes screen.

183

Merging Documents

Exercise 5.4: Entering the Formatting Codes for Printing the Address

To enter the formatting codes for printing the address, follow these steps:

1. From the Document Initial Codes screen, press ⇧Shift + F8 (Format), choose **L**ine (**1**), and choose **M**argins Left/Right (**7**).

    ⌨ Access the Layout pull-down menu, choose Line, and choose Margins Left/Right (7).

2. Type **4.5"** for the left margin, and press ↵Enter. Then type **0.5"** for the right margin, and press ↵Enter.

3. Press ↵Enter to return to the Format menu.

4. Choose **P**age (**2**), and choose **M**argins Top/Bottom (**5**).

    ⌨ Access the Layout pull-down menu, choose Page, and choose Margins Top/Bottom (5).

5. Type **0** for the top margin, and press ↵Enter. Then type **0** for the bottom margin, and press ↵Enter.

6. Press F7 (Exit) three times to return to the editing screen.

7. Press ⇧Shift + F8 (Format), and choose **O**ther (**4**).

    ⌨ Access the Layout pull-down menu, and choose Other.

8. Choose **A**dvance (**1**), choose **L**ine (**3**), type **2"**, and press ↵Enter.

9. Press F7 (Exit) to return to the editing screen.

Exercise 5.5: Entering the Merge Codes for Printing the Envelopes

To enter the merge codes for printing the envelopes, follow these steps:

1. Press ⇧Shift + F9 to activate the Merge Codes command, and choose **F**ield (**1**).

    ⌨ Access the Tools pull-down menu, choose Merge Codes, and choose Field.

2. At the `Enter Field` prompt, type **FullName** (the name of the first field in the secondary file), and press ↵Enter.

3. Press ↵Enter to move the cursor to a new line.

4. Enter the rest of the fields from the secondary file for the envelope's address. Follow the procedures you use entering fields for any merge file.

To Address Envelopes

5. Press Shift+F9 (Merge Codes), and choose **P**age Off (**4**).

    ⌨ Access the Tools pull-down menu, choose Merge Codes, and choose Page Off.

    A {PAGE OFF} code appears in the document, just below the field names.

6. Press Shift+F9 again, and choose **M**ore (**6**).

    ⌨ Access the Tools pull-down menu, choose Merge Codes, and choose More.

7. Highlight the {PRINT} code in the Merge Codes selection box.

    ⌨ Move the mouse pointer to the Merge Codes selection box. Drag the mouse to move the highlight bar to the {PRINT} code.

8. With the highlight bar on {PRINT}, press Enter.

    ⌨ Double-click the {PRINT} code.

    A {PRINT} code appears in the document (see fig. 8.9).

9. Press F7 (Exit), and then save the file under the name ENVELOPE.PMF.

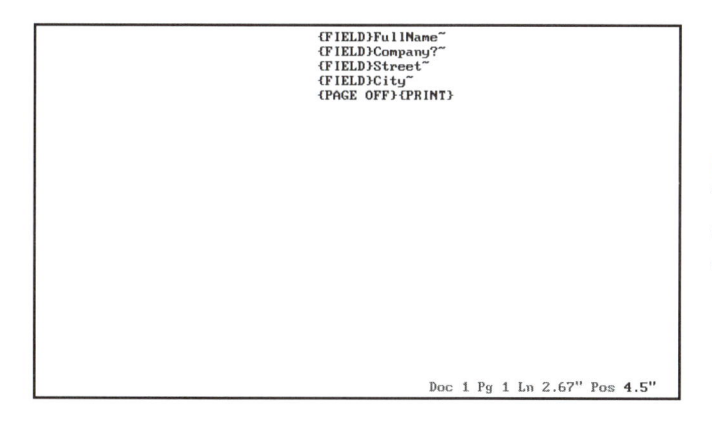

```
{FIELD}FullName~
{FIELD}Company?~
{FIELD}Street~
{FIELD}City~
{PAGE OFF}{PRINT}




                              Doc 1 Pg 1 Ln 2.67" Pos 4.5"
```

Fig. 8.9
The completed envelope document.

Merging Files To Print Envelopes

Now that you have created the envelope definition, selected it, and created a primary file for printing envelopes, you can merge the ENVELOPE.PMF file with the ADDRESS.SMF file. (*Note:* Be sure to open the back of your printer so that the envelopes can flow out easily.)

185

Merging Documents

Exercise 5.6: Merging the Address and Envelope Files and Sending the Results Directly to the Printer

Follow these steps to merge the address and envelope files and to send the results directly to the printer:

1. Clear the screen.
2. Press [Ctrl]+[F9] to activate the Merge/Sort command, and choose **M**erge (**1**).

    ⌨ Access the Tools pull-down menu, and choose Merge.
3. At the `Primary file` prompt, type the name of the primary file. For this example, type **envelope.pmf** and press [↵Enter].
4. At the `Secondary file` prompt, type the name of the secondary file. In this case, type **address.smf** and press [↵Enter].

WordPerfect merges the files and sends the results directly to the printer. After printing each envelope, the printer pauses and prompts you to load another envelope.

Objective 6: To Print Mailing Labels

Mailing labels are one of the classic applications of merge capabilities. The first step is to create a label definition. You can do this through the Format: Labels menu by defining a paper size and type, showing the number of labels, the dimensions of each label, the arrangement of labels on the paper, and the margins you want to maintain on each label.

If you are using standard-sized labels, however, an easier method is to create the label definition with a macro. WordPerfect provides a macro, LABELS.WPM, that automatically creates label definitions for a variety of popular label sheets. You can run this macro and, if your labels are listed on the menu that appears, create the label definition you need.

After you create the label definition, you need to create a primary file that chooses the label definition and specifies which fields should be merged from the secondary file. Then you can merge the primary file with the secondary file of addresses and print your labels.

Suppose that you want to create mailing labels on a label sheet that is 8 1/2 by 11 inches in size and that holds 30 labels arranged in 3 columns. And you want to print the labels on a Hewlett-Packard LaserJet Series II printer. Note that these instructions may vary depending on your printer.

Exercise 6.1: Using the LABELS Macro To Create a Label Form Definition

To use the LABELS macro to create a label form definition, follow these steps:

1. Press `Alt`+`F10` to activate the Macro command.

    🖰 Access the Tools pull-down menu, choose Macro, and choose Execute.

2. Type **labels** and press `↵Enter`.

    The macro displays a list of standard label sizes.

3. Choose 3-up labels for this example, and press `↵Enter`.
4. At the Location prompt, choose Continuous (**1**).

    The definition you created for labels is highlighted.

5. Choose Exit (**2**) to return to the editing screen.

Creating the Labels Primary File

After you have created the label definition, you need to create the primary file. In that file, you first must choose the definition. You then can specify which fields should be used from the secondary file (in this example, ADDRESS.SMF) for merge printing the addresses.

Exercise 6.2: Choosing the Label Form Definition

To choose the label form definition, follow these steps:

1. Begin a new document. This document will become the primary file.
2. Press `⇧Shift`+`F8` to activate the Format command, choose Document (**3**), and choose Initial Codes (**2**).

    🖰 Access the Layout pull-down menu, choose Document, and choose Initial Codes (2).

3. Press `⇧Shift`+`F8` again, and choose Page (**2**).

    🖰 Access the Layout pull-down menu, and choose Page.

4. Choose Paper Size/Type (**7**).

    The Format: Paper Size/Type menu appears.

5. Use the arrow keys to highlight the new definition for labels.
6. Choose Select (**1**).
7. Press `F7` (Exit) three times to return to the editing screen.

Merging Documents

Now you can enter the {FIELD} codes (and other merge codes as well) for your mailing-label merge.

Exercise 6.3: Entering the Merge Codes

To enter the merge codes, follow these steps:

1. Press `Shift` + `F9` to activate the Merge Codes command, and choose **F**ield (**1**).

   Access the Tools pull-down menu, choose Merge Codes, and choose Field.

2. At the `Enter Field` prompt, type **FullName** (the name of the first field in the secondary file) and press `Enter`.
3. Press `Enter` to move the cursor to a new line.
4. Enter the rest of the fields from the secondary file for the envelope's address.
5. Press `F7` (Exit) and then save the file under the name LABELS.PMF.

Merging Files To Print Labels

Now that you have created the primary file for printing labels, you can merge the LABELS.PMF file with the ADDRESS.SMF file. The following exercise explains how to merge the two files.

Exercise 6.4: Merging the Labels and Address Files to the Screen

Follow these steps to merge the labels and address files to the screen:

1. Clear the screen.
2. Press `Ctrl` + `F9` to activate the Merge/Sort command, and choose **M**erge (**1**).

   Access the Tools pull-down menu, and choose Merge.

3. At the `Primary file` prompt, type the name of the primary file. For this example, type **labels.pmf** and press `Enter`.
4. At the `Secondary file` prompt, type the name of the secondary file. In this case, type **address.smf** and press `Enter`.

To Print Mailing Labels

WordPerfect merges the files to the screen. On the editing screen, the records appear consecutively, separated by hard page breaks (see fig. 8.10).

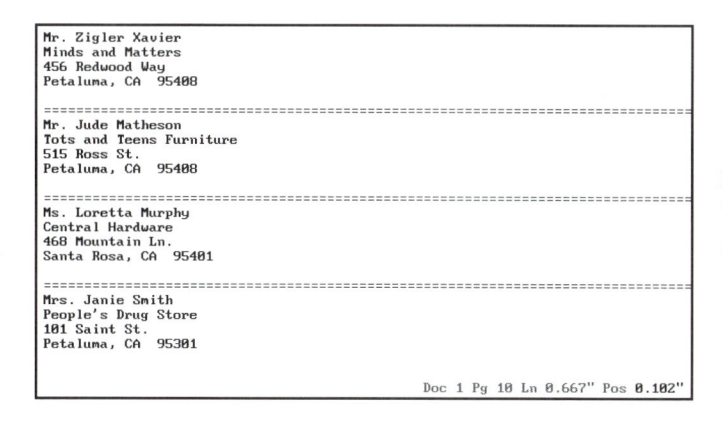

```
Mr. Zigler Xavier
Minds and Matters
456 Redwood Way
Petaluma, CA  95408
==========================================================================
Mr. Jude Matheson
Tots and Teens Furniture
515 Ross St.
Petaluma, CA  95408
==========================================================================
Ms. Loretta Murphy
Central Hardware
468 Mountain Ln.
Santa Rosa, CA  95401
==========================================================================
Mrs. Janie Smith
People's Drug Store
101 Saint St.
Petaluma, CA  95301

                                  Doc 1 Pg 10 Ln 0.667" Pos 0.102"
```

Fig. 8.10
The merged files on-screen.

Now you are ready to print the labels. Before you do, however, a good practice is to preview the labels on-screen.

Exercise 6.5: Previewing and Printing the Labels

Follow these steps to preview the labels and then print them:

1. Press [Shift] + [F7] to activate the Print command.

   Access the File pull-down menu, and choose Print.

2. Choose **V**iew Document (**6**).

3. To see the arrangement of the labels in this example, choose 100% (**1**).

4. Press [F7] to exit the View Document screen and return to the editing screen.

   If the labels are not arranged properly on-screen, check the primary and secondary files for possible errors in the codes or settings.

5. If the labels are arranged properly, load the label sheets face up into the paper tray.

6. Choose [Shift] + [F7] (Print), and choose **F**ull Document (**1**) to print the labels.

   Access the File pull-down menu, choose Print, and choose Full Document (1).

WordPerfect prints the labels.

189

Merging Documents

Chapter Summary

This chapter introduces WordPerfect's powerful Merge feature. You have learned how to use Merge by combining primary and secondary merge files. The text shows you how to merge these files to either the screen or to the printer. And you have learned how to use Merge to create and print envelopes and mailing labels. In the next chapter, you learn about WordPerfect's Sort and Select features for handling record-keeping tasks and extracting particular data from a large database.

Testing Your Knowledge

True/False Questions

1. A merge operation requires a primary and secondary merge file.
2. The secondary merge file contains fixed text, graphics, and merge codes.
3. Each record in a secondary merge file contains a number of fields.
4. When you merge files to the screen, you can check for errors in the merge before printing.
5. After you have created a primary file, you can automate addressing envelopes and printing mailing labels.

Multiple Choice Questions

1. A merge operation requires
    A. a primary file.
    B. a secondary file.
    C. an initial file.
    D. a list file.
    E. both A and B.
2. Which of the following is *not* a field in the record of a secondary file?
    A. FNAME
    B. TITLE
    C. CITY

Testing Your Knowledge

    D. TOM BLUES
    E. STATE
3. To activate the Merge Codes command, you
    A. press [Ctrl]+[F9].
    B. press [F9].
    C. press [Alt]+[F9].
    D. press [Shift]+[F9].
    E. press none of the above.
4. When you have finished entering all fields for the record, from the Merge Codes menu, press
    A. [Shift]+[F9] and choose Field (1).
    B. [Shift]+[F9] and choose End Record (2).
    C. [F9] and choose End Record (2).
    D. [Shift]+[F9] and choose Next Record (5).
    E. [Alt]+[F9] and choose Field (1).
5. A primary and secondary file can be merged to
    A. the printer.
    B. the printer or the screen.
    C. a disk.
    D. the screen.
    E. the printer or a disk.

Fill-in-the-Blank Questions

1. The _____ merge file contains data that is merged into the _____ document.
2. A text file combines a _____ merge file and a _____ merge file.
3. The merge codes menu is displayed by pressing _____.
4. After you create the primary and secondary files, you can merge to the _____ or _____.
5. Pressing [Shift]+[F9] and choosing More (6) displays the _____ codes selection box.

191

Merging Documents

Review: Short Projects

1. Creating a Secondary File

   Use a list of five friends to create a secondary file and include the following fields: Name, Address, City, State, ZIP, Phone. Save the file as FRIENDS.SMF.

2. Creating a Primary File

   Type the following:

   {DATE}

   {Field Name}

   {Field Address}

   {City}, {State} {Zip}

   Call me at {PHONENO}.

   Hint: Be sure that field names match the names used in Short Project 1.

   Save the document as FRIENDS.PMF.

3. Merge Printing

   Do a merge print of Projects 1 and 2 to the printer.

Review: Long Projects

1. Creating a Primary and a Secondary Document, Performing a Print Merge to the Printer

   Create an envelope definition, envelope primary file, and print envelopes for the same five people.

2. Creating Mailing Labels

   Create mailing labels for five people.

Sorting and Selecting

9

Although WordPerfect's Sort and Select features cannot compete with specialized database management programs in all respects, these features provide enough power and flexibility to handle many of your data management needs. When you combine Sort and Select with other WordPerfect features—such as Search, Replace, and Merge—you create a powerful data management tool.

Examples of two simple applications of the Sort command are sorting lines to create alphabetical phone lists or rosters, and sorting mailing lists by ZIP code to conform with postal service rules for bulk mailings. An example of the use of the Select command is to find records that meet certain criteria—such as all the customers who live in Indianapolis and have a ZIP code of 46260. WordPerfect can work with four kinds of data: a line, a paragraph, a secondary merge file, or a table. This chapter shows you how to sort the first three kinds of records. Sorting tables, a slightly different procedure, is beyond the scope of this book.

Objectives

1. To Understand the Sort Screen
2. To Sort Lines and Paragraphs
3. To Sort Secondary Merge Files
4. To Choose Particular Data

Sorting and Selecting

Key Terms in This Chapter	
Sort keys	The characters or numbers in a specific file location, which WordPerfect uses to sort and select.
Record	A collection of related information in a file: a line of data, a paragraph, or a name and address in a secondary merge file.
Fields	The components that make up a record. Each field contains the same type of information, such as a person's first name, the name of a city, or a ZIP code.
Input file	The file you intend to sort, which can be on-screen or on disk.
Output file	The sorted (or selected) file, which you can display on-screen or save to disk.

Objective 1: To Understand the Sort Screen

You can sort files displayed on-screen or stored on disk, and you can return the sorted results to the screen or to a new file on disk. The Sort feature offers options for four types of sort operations based on the kind of data. Use a *line sort* when records are lines (for example, a name or an item). Use a *paragraph sort* when records are paragraphs (as in a standard legal clause or a bibliography). Use a *merge sort* when records are in a secondary merge file (such as a list of names and addresses). As previously mentioned, this book does not cover sorting tables.

Before you perform a sort, you must be sure that your data is set up properly. A line record must end with a hard or soft return, and records should be formatted with one tab per field. A paragraph record must end with two hard returns.

All the sort operations begin from the Sort screen.

Exercise 1.1: Displaying the Sort Screen

Before beginning the sort, type the text in figure 9.1. Remember to use tab stops in formatting the lines of text.

To Understand the Sort Screen

```
Peggy O'Brien      890 Geyser Peak     Bodega Bay, CA     95301
John Bartleet      213 Oak Pass        Bodega Bay, CA     95301
Jim Daniels        1910 Vine Trail     Santa Rosa, CA     95401
Zigler Xavier      456 Redwood Way     Petaluma, CA       95408
Jude Matheson      515 Ross St.        Petaluma, CA       95408
Loretta Murphy     468 Mountain Ln.    Santa Rosa, CA     95401
Janie Smith        101 Saint St.       Petaluma, CA       95301




C:\WP51\BOOK\LINESORT.TXT                    Doc 1 Pg 1 Ln 2" Pos 7.5"
```

Fig. 9.1
The data used in the sort.

Follow these steps to display the Sort screen:

1. Press Ctrl+F9 to activate the Merge/Sort command, and choose **S**ort (**2**).

   Access the Tools pull-down menu, and choose Sort.

2. At the prompt Input file to sort: (Screen), press Enter if you want to sort the data already displayed on-screen. Alternatively, type the name of the input file on disk, and press Enter.

3. At the prompt Output file for sort: (Screen), press Enter if you want the sorted results to replace the screen display. Alternatively, type the name of the output file, and press Enter if you want to save the results to disk in a new file.

   Caution: If the input file and output file have the same names, the sorted data will replace the unsorted data.

The Sort screen appears. Notice that the screen is divided into five parts (see fig. 9.2).

The heading displays the current Sort type. The default is Sort by Line. The key definition area determines what criteria control the sort. Note that you can specify criteria for nine sort keys. In the Select area, you enter the formulas to select (extract) certain records from the data. The area toward the bottom of the screen indicates the Action, Order, and Type (which coincides with the heading) of the sort. The seven options on the Sort and Select menu enable you to specify the type of sort, the order, and the sort criteria. After you enter this information, you start the sort from this menu.

Sorting and Selecting

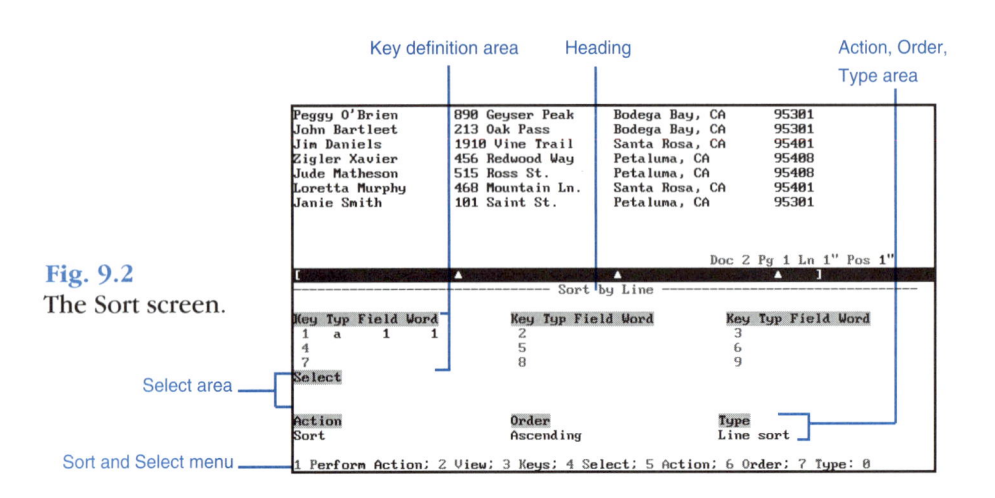

Fig. 9.2
The Sort screen.

```
                        Key definition area   Heading                    Action, Order,
                                                                         Type area

        Peggy O'Brien          890 Geyser Peak      Bodega Bay, CA    95301
        John Bartleet          213 Oak Pass         Bodega Bay, CA    95301
        Jim Daniels            1910 Vine Trail      Santa Rosa, CA    95401
        Zigler Xavier          456 Redwood Way      Petaluma, CA      95408
        Jude Matheson          515 Ross St.         Petaluma, CA      95408
        Loretta Murphy         468 Mountain Ln.     Santa Rosa, CA    95401
        Janie Smith            101 Saint St.        Petaluma, CA      95301

                                                                Doc 2 Pg 1 Ln 1" Pos 1"
        [                         ▲                   ▲                        ▲      ]
        ───────────────────────────── Sort by Line ──────────────────────────────
        Key Typ Field Word       Key Typ Field Word          Key Typ Field Word
         1   a    1     1         2                           3
         4                        5                           6
         7                        8                           9
Select area ──── Select

                Action                    Order                       Type
                Sort                      Ascending                   Line sort

Sort and Select menu ──── 1 Perform Action; 2 View; 3 Keys; 4 Select; 5 Action; 6 Order; 7 Type: 0
```

The Sort and Select menu offers the following options:

Option	Action
Perform Action (1)	Instructs WordPerfect to begin sorting or selecting
View (2)	Moves the cursor from the Sort screen into the document to be sorted. Use this option to change the tab settings on the menu to those in the document. You can move the cursor to view the data, but you cannot edit it. You press F7 (Exit) to return to the Sort screen.
Keys (3)	Moves the cursor into the key definition area so that you can define and change the sort keys (criteria) for the sort operation. When you choose this option, the bottom of the screen displays the Keys menu, from which you can choose an alphanumeric sort or a numeric sort.
Select (4)	Moves the cursor to the Select area, where you can enter the Select statement (a formula), containing the information you want to select. This statement directs WordPerfect to choose certain records.

Option	Action
Action (5)	This option is activated only when you choose Select (4). You can choose Select and Sort (1) to select and sort the data, or you can choose Select Only (2) just to select the data.
Order (6)	Offers a choice of Ascending (1), A-to-Z order; or Descending (2), Z-to-A order
Type (7)	Offers a choice of sorting by line, paragraph, or secondary merge file

Objective 2: To Sort Lines and Paragraphs

WordPerfect can sort the lines and paragraphs in any standard text file. The Sort feature is useful, for example, when you want to sort the data in office phone lists, personnel rosters, columns on charts, or dated paragraphs.

Display the Sort screen, using the procedure already described, and then continue with the procedure according to the text that follows.

Choosing the Sort Type

Be sure that the Sort Screen is displayed as shown in figure 9.2. You can choose to sort by lines or paragraphs. Use a line sort when you want to sort rosters and lists. Use a paragraph sort for notes or reports.

Exercise 2.1: Sorting Lines

Sort by Line is WordPerfect's default setting. If the heading on the Sort screen shows something other than `Sort by Line`, do the following:

1. Choose Type (7).
2. Choose Line (2).

    Notice that the key definition area shows `Field` and `Word`. You identify the location of key words by their Field and Word positions in each line. Fields are separated by tabs, and words are separated by spaces.

Sorting and Selecting

Also notice the tab ruler above the heading `Sort by Line`. The tab settings shown on the tab ruler must be set one tab per field, with no unused tabs between fields. If the tabs shown on the tab ruler do not reflect your one-tab-per-field setting, choose **V**iew (2). When the cursor moves into the document, place the cursor in the middle of a line of data. The tab ruler changes to reflect your tab settings.

3. Press F7 (Exit) to return to the Sort screen.

Exercise 2.2: Sorting Paragraphs

To sort by paragraph, follow these steps:

1. Choose **T**ype (7).
2. Choose **P**aragraph (3).

The title on the Sort screen displays `Sort by Paragraph`, and the key location headings are `Field`, `Line`, and `Word`. You identify the location of key words by their Field, Line, and Word positions in each paragraph. Paragraphs are separated by two or more hard returns.

Exercise 2.3: Choosing the Sort Order

Most of your sorts will be in ascending order—that is, from A to Z or from 0 to 9. At times, however, you may want to sort in descending order—from Z to A or from 9 to 0. To change the sort order, do the following:

1. Choose **O**rder (6) to display the Order menu.
2. Choose either **A**scending (1) for A-to-Z sort order, or **D**escending (2) for Z-to-A sort order (see fig. 9.3).

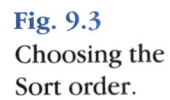

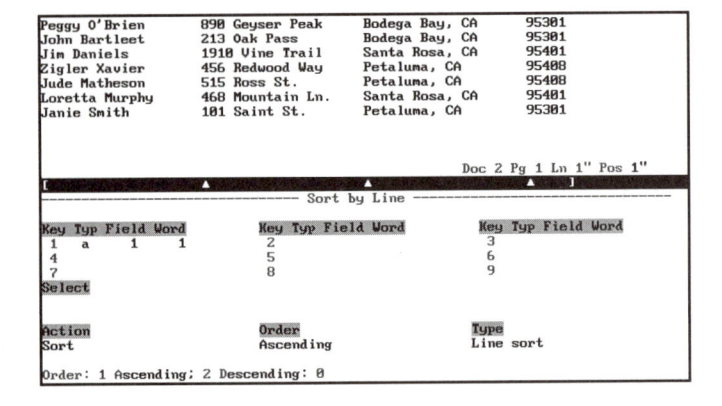

Fig. 9.3
Choosing the Sort order.

Defining the Sort Keys

WordPerfect uses sort keys to reorganize or select the information to be sorted. For example, to organize a list of names in alphabetical order, you use the last name as the sort key. In performing sort operations, you will soon discover, however, that you often need more than one key to organize your data. If, for example, you have several *Smiths* in your list, sorting by last name only is not sufficient. You need a key to sort by first name as well. In that case, you can define the first key to be the last name, and the second key to be the first name. In WordPerfect, you can define nine sort keys.

Unfortunately, you cannot simply tell WordPerfect that a sort key is the "first name." You must instead specify the location of the key by telling WordPerfect which field, line, and word contains the information to sort by. When defining each key, you also must specify whether the information is alphanumeric or numeric.

In an *alphanumeric sort*, numbers are evaluated as normal text. If, therefore, you are sorting a column of numbers with an alphanumeric sort, all the numbers (such as ZIP codes or telephone numbers) must be the same length.

In a *numeric sort*, the information is evaluated as numbers only. Any text in the sort key is ignored. You use a numeric sort for numbers that are not the same length (in other words, for most of your sorts involving numbers).

Exercise 2.4: Displaying the Keys Menu

To display the Keys menu, follow these steps:

1. Choose **K**eys (**3**). The cursor moves under the *a* in the Typ column so that you can enter the location of each sort key.

2. Type **a** to specify an alphanumeric sort for Key 1, or type **n** to specify a numeric sort for Key 1 (see fig. 9.4).

3. Enter the location of Key 1. The default values in Key 1 are preset at a 1 1. These values mean that the Sort type is alphanumeric and that the first word in the first field will be used as the basis for sorting. You can enter negative values in each key. If you want to use the third word from the end of the field, for example, enter –3 under Word.

    If sorting by Key 1 results in ties (equal values, such as the same names or numbers), you can sort on more than one field by using Key 2, Key 3, and so on. Press ⏎ to move to Key 2, and then enter the values for this key.

    Suppose that you want to sort the lines in the example by ZIP code and also by last name within each ZIP code.

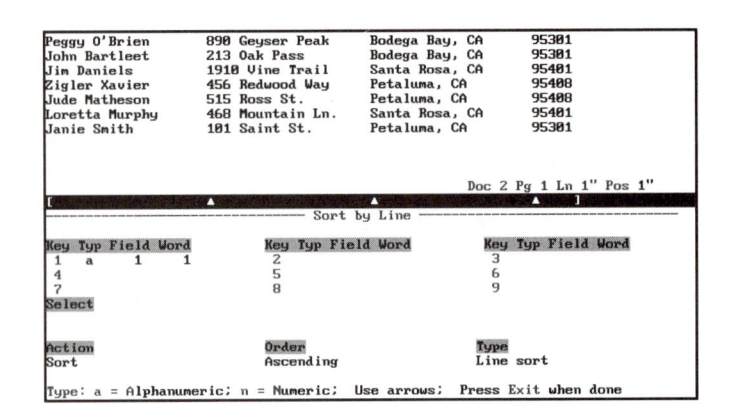

Sorting and Selecting

Fig. 9.4
Choosing an alphanumeric or numeric sort.

```
Peggy O'Brien      890 Geyser Peak     Bodega Bay, CA    95301
John Bartleet      213 Oak Pass        Bodega Bay, CA    95301
Jim Daniels        1910 Vine Trail     Santa Rosa, CA    95401
Zigler Xavier      456 Redwood Way     Petaluma, CA      95408
Jude Matheson      515 Ross St.        Petaluma, CA      95408
Loretta Murphy     468 Mountain Ln.    Santa Rosa, CA    95401
Janie Smith        101 Saint St.       Petaluma, CA      95301

                                              Doc 2 Pg 1 Ln 1" Pos 1"
─────────────────────── Sort by Line ───────────────────────
Key Typ Field Word     Key Typ Field Word     Key Typ Field Word
 1   a    1     1       2                      3
 4                      5                      6
 7                      8                      9
Select

Action                 Order                  Type
Sort                   Ascending              Line sort
Type: a = Alphanumeric; n = Numeric; Use arrows; Press Exit when done
```

4. The ZIP code is specified by Key 1 as the first word in field number 4.

5. The last name is specified by Key 2 as the second word in the first field (see fig. 9.5).

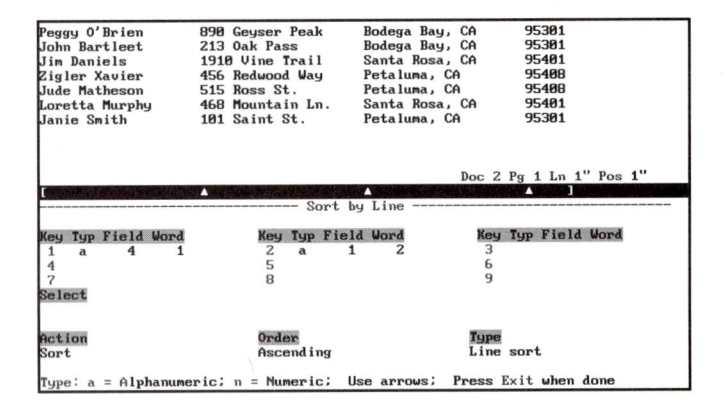

Fig. 9.5
Specifying Key 1 and Key 2.

```
Peggy O'Brien      890 Geyser Peak     Bodega Bay, CA    95301
John Bartleet      213 Oak Pass        Bodega Bay, CA    95301
Jim Daniels        1910 Vine Trail     Santa Rosa, CA    95401
Zigler Xavier      456 Redwood Way     Petaluma, CA      95408
Jude Matheson      515 Ross St.        Petaluma, CA      95408
Loretta Murphy     468 Mountain Ln.    Santa Rosa, CA    95401
Janie Smith        101 Saint St.       Petaluma, CA      95301

                                              Doc 2 Pg 1 Ln 1" Pos 1"
─────────────────────── Sort by Line ───────────────────────
Key Typ Field Word     Key Typ Field Word     Key Typ Field Word
 1   a    4     1       2   a    1     2       3
 4                      5                      6
 7                      8                      9
Select

Action                 Order                  Type
Sort                   Ascending              Line sort
Type: a = Alphanumeric; n = Numeric; Use arrows; Press Exit when done
```

6. Press **F7** (Exit).

7. Choose **P**erform Action (**1**) to sort the file.

The lines are sorted by ZIP code. Within each ZIP code, the last names are listed alphabetically (see fig. 9.6).

If you specified that the output goes to the screen, the results appear on-screen. If you specified that the output goes to the file, the results are sent to the file. Save the document as LIST and exit the document.

To Sort Lines and Paragraphs

```
John Bartleet      213 Oak Pass        Bodega Bay, CA    95301
Peggy O'Brien      890 Geyser Peak     Bodega Bay, CA    95301
Janie Smith        101 Saint St.       Petaluma, CA      95301
Jim Daniels        1910 Vine Trail     Santa Rosa, CA    95401
Loretta Murphy     468 Mountain Ln.    Santa Rosa, CA    95401
Jude Matheson      515 Ross St.        Petaluma, CA      95408
Zigler Xavier      456 Redwood Way     Petaluma, CA      95408




C:\WP51\BOOK\LINESORT.TXT                    Doc 1 Pg 1 Ln 1" Pos 1"
```

Fig. 9.6
A list sorted by ZIP code and name.

Exercise 2.5: Sorting by Paragraph

Now suppose that you want to sort the bibliography shown in figure 9.7. Because some authors have the same last name, you need to sort by the author's initials in addition to last name. Finally, because you have multiple works by some authors, you want to sort the works by date.

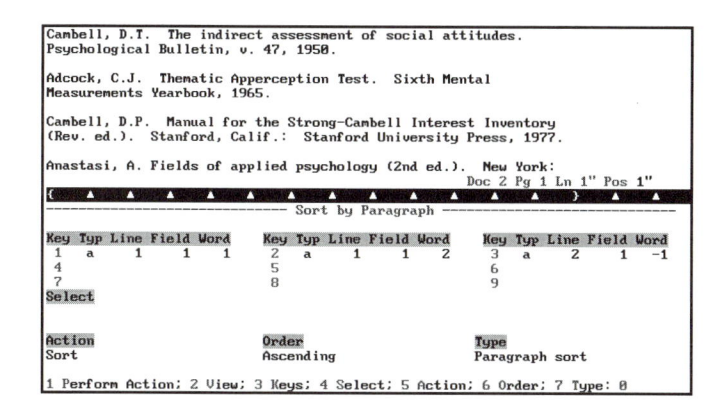

```
Cambell, D.T.  The indirect assessment of social attitudes.
Psychological Bulletin, v. 47, 1950.

Adcock, C.J.  Thematic Apperception Test.  Sixth Mental
Measurements Yearbook, 1965.

Cambell, D.P.  Manual for the Strong-Cambell Interest Inventory
(Rev. ed.).  Stanford, Calif.:  Stanford University Press, 1977.

Anastasi, A. Fields of applied psychology (2nd ed.).  New York:
                                             Doc 2 Pg 1 Ln 1" Pos 1"
{    ▲    ▲    ▲    ▲    ▲    ▲    ▲  }  ▲    ▲
─────────────────── Sort by Paragraph ─────────────────────────
Key Typ Line Field Word    Key Typ Line Field Word    Key Typ Line Field Word
 1   a   1    1     1       2   a   1    1     2       3   a   2    1    -1
 4                          5                          6
 7                          8                          9
Select

Action                Order                  Type
Sort                  Ascending              Paragraph sort

1 Perform Action; 2 View; 3 Keys; 4 Select; 5 Action; 6 Order; 7 Type: 0
```

Fig. 9.7
A bibliography to sort.

Note: Before you begin, type the text in figure 9.8. Make sure that you have changed the Sort type on the Sort screen to a Paragraph sort.

The author's name is specified by Key 1 as the first word in the first field of the first line. The author's initials are specified by Key 2 as the second word in the first field of the first line. The work's date is specified by Key 3 as the last word of the first field of the second line. The paragraphs are sorted alphabetically by the author's last name and initials and numerically by date.

Objective 3: To Sort Secondary Merge Files

A secondary merge file is nothing more than a database with merge codes. WordPerfect can sort your secondary merge files so that form letters, mailing lists, or labels will print in any order you choose.

Before you perform the sort, you must be sure that your data is set up properly. A secondary merge file contains records, each of which contains fields. Each field must end with an {END FIELD} code, and each record must end with an {END RECORD} code.

Begin by retrieving a secondary merge file created in Chapter 8. Then display the Sort screen, and continue with the procedure according to the text that follows.

Exercise 3.1: Choosing the Sort Type and Order

From the Sort and Select menu, do the following:

1. Choose **T**ype (**7**).
2. Choose **M**erge (**1**) to sort a secondary merge file.

   The screen heading becomes Sort Secondary Merge File, and the location headings for each sort key become Field, Line, and Word.
3. Choose **O**rder (**6**) to display the Order menu.
4. Choose either **A**scending (**1**) for A-to-Z sort order or **D**escending (**2**) for Z-to-A sort order.

Exercise 3.2: Defining the Sort Keys

Now define the sort keys by following these steps:

1. Choose **K**eys (**3**) to display the Keys menu. The cursor moves under the *a* in the Typ column so that you can enter the location of each sort key.
2. Type **a** to specify an alphanumeric sort for Key 1, or type **n** to specify a numeric sort for Key 1.
3. Enter the location of Key 1. The default values in Key 1 are preset at a 1 1 1. These values mean that the Sort type is alphanumeric and that the first word on the first line in the first field will be used as the basis for sorting.

To Choose Particular Data

If sorting by Key 1 results in ties (equal values, such as the same names or numbers), you can sort on more than one field by using Key 2, Key 3, and so on.

4. Press ← to move to the entry area for Key 2.

   Suppose that you want to sort the secondary merge file by state. You also want to sort entries for each state by last name and then by first name.

   Key 1 is the state abbreviation (the first word from the right in the third field).

   Key 2 is the last name (the first word from the right in the first field).

   Key 3 is the first name (the first word in the first field).

5. For all three keys, choose alphanumeric sorting—**a** (see fig. 9.8).

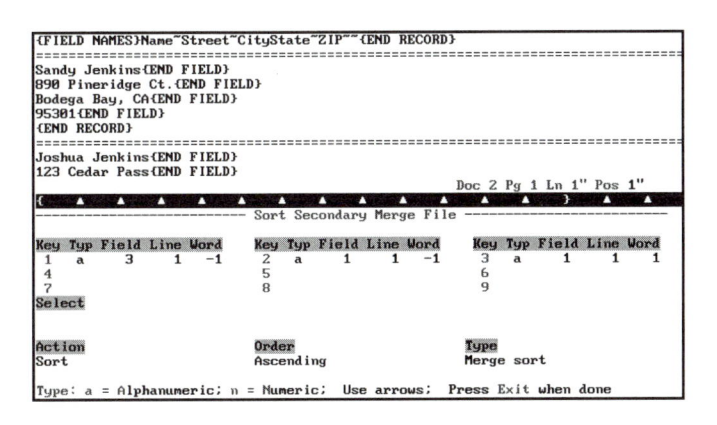

Fig. 9.8
Setting up the sort keys.

Exercise 3.3: Performing the Sort

To perform the sort, follow these steps:

1. Press F7 (Exit) to return to the Sort and Select menu.
2. Choose **P**erform Action (**1**) to start the sort operation.

WordPerfect sorts the data based on your sort criteria.

Objective 4: To Choose Particular Data

When you are working with a large database, you often need to choose particular data. Using the Select feature (accessed through the Sort and Select menu), you can choose only the paragraphs, lines, or secondary merge

203

Sorting and Selecting

records that contain a specific combination of data—for example, the names of customers who live in California. The steps in selecting are the same as those used in sorting, but you must include a statement that describes the records you want to choose.

Display the Sort screen, and then continue with the procedure according to the text that follows.

Exercise 4.1: Choosing the Sort Type and Sort Order

First, choose the sort type and sort order by doing the following:

1. Choose **T**ype (**7**).
2. Specify whether you are selecting records from a line, paragraph, or secondary merge file.
3. Choose **O**rder (**6**).
4. Choose **A**scending (**1**) or **D**escending (**2**).

Exercise 4.2: Defining the Sort Keys

To define the sort keys, follow these steps:

1. Choose **K**eys (**3**). Even though you may not want to sort your data, you must use sort keys to tell the program where to find the data you want.
2. Type **a** to specify an alphanumeric sort for Key 1, or type **n** to specify a numeric sort for Key 1.
3. Type the location for Key 1.

Press ← to move to the Key 2 entry area, and type the location for that key. Move to other Key entry areas and type their locations, if necessary.

In this example, enter a sort key as the specification for Key 1: Type = **a** (alphanumeric), Field = **3** (city and state), and Word = **1** (city). This information tells WordPerfect where to look for the select key.

Exercise 4.3: Entering the Selection Criteria

To return to the Sort and Select menu, follow these steps:

1. Press F7 (Exit).

204

To Choose Particular Data

2. Choose **S**elect (**4**).

   You are now ready to provide the Select statement, which consists of the following items:

   - A defined key in the form Key#. The # is replaced by the number of the key you want to use.
   - A comparison operator, indicating that the key must be one of the following in relation to the condition:

     Equal to (=)

     Not equal to (<>)

     Greater than (>)

     Less than (<)

     Greater than or equal to (>=)

     Less than or equal to (<=)

   - A condition

   After you choose **S**elect (**4**), WordPerfect moves the cursor under the word Select and displays a list of comparison operators at the bottom of the screen.

3. Under Select, enter **Key1=petaluma**. This Select statement tells WordPerfect to choose only records in which the city is *petaluma* or *Petaluma* (see fig. 9.9). (WordPerfect's Sort and Select features do not differentiate between upper- and lowercase.)

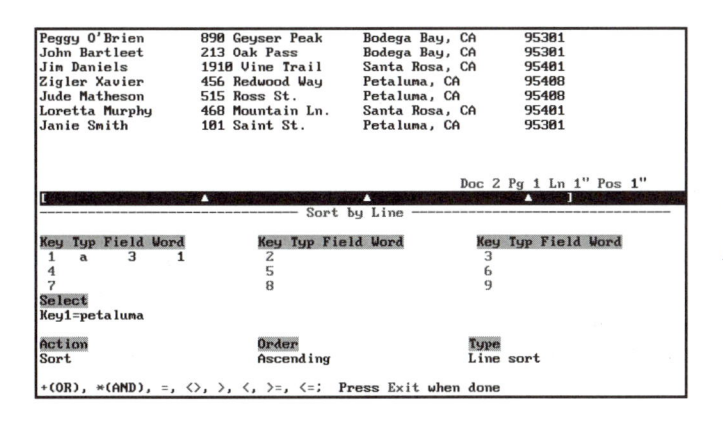

Fig. 9.9
Sorting on *petaluma*.

205

Sorting and Selecting

4. Press F7 (Exit) to return to the Sort and Select menu.
5. Choose Action (5) to display the Action menu.
6. Choose Select and Sort (1) if you want to sort and choose the records. Alternatively, choose Select Only (2) if you want to choose records without sorting them.

   WordPerfect returns you to the Sort and Select menu.

7. In the Select statement, you also can define multiple criteria. You must join the items with a logical operator to specify whether both conditions must be met or whether either condition is acceptable. To specify that both conditions must be met, use AND (indicated with an asterisk—*). To specify that either condition is acceptable, use OR (indicated with a plus sign —+).
8. Choose Perform Action (1).

The selected records are sent to the screen or to a disk file, as you requested (see fig. 9.10).

Fig. 9.10
The selected records.

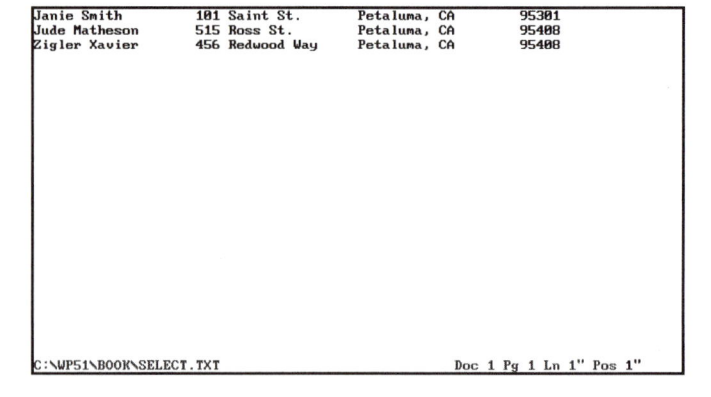

```
Janie Smith      101 Saint St.    Petaluma, CA    95301
Jude Matheson    515 Ross St.     Petaluma, CA    95408
Zigler Xavier    456 Redwood Way  Petaluma, CA    95408




















C:\WP51\BOOK\SELECT.TXT                     Doc 1 Pg 1 Ln 1" Pos 1"
```

Chapter Summary

In this chapter, you have learned how to use WordPerfect's Sort feature to handle some simple data management tasks. You explored WordPerfect's capabilities to sort by line, paragraph, and secondary merge file. And you learned how to use the Select feature to extract particular data from a large database.

Testing Your Knowledge

True/False Questions

1. Some Sort operations begin from the Sort Screen.
2. The Sort Screen is divided into the heading, the key definition, the Sort and Select menu, and the Action, Order, and Type areas.
3. WordPerfect can sort the lines and paragraphs in any standard text file.
4. In a numeric sort, the information is evaluated as normal text.
5. A secondary merge file is nothing more than a database with merge codes.

Multiple Choice Questions

1. The Sort feature offers options for four types of sort operations, based on the kind of data:
    A. a line, a phrase, a secondary merge file, or table.
    B. a line, a paragraph, a primary merge, or a table.
    C. a line, a paragraph, a secondary merge file, or a table.
    D. a sentence, a line, a primary merge, or a paragraph.
    E. a paragraph, a line, a secondary merge, or a segment.
2. Pressing Ctrl + F9 and choosing 2 activates
    A. the Merge command.
    B. the Merge/Sort command.
    C. the Sort command.
    D. the prompt for the Input file to sort.
    E. the Sort screen.
3. Which of the following is not a Sort Type?
    A. Line
    B. Paragraph
    C. Merge
    D. Table
    E. None of the above

Sorting and Selecting

4. The Select statement consists of
    A. a defined key in the form key number.
    B. a comparison operator.
    C. a condition.
    D. both A and B.
    E. A, B, and C.
5. To perform the Select or Select and Sort, choose
    A. **v**iew (**2**).
    B. **s**elect (**4**).
    C. **p**erform Action (**1**).
    D. **o**rder (**6**).
    E. **T**ype (**8**).

Fill-in-the-Blank Questions

1. The _____ definition area determines what criteria will control the sort.
2. To sort by Paragraph, choose _____ and choose _____.
3. A secondary merge file is nothing more than a _____ with _____ codes.
4. In an _____ sort, numbers are evaluated as _____ text.
5. You may specify that the output goes to the _____ or to the _____.

Review: Short Projects

1. Sort by Line and Output to the Screen

    Type the following, sort by line, and send the output to the screen.

Pears	2 pounds	$6.00
Apples	4 pounds	$7.00
Grapes	3 pounds	$7.00

2. Sort by Paragraph

    Type two paragraphs from your text and sort by paragraph. Send the sorted file to the screen.

Testing Your Knowledge

3. Retrieve, Sort, and Select

    Retrieve the secondary file from Chapter 8, sort the file, and select the records with the State = NY.

Review: Long Projects

1. Create, Sort, and Send to Disk

    Type a list of 10 lines that contain name, address, city, state, and ZIP code. Sort the file, and send it to disk as NAMES. From this file, choose a common field and send this file to disk as SILNAMES, and print the file.

2. Create and Sort a Secondary File

    Create a secondary file with 10 records. Be sure to have three records with one field the same. For example, Dept = 1, State = CT. First, sort the file to the screen, and then select by the common field. Send the selected file to the printer. Save the secondary file. Using the same file, choose multiple conditions, again using common fields, and print this file.

Graphics

With WordPerfect's Graphics feature, you can enhance the appearance of a document with graphics boxes and lines. You can use five types of boxes: figure, table, text, user-defined, and equation.

As you create the boxes, you can insert text; graphics from the PTR Program/Graphics disks; or graphics, charts, and graphs created with external programs, such as Harvard Graphics, PC Paintbrush, DrawPerfect, and 1-2-3. If you prefer, you can create an empty box and enter text or graphics later. Graphics boxes can be placed in the body of a document as well as in headers, footers, and endnotes.

To create a graphics box, you must complete these basic procedures:

- Choose the type of box you want.
- Determine the appearance of the box.
- Create the box and define its contents.

Each of these procedures is described in this appendix.

Choosing the Box Type

Each of WordPerfect's five box types has a default definition. The *definition* includes the border of the box, the inside and outside border space, the caption-numbering method and style, the minimum offset, and the box shading. You can use the default box styles, or you can define your own. Defining boxes gives you a consistent set of boxes to use in your documents. Although anything you put in one type of box can be put in any other type, you may want to reserve each type of box for a specific use.

To choose the type of box you want to create, follow this procedure:

1. Press Alt + F9 to activate the Graphics command. The Graphics menu appears at the bottom of the screen.

    Access the Graphics pull-down menu.

2. Choose one of these box types:

    Figure (**1**)

    Table Box (**2**)

    Text **B**ox (**3**)

    User Box (**4**)

    Equation (**6**)

WordPerfect then displays a menu similar to the following:

   Figure: 1 Create; **2 E**dit; **3** **N**ew Number; **4 O**ptions: **0**

The first word of this menu will vary, depending on what type of box you choose.

   If you are using the Graphics pull-down menu, choosing a box type from that menu displays a pop-out menu that shows the preceding options.

Changing the Box Options

After you choose the box type, you can change the default options that determine how the box should look. If you want to change the options, you should do so before creating the box. Among the options you can change are the border styles, the spacing between the border and contents, the style and position of the caption, and the box shading.

To change the appearance of a box, follow this procedure:

1. Choose **O**ptions (**4**).

    Choose Options from the pop-out menu.

2. Choose the options you want to change, and enter the necessary information.
3. Press `F7` (Exit) to return to the document.

You can choose any (or all) of nine options to determine the appearance of the box.

- To specify a border for each side of the box, choose **Border Style** (**1**), and then choose a border (none, single, double, dashed, dotted, thick, or extra thick).

- To change the space between the border of the box and the text, choose **Outside Border Space** (**2**), and type a distance for each side.

- To change the space between the border and the contents of the box, choose **Inside Border Space** (**3**), and type a distance for each side.

- To choose the numbering for the caption, choose First Level Numbering Method (**4**), and indicate your choice (off, numbers, letters, or Roman numerals).

    WordPerfect automatically numbers the caption for the box. This option determines *only* the numbering style; you must add the caption when you create the box.

- If you want two levels of numbering for the caption, choose **S**econd Level Numbering Method (**5**), and indicate your choice. If you choose letters or Roman numerals, they are printed in lowercase.

- To specify the text for the caption number, choose **C**aption Number Style (**6**), and type the text you want. Press 1 to include first-level numbering; press 2 to include second-level numbering.

    You can include formatting codes within the caption number style. Keep in mind that this option defines only the caption number style; you must add the caption when you create the box.

- To specify where the caption appears, choose **P**osition of Caption (**7**), and choose whether to place the caption above or below the box, as well as outside or inside the border.

- To set the minimum paragraph offset, choose **M**inimum Offset from Paragraph (**8**), and type the minimum offset.

    A paragraph-type box is offset from the top of a paragraph by the amount you specify. If the paragraph falls at the end of the page, the box may not fit. This option specifies how much the offset can be reduced to fit the box on the page.

- To add a gray shade to the box, choose **G**ray Shading (% of Black) (**9**), and type a percentage from 1 to 100. Zero percent shading is white; 100 percent shading is black.

When you change any of the options, WordPerfect inserts into the document a code for the new box appearance. All boxes of this type will have the same appearance until you change the options again.

Creating the Box and Defining its Contents

After you choose the type of box and the options you want, you can create it. Note that if you create the box without first choosing options, WordPerfect uses the default box settings. When you *create* a box, you specify the type of box, its contents, the text for the caption, the placement on the page, and the size of the box.

To create a graphics box, follow this procedure:

1. Move the cursor to the place where you want the box to appear. If you have changed the options, be sure that the cursor is below the options code.
2. Press `Alt`+`F9` to activate the Graphics command, and choose a box type.

    🖰 Access the Graphics pull-down menu, and choose the box type you want to create.

3. Choose **C**reate (**1**) to display the Definition menu.
4. Choose the options you want and enter the changes, or press `⏎Enter` to accept the default definitions.

    The options you can choose are the same for all box types; only the menu heading varies.

5. Press `F7` (Exit) to return to the document.

Only an outline appears on-screen. To view the document as it will appear when printed, use View Document.

You can specify the following options on the Definition menu:

- Choose **F**ilename (**1**) if you want to import a file (for example, a text or graphics file). Then type the name of the file, and press `⏎Enter`. WordPerfect inserts the file into the box. To create an empty box and enter the contents later, leave this option blank.

- Choose **C**ontents (**2**) to tell WordPerfect what type of material the box should contain. The box can contain a graphics image, a block of text, or an equation. Usually, when you retrieve a file into the box by using **F**ilename (**1**), WordPerfect automatically fills in the Contents option.

- Choose **C**aption (**3**) to add a caption to the box. An editing screen appears with the caption number displayed in the style you set when you specified the box options. You can delete, change, or add text to the caption number. Captions conform to the width of the current box.

- Choose Anchor Type (4) to specify the way you want the box to be anchored. A paragraph-type box stays with the paragraph to which it is assigned. If the paragraph moves, the box moves. A page-type box is anchored to the page and stays in that position regardless of any editing changes. If you choose a page-type box, WordPerfect prompts you to indicate whether you want the box to appear on the current page or whether you want to skip some pages before inserting the box. A character-type box is treated as a character and wraps with the line of text to which the box is anchored.

- Choose Vertical Position (5) to specify the vertical alignment of the box. The type of box determines the placement options. For a paragraph-type box, enter the offset from the top of the paragraph. For a page-type box, choose one of five types of alignment: full page, top, center, bottom, or set position (enter an exact position). For a character-type box, choose to align the text with the top, center, or bottom of the box. Or choose Baseline (4) to align the last line of text in the box with the line of text where the character-type box is located.

- Choose Horizontal Position (6) to specify where the box is positioned horizontally. Again, the type of box determines the placement options. For a paragraph-type box, choose to align the box with the left or right margin, centered between the margins, or extended from margin to margin. For a page-type box, choose to align the box with the margins or the columns (left, right, center, or from the left to the right margin or column); or use Set Position (3) to enter an exact location. A character-type box is aligned vertically only.

- Choose Size (7) to choose the size of the box. You can enter the width, height, or both. If you enter only the width or height, WordPerfect calculates the other dimension. The Auto Both (4) option (the default setting) calculates both the height and width automatically.

- Choose Wrap Text Around Box (8) if you want the text to wrap automatically around the box. If you want text to flow through the box, choose this option, and change the default from Yes to No.

- Choose Edit (9) to insert text into the box or to edit a graphics image retrieved into the box. When an editing screen appears, type the text, or edit the image.

Importing a Graphics Image

WordPerfect's PTR/Graphics disks contain clip-art files (with a WPG extension) you can import. Check your WordPerfect manual to review the other types of file formats you can import into WordPerfect.

Suppose that you want to import the image of a printer from the WordPerfect PTR/Graphics disks. Follow these steps to import the image:

1. Move the cursor to the place in the document where you want the image to appear.
2. Press [Alt]+[F9] to activate the Graphics command, and choose a box type.

    🖰 Access the Graphics pull-down menu, and choose Figure.
3. Choose **C**reate (**1**) to display the Definition menu.
4. Choose **F**ilename (**1**).
5. Type the name of the graphics file, and press [⏎Enter].
6. Press [F7] (Exit) to return to the document.
7. To display an outline of the image, position the cursor after the box.
8. To view the document as it will appear when printed, press [⇧Shift]+[F7] (Print), and choose **V**iew Document (**6**).

    🖰 Access the File pull-down menu, choose Print, and choose View Document (6).
9. Press [F7] (Exit) to return to the editing screen.

    Note: If you do not specify the box size, WordPerfect calculates an initial box size based on the space remaining on the page. When you import a graphics image, WordPerfect adjusts the proportions of the box to suit the image. You can modify the size of the box at any time.

Entering Text into a Box

When you create a box, you can fill it with text by specifying on the Definition screen the name of an existing text file. If, however, you prefer to type text directly into the box, you can do that as you create the box, or you can go back later and type the text into an empty box.

To enter text directly into a box, follow these steps:

1. Press [Alt]+[F9] to activate the Graphics command, and choose **T**ext **B**ox (**3**).

    🖰 Access the Graphics pull-down menu, and choose Text Box.

2. To enter text as you create the box, choose **C**reate (**1**). To enter text into an empty existing box, choose **E**dit (**2**), type the box number, and press `⏎Enter`.
3. From the Definition menu, choose **E**dit (**9**).

   A screen for entering text appears.
4. Type the text, using any of WordPerfect's text-formatting features.
5. Press `Alt`+`F9` (Graphics) if you want to rotate the text, and choose a degree of rotation: 0, 90, 180, or 270.
6. Press `F7` (Exit) twice to return to the document.

Using Line Draw

If you plan to edit your document, use the Graphics feature to draw lines and boxes so that you don't inadvertently change the images as you edit. You can use the Line Draw feature to draw a line or box by simply moving the cursor. Keep in mind that lines and boxes drawn with Line Draw are composed of characters and are part of the text. You cannot type over them or around them without disturbing them.

To draw a line or box with Line Draw, complete these steps:

1. Press `Ctrl`+`F3` to activate the Screen command, and choose **L**ine Draw (**2**).

   🖱 Access the Tools pull-down menu, and choose Line Draw.

   A menu of line-drawing options appears.
2. Choose one of the following options:
   - Choose **1** to draw a single line.
   - Choose **2** to draw a double line.
   - Choose **3** to draw a line of asterisks (****).
   - Choose **4** to display a menu of alternative line styles, and then choose the style you want.
   - Choose **5** to erase a line you have drawn.
   - Choose **6** to move the cursor to a new location without drawing a line.
3. Use the cursor keys to draw the line or box.
4. Press `F7` to quit Line Draw.

Index

A

accessing
   menus, pull-down, 24
   screens, 159-160
adding
   tab stops
      multiple, 85-86
      single, 85
   text with Insert mode, 45-46
addressing envelopes, 181
   envelope definition, 183
   envelope form, 182-183
   formatting codes, 184
   merge codes, 184-185
   primary files, 183
adjusting screens after editing, 52
alignment
   boxes, 215
   text, 93-95
alphanumeric keys, 11, 13
alphanumeric sort, 199
alternatives list, correct spellings, 143-147

anchoring boxes, 215
antonyms, 134
appearance of fonts, 103-104
appending text blocks, 68
arrow keys, moving cursors, 18
attributes of fonts, 102-104
automatic backups, 28
automatic page breaks, 126
automatic page numbering, 122-126

B

backups, 28
base fonts, 104-105
binding edge, 115
blank lines, 47
blank spaces, 47
block cursor, 14
blocks of text, 60-61, 63
   appending, 68
   backing out of operation, 62
   boldfacing, 69-70
   centering, 70-71
   checking spelling, 146-147

copying, 64-65
deleting, 65-66
highlighting, 61-62
moving, 63-64
printing, 68
saving, 67
underlining, 69-70
boldface, 69-70, 101
boxes
   alignment, 215
   anchoring, 215
   borders, 213
   captions, 213-214
   contents, 214
   creating, 212-215
   definition, 212
   importing text, 214
   lines, 217
   options, 212-214
   shading, 212
   size, 215
   text, 215-217
braces, 83
brackets, 83
buttons, mouse, 14

C

Cancel command (F1), 25
canceling printing, 160
captions (boxes), 213-214
center justification, 91
center tab stops, 84, 86
centering
   pages, 119-120
   text, 95
      blocks, 70-71
      lines, 93-94

character strings, 134
characters, deleting, 47-48
checking spelling, 142-147
clearing documents from screen, 31
clicking with mouse, 14
clip art, 216
codes
   formatting, printing addresses, 184
   hidden, 52-53
      deleting, 54
      displaying, 53
      replacing, 140
      searching for, 136
   merge, 169, 173-175
      labels, 188
      printing addresses, 184-185
   paired, searching for, 137
commands, 11
   Append, 68
   Block, 61-62, 64, 67-69
   Cancel (F1), 25
   Center, 70, 93-95
   Columns/Table, 87
   Copy, 64
   Exit (F7), 26, 30-31
   Flush Right, 95-96
   Font, 102-103
   Format, 77-78, 81-83, 93, 111
   GoTo, 62
   Graphics, 212, 214
   List, 39
   Merge Codes, 170, 174, 177, 179
   Merge/Sort, 176, 195, 197
   Move, 64, 65
   Print, 26-27, 40, 68, 154, 156, 159, 161
   Replace, 138, 140
   Restore, 66

Index

Retrieve, 38-39
Reveal Codes, 38, 53
Save, 29, 67
Screen, 82, 217
Setup, 10, 79
Spell, 142
View Document, 26
contents (boxes), 214
copies, number printing, 155-156
copying
  documents, 43-44
  text, 60
    blocks, 64-65
    sentences, paragraphs, or pages, 65
creating
  boxes, 212-217
  documents, 15-26
  headers and footers, 120-121
  tables, 86-88
current fonts, 101
cursor, 6
  horizontal position (Pos), 10
  moving, 17
    with arrow keys, 18
    with keyboard, 17-18
    with mouse, 20, 21
  vertical position (Ln), 10
cursor-movement keys, 11, 13

D

data, selecting combination, 204
decimal tab stops, 84, 86
defaults, 6
  base fonts, 101
  directory, 15, 45
  settings, 16

deleting
  codes, hidden, 54
  documents, 43
  hard page breaks, 127
  tab stops, 84-85
  text
    blocks, 65-66
    end of pages, 49
    lines, 49
    restoring, 51-52, 66
    sentences, paragraphs, and pages, 50-51
    single characters, 47-48
    with mouse, 51
    words, 48
dictionaries, 141-142
  see also Speller
directories
  default, 15, 45
  disk, printing, 158-159
disks
  documents, saving, 29-31
  printing documents from, 156-159
displaying
  codes, hidden, 53
  documents, 44
  menus, Keys, 199-201
  screens, Sort, 194-197
  tab ruler, 82-83
Document Initial Codes screen, 78-79
documents
  checking spelling, 142-147
  clearing from screen, 31
  copying, 43-44
  creating, 15-26
  deleting, 43
  displaying, 44
  navigating, 19
    GoTo (Ctrl+Home), 19
    Repeat (Esc) key, 19-20

221

previewing, 26-27, 160-161
printing, 27-28, 44, 154
    marking, 158
    number of copies, 155-156
    print queues, 155
    screen print, 155
    selected pages, 154-155
    single pages, 154
retrieving, 42-43
saving, 28-31
text, entering, 16
documents (Doc), 10
dot leaders, 84, 86
double-clicking with mouse, 14
dragging with mouse, 14
dual-floppy disk system, starting WordPerfect, 9
duplex printing, 115

E

editing
    envelope form definition, 182
    headers and footers, 121-122
    in Reveal Codes, 54
    screen 10-11
    tables, 87, 88
end of pages, deleting text, 49
entering text, 16
envelopes
    addressing, 181
        envelope definition, 183
        envelope form, 182-183
        formatting codes, 184
        merge codes, 184-185
        primary files, 183
    printing, 185-186

exiting
    menus, 26
    WordPerfect, 30-31

F

fields, 168-169, 194
files
    input, 194
    lists, List Files screen, 40-41
    marking to print, 158
    merging, 168-169
        to print envelopes, 185-186
        to print labels, 188
        to screen, 188-189
    naming, 6, 28-29
    output, 194
    primary
        creating, 183
        labels, 187
    primary merge, 168, 173-178
    retrieving, 38
        with List Files screen, 39-41
        with Retrieve command, 38-39
    searching for, 41-42
    secondary merge, 168, 170
        records, 170-173
        sorting, 202-203
    sorting, 197
        lines, 197-198
        paragraphs, 198, 201
        sort order, 198
    see also text files
floppy disk system, starting WordPerfect, 9
flush-right text, 95-96
font type, 114

Index

fonts, 101
    attributes, 102-104
    initial, 76
footers, 110
    automatic page numbering, 122
    creating, 120-121
    editing, 121-122
form definition of pages, 110-117
formatting codes, 184
full justification, 91
full-screen menus, 21-23
function keys, 11-13

G

GoTo (Ctrl+Home) key, 19
graphics, 211
    boxes, 212-215
    contents, 214-215
    definition, 214-215
    importing, 216-217

H

hanging indents, 90-91
hard copies, 153
hard disk system, starting
  WordPerfect, 8-9
hard hyphens, 99
hard page breaks, 110, 127
hard returns, 6, 99-100
hard spaces, 100
headers, 110
    automatic page numbering, 122
    creating, 120-121
    editing, 121-122
heading, List Files screen, 40

headwords, Thesaurus, 134
Help, 14
hidden codes, 52-53
    deleting, 54
    displaying, 53
    replacing, 140
    searching for, 136
hiding tab ruler, 83
highlighting blocks of text, 61-62
hyphen characters, 99
hyphenation, 96-99

I

importing
    graphics, 216-217
    text to boxes, 214
indenting text, 88
    existing, 90
    hanging indents, 90-91
    with Left Indent key, 89
    with Left-Right Indent key, 89-90
    with Tab key, 89
initial fonts, 76, 101
input files, 194
Insert mode, 38, 45-47
inserting
    blank lines, 47
    blank spaces, 47

J–K

justification of text, 91-93

keyboards, 11-13
    merging primary and secondary
      files, 178-181
    moving cursors, 17-18
    highlighting text, 61

keys
    alphanumeric, 11, 13
    arrow, moving cursors, 18
    cursor-movement, 11, 13
    function, 11-13
    GoTo (Ctrl+Home), 19
    numeric, 11
    Repeat (Esc), 19-20
    sort, 194, 199
        secondary merge files, 202
        selecting combination of data, 204
Keys menu, 199-203

L

label form definition, 187-188
LABELS macro, 187
labels, *see* mailing labels
Landscape orientation, 114
left and right margins
    centering text between, 70-71
    changing
        for current document, 76
        in Document Initial Codes screen, 78-79
        permanently, 79-81
        within documents, 77-78
left justification, 91
left tab stops, 84-85
line breaks, 99-100
Line Draw, 217
line sorts, 194
lines, 217
    centering, 93-94
    deleting, 49
    sorting, 197-198
    spacing, 81-82

List Files menu, 41-45
List Files screen
    files, retrieving, 39-41
    printing from, 157-158

M

macros, 187
mailing labels
    previewing, 189
    printing, 186-189
        label form definition, 187-188
        LABELS macro, 187
        merge codes, 188
        primary file, 187
margins
    left and right
        centering text between, 70-71
        changing for current document, 76
        changing in Document Initial Codes creen, 78-79
        changing permanently, 79-81
        changing within document, 77-78
    top and bottom, 117-118
        centering pages between, 119-120
marking files to print, 158
menus, 21
    exiting, 26
    full-screen, 21-23
    one-line, 21-23
    pull-down, 23-25
merge codes, 169, 173-175
    entering, printing addresses, 184-185
    labels, 188

Index

merge files, secondary, 202-203
merge sorts, 194
merging files, 168-169
    from keyboards, 178-181
    text, 169
    to print envelopes, 185-186
    to print labels, 188
    to printers, 176-178
    to screen, 176, 188-189
modes
    Insert, 38, 45-47
    Typeover, 38, 46-47
mouse, 13-14
    moving cursors, 20-21
    deleting text, 51
    highlighting text, 61-62
moving
    cursors, 17
        with arrow keys, 18
        with keyboard, 17-18
        with mouse, 20-21
    text, 60
        blocks, 63-64
        sentences, paragraphs, or pages, 65
moving around, *see* navigating documents

N

naming files, 29
navigating documents, 19-20
numbering pages
    position, 123-124
        starting number, 124
        suppressing, 125-126
numeric keys, 11
numeric sort, 199

O

on-line Help, 14
one-line menus, 21-23
order of sorting
    alphanumeric, 199-200
    combination of data, 204
    lines and paragraphs, 198
    numeric, 199-200
    secondary merge files, 202
orientation, Portrait or Landscape, 114
orphans, 110
output files, 194

P

page (Pg), 10
page breaks
    automatic, 126
    hard, 127
page numbering
    automatic, 122-126
    position, 123-124
    starting number, 124
    suppressing, 125-126
pages
    centering between top and bottom margins, 119-120
    copying, 65
    deleting, 49-51
    moving, 65
    numbering automatically, 122-126
    printing, 154-155
    size and type, 110-117
paired codes, searching for, 137

225

paper
    size, 113
    type, 112
paragraphs
    copying, 65
    deleting, 50-51
    moving, 65
    sorting, 194, 198, 201
phrases, checking spelling, 142-147
Portrait orientation, 114
previewing
    documents, 26-27, 160-161
    mailing labels, 189
primary merge files, 168, 173-175
    creating, 183
    keyboard merge, 178-180
    labels, 187
    merging with secondary, 175-178
Print menu
    previewing documents, 160-161
    printing from, 157
print queues, 154-155
Print: Control Printer screen
    accessing, 159-160
    printing
        canceling, 160
        suspending, 160
printers
    merging primary and secondary files, 176-178
    Print: Control Printer screen, 159-160
printing
    addresses
        formatting codes, 184
        merge codes, 184-185
    canceling, 160
    directories, disk, 158-159
    documents, 27-28, 44, 154
        marking, 158
        number of copies, 155-156
        previewing first, 160-161
        print queues, 155
        screen print, 155
        selected pages, 154-155
        single pages, 154
    envelopes, 185-186
    from List Files screen, 157-158
    from Print menu, 157
    mailing labels, 186-189
        label form definition, 187-188
        LABELS macro, 187
        merge codes, 188
        primary file, 187
    suspending, 160
    text blocks, 68
pull-down menus, 23-25

Q–R

queues, print, 155

records, 168-173, 194
Repeat (Esc) key, 19-20
replacing
    hidden codes, 140
    text strings, 137-141
restoring
    deleted text, 51-52, 66
    font attributes, 103-104
Retrieve command, 38-39
retrieving
    documents, 42-43
    files, 38
        with List Files screen, 39-41
        with Retrieve command, 38-39

Index

Reveal Codes, editing in, 54
right justification, 91
right tab stops, 84, 86
right-aligning text, 95-96

S

saving
   documents, 28-31
   text blocks, 67
screens
   adjusting after editing, 52
   documents, clearing from, 31
   editing, 10-11
   List Files, 39-41
      printing from, 157-158
   merging primary and secondary files, 176
   Print: Control Printer screen
      accessing, 159-160
      canceling printing, 160
      suspending printing, 160
   printing, 154-156
   Sort, 194
      displaying, 194-197
      selecting data combinations, 204-206
searching
   for files, 41-42
   text for strings, 134-137
secondary merge files, 168-170
   merging with primary, 175-178
   records, 170-173
   sorting, 202-203
      order and types, 202
      sort keys, 202-203
selecting data combinations, 204-206

sentences
   copying, 65
   deleting, 50-51
   moving, 65
settings, default, 16
shading boxes, 212
single characters, deleting, 47-48
size
   boxes, 215
   fonts, 102-104
soft hyphens, 99
soft page breaks, 110
soft returns, 6, 99-100
Sort and Select menu, 202-206
sort keys, 194, 199
   secondary merge files, 202
   selecting combination of data, 204
Sort screen, 194
   displaying, 194-197
   selecting data combinations, 204-206
sorting files, 197
   lines, 197-198
   paragraphs, 198, 201
   secondary merge, 202-203
   sort order, 198
Speller, 141-142
   alternatives list, correct spellings, 143-147
   checking words, phrases, and documents, 142-147
   checking capitalization, 146
   double words, 145-146
starting WordPerfect
   on dual-floppy disk system, 9
   on hard disk system, 8-9
status line, 10

strings (text), 134
    replacing, 137-141
    searching for, 134-137
subscript, 110
superscript, 110
supplemental dictionary, 141
suspending printing, 160
synonyms, 134

T

tab ruler
    displaying, 82-83
    hiding, 83
tab stops, 82
    adding
        multiple center, right, or decimal, 86
        multiple left, 85
        single, 85
    changing, 83
    deleting, 84-85
    dot leaders, 84
    viewing on tab ruler, 82-83
tables
    creating, 86-88
    editing, 87, 88
text
    adding with Insert mode, 45-46
    alignment, 52
        centering, 93-95
        right, 95-96
    blocks, 60-63
        appending, 68
        backing out of operation, 62
        boldfacing, 69-70
        centering, 70-71
        checking spelling, 146-147
        copying, 60, 64-65
        deleting, 65-66
        highlighting, 62
        highlighting with keyboard, 61
        highlighting with mouse, 61-62
        moving, 60, 63-64
        printing, 68
        saving, 67
        underlining, 69-70
    boldfacing, 101
    boxes, 216-217
    captions (boxes), 213
    checking spelling, 142-147
    deleting
        lines, 49
        restoring, 51-52
        sentences, paragraphs, and pages, 50-51
        single characters, 47-48
        to end of pages, 49
        with mouse, 51
        words, 48
    entering, 16
    fonts, 101-105
    hidden codes, replacing, 140
    hyphenation, 96-99
    importing to boxes, 214
    indenting, 88
        existing, 90
        hanging indents, 90-91
        with Left Indent key, 89
        with Left-Right Indent key, 89-90
        with Tab key, 89
    inserting
        blank lines, 47
        blank spaces, 47
    justification, 91-93

Index

    restoring deleted, 66
    strings
        replacing, 137-141
        searching for, 134-137
    typing over existing text, 46
    underlining, 101
    wrapping around boxes, 215
text files, merging, 169
Thesaurus, 134, 147-149
toggle switches, 12, 101
top and bottom margins, 117-120
Typeover mode, 38, 46-47
types, sorting
    combination of data, 204
    secondary merge files, 202
typing text over existing text, 46

U–W

underlining text, 69-70, 101

widow/orphan protection, 127-128
widows, 110
word wrap, 6, 13, 16
WordPerfect
    exiting, 30-31
    features, 6-7
    starting
        on dual-floppy disk system, 9
        on hard disk system, 8-9
words
    checking spelling, 142-147
    deleting, 48
wrapping text around boxes, 215

229

Using WordPerfect Is Easy When You're Using Que

Using WordPerfect 6, Special Edition
Que Development Group
The classic, #1 best-selling word processing book—only from Que! Includes tear-out command map, icons, margin notes, and cautions.
WordPerfect 6
$27.95 USA
1-56529-077-1, 1,200pp., 7 3/8 x 9 1/8

WordPerfect 6 QuickStart
Que Development Group
A graphics-based, fast-paced introduction to 6 essentials! Numerous illustrations demonstrate document production, table design, equation editing, and more.
WordPerfect 6
$21.95 USA
1-56529-085-2, 600 pp., 7 3/8 x 9 1/8

WordPerfect 6 Quick Reference
Que Development Group
Instant reference for the operations of WordPerfect 6. Alphabetical listings make information easy to find!
WordPerfect 6
$9.95 USA
1-56529-084-4, 160 pp., 4 3/4 x 8

Easy WordPerfect 6
Shelley O'Hara
The perfect introduction for new WordPerfect users—or those upgrading to Version 6.
WordPerfect 6
$16.95 USA
1-56529-087-9, 256 pp., 8 x 10

Check Out These Other Great Titles!

Using WordPerfect 5.1, Special Edition
Que Development Group
WordPerfect 5.1
$27.95 USA
0-88022-554-8, 900 pp., 7 3/8 x 9 1/4

WordPerfect 5.1 QuickStart
Que Development Group
WordPerfect 5.1
$21.95 USA
0-88022-558-0, 427 pp., 7 3/8 x 9 1/4

WordPerfect 5.1 Quick Reference
Que Development Group
WordPerfect 5.1
$9.95 USA
0-88022-576-9, 160 pp., 4 3/4 x 8

Easy WordPerfect
Shelley O'Hara
WordPerfect 5.1
$19.95 USA
0-88022-797-4, 200 pp., 8 x 10

Using WordPerfect 5
Charles O. Stewart III, et. al.
WordPerfect 5
$27.95 USA
0-88022-351-0, 867 pp., 7 3/8 x 9 1/4

Using WordPerfect 5.2 for Windows, Special Edition
Que Development Group
WordPerfect 5.2 for Windows
$29.95 USA
1-56529-166-2, 850 pp., 7 3/8 x 9 1/4

WordPerfect 5.1 Tips, Tricks, and Traps
Charles O. Stewart III, Daniel J. Rosenbaum, & Joel Shore
WordPerfect 5.1
$24.95 USA
0-88022-557-2, 743 pp., 7 3/8 x 9 1/4

WordPerfect for Windows Quick Reference
Que Development Group
Version 5.1 for Windows
$9.95 USA
0-88022-785-0, 160 pp., 4 3/4 x 8

WordPerfect 5.1 Office Solutions
Ralph Blodgett
Version 5.1
$49.95 USA
0-88022-838-5, 850 pp., 8 x 10

que

**To Order, Call: (800) 428-5331
OR (317) 573-2500**